WILLIAMS

WILLIAMS
A DIFFERENT KIND OF LIFE

Virginia Williams

with Pamela Cockerill

ECHO POINT BOOKS & MEDIA, LLC
BRATTLEBORO, VERMONT.

Published by Echo Point Books & Media
Brattleboro, Vermont
www.EchoPointBooks.com

Williams
ISBN: 978-1-63561-080-2 (paperback)

Cover design by Adrienne Núñez
Cover images courtesy of the author except
Frank Williams (top) and Virginia and Frank Williams (center)
courtesy of Minnow / BBC Films / Curzon Artificial Eye

PREFACE

I am not usually given to making New Year's resolutions, but at the end of 1988, I decided that I would spend the following year setting down everything that has happened to Frank and me in the last two decades, both before and after the car accident which left him permanently paralysed from the neck down. I felt it might act as an exorcism, a way to put it all behind me and start to look forward again.

There were other reasons too. One was selfish. I have changed in the last few years. Responsibility has altered my personality: once I would have been content to be a footnote in someone else's biography – now I feel differently. Frank has achieved so much in his life. I wanted, in this small way, to achieve something as well.

But by far the most important reason for writing the book is Frank himself. I'm sure that if I had asked him, he would have said he did not want me to write it. Yet I truly hope he reads it. His memory of the early days after his accident is blurred and vague, he has never asked me what it was like in France or in the London Hospital or what it has been like for me these past few years. Now he will know.

WILLIAMS

INTRODUCTION

*T*here are very few days in my life that I can recall with absolute clarity. I cannot describe the weather on my wedding day. I am pretty hazy over what I did and said during the hours following the birth of my first son. Although, like most people, I do remember what I was doing when John Kennedy was shot, I cannot picture even that day very vividly. But I can recollect every single detail of the events of Saturday 8 March 1986.

Frank had left home early that morning to join his team at the Paul Ricard circuit in the south of France where they were testing the FW 11, the new Williams Formula One car. It was a routine trip. The cars would usually test at Ricard five or six times a year. The Riviera climate was more predictable than that of Northamptonshire so they were less likely to be held up by rain than if they tested at Silverstone. In two weeks' time in Brazil the curtain would go up on the new Grand Prix season and everyone's adrenaline was beginning to build up in anticipation of that first race.

It looked as though the Williams team was set for a competitive season. Not only was the new car looking quick, but this year we would have two top-class drivers: Nigel Mansell, who had been with us the previous season, and Nelson Piquet whom Frank had signed up from Brabham. Frank liked and respected them both as men, as well as drivers, which augured well for team harmony. Our prospects looked good.

Frank had been running a Grand Prix team since 1969. It had taken him a long ten years of competing to achieve his first win in a Formula One race but after that first success in 1979 he had gone from strength to strength. He had surprised the motor racing world the following year by winning both the Drivers and Constructors Championships. After a decade of being professional also-rans, Williams had almost overnight joined the upper echelons of the sport, ranking alongside Ferrari, McLaren and Brabham as a major force in Grand Prix racing.

The championships had eluded us over the last couple of seasons and Frank wanted them back. It was widely felt that Williams would be a very hard team to beat in 1986.

It wasn't universal practice for team managers to be present for circuit tests but Frank, who loved travelling, rarely missed an opportunity to be at the track when his cars were running. He liked test sessions and had a good working knowledge of all the different circuits. If Patrick Head, Frank's partner and Williams chief engineer, wasn't there, then almost invariably Frank would be. Not as an observer, but as a fully employed member of the team, debriefing the drivers, and noting down their comments on engines, tyres and track conditions for analysis afterwards.

That Saturday I was at home with our two younger children, Claire and Jaime, at our new house in Boxford, near Newbury. Jonathan, our eldest boy, was away at boarding school.

One of the rewards of Frank's success had been the freedom to buy and renovate our own houses. After years of living in rented accommodation I enjoyed being a home-owner. I'd always loved doing places up and having the painters and decorators in, but there had been very little opportunity to indulge my passion in the early days of Frank Williams (Racing Cars) Ltd. In recent years I had made up for it. We had moved house three times since 1980.

Boxford House was a dream home; a big secluded mansion with creepers and wonderful gargoyles on the front which I had seen advertised in *Country Life* in 1984. We had gone to view it on a glorious day and the moment I glimpsed it through the trees, imposing and gothic in the autumn sunshine, I had been entranced. 'This is it, isn't it?' I'd exclaimed. Frank was as captivated as I was. Within six months we had moved in.

Both house and garden were in a dire state when we bought the place but it was obvious that there was huge potential if enough energy and love were spent on it. It had taken the builders nine months to complete the renovations which had included re-roofing and putting in new bathrooms and kitchens. Just before Christmas they had moved out and now, at last, we were starting to appreciate what we had created. In September, in anticipation of spring days like this, I had planted hundreds of my favourite white Mount Hood daffodils around the garden. That morning as I looked out of the kitchen window I could see the first pale buds peeping out of the dark-green clumps scattered under the trees. Above the bare branches of the chestnuts and oaks bordering the lawn, the sky was blue.

I stood at the window for several minutes surveying my world, feeling totally happy and content. What more could anyone want? I had an idyllic house, three lovely healthy children, and a husband who was more successful than he, or I, had ever dreamed possible. On top of that I was still helplessly in love with Frank. How many women could still say that of their husbands after nearly twelve years of marriage? I thought that morning that I was the luckiest person in England.

It was an unusually warm day for March so I packed a picnic lunch, and the children and I went out on our bicycles. Jaime who was only three, and too small to ride by himself, sat on the child seat on my bike, while Claire, nine years old and excited at the prospect of eating outside, cycled off in front to find a picnic spot. We ate our sandwiches on some open fields at the edge of the Downs before pedalling lazily back home. The afternoon was spent recovering from our exertions. Jaime and Claire watched television in the playroom while I sat with them on the sofa reading a new book. Outside on the lawn Fred, our black labrador, lay snoring in the sun, sleeping off his lunch of crisps and beer, scrounged from the regulars at Boxford's village pub, The Bell.

At about five o'clock the phone rang and I walked into the kitchen to answer it.

'Hi! It's me.' Frank's voice at the other end of the line was cheerful. Typically, he sounded in a hurry. 'I'm just leaving the circuit. Peter Windsor's coming with me.' (Peter was head of public relations at Williams.) 'I'll be home in a couple of hours – I hope you've got pasta for supper.'

'It's tagliatelle.'

'Great. Okay. Lots of love.' Frank never said goodbye to me on the phone, always 'Lots of love'. He still does.

After I put the phone down I went into the kitchen to sort out the ingredients for supper. Frank was running a half-marathon at

Portsmouth the next day which explained his interest in the menu. He always ate pasta on the evening before a race, to give himself reserves of energy to call on during the run, and just to make sure he usually followed it up with a couple of bowls of cornflakes. He had started running about sixteen years earlier, long before jogging had become a fashionable thing to do and he took it very seriously – next to motor racing it had become his biggest obsession. In 1986 he was running about seventy miles a week, and doing a half-marathon every third or fourth week, putting up respectable times of around one hour twenty minutes.

The attraction of running had initially lain in the fact that it helped him unwind and gave him thinking time, but he had come to regard it also as a challenge. Frank has always had an intensely competitive nature and thrives on working towards self-imposed targets. Running provided all sorts of rewards for that side of his personality.

I made a cream sauce with lots of Parmesan cheese to go with the tagliatelle and mixed what Frank calls my 'magic' salad sprinkled with pine nuts, avocado and pieces of bacon. As I laid the table I was already planning a schedule in my head for the next day when I planned to take Claire and Jaime to Portsmouth to see Frank run.

The children and I were back in the playroom when, some forty-five minutes after the first call, the phone rang again. I retraced my steps to the kitchen and picked up the receiver. I recognized Peter Windsor's voice on the line though he sounded rather muffled.

'Ginny? I'm ringing from Nelson's car phone. Listen, we've had a bit of an accident but there's no need to worry. Frank's okay. I was in the car with him.'

'Oh no,' I thought. 'Not again.' Frank was regularly involved in minor skirmishes in cars, usually as a consequence of employing race-driving techniques on the public roads. He hadn't driven competitively since his Formula Three days twenty years ago but old habits die hard.

'Are you all right?' I asked Peter anxiously.

'Yes, I'm fine.'

'What's Frank done to himself?'

Peter hesitated, 'He's okay I think. He's conscious and he's talking to me but we're taking him to the hospital to be checked over.'

'You won't be back tonight then?' I thought how cross Frank would be to miss his half-marathon.

'I shouldn't think so. Look, I've got to go. I'll ring you again when we find out some more, all right?'

I put the phone down telling myself that it probably wasn't all that bad. In the motor racing world where people are crashing cars all the time you don't want to sound like a panicking wife and I was determined not to overreact to what was probably just another of Frank's little incidents. I'd had a fair bit of practice at dealing with them.

I recalled a few years earlier, Frank walking into the house with Jacques Laffite, both of them with bleeding heads and Jacques, not the most easily frightened of racing drivers, declaring, 'F—ing awful driver! I'll never drive anywhere with him again.'

But even so I'd never had a phone call saying that Frank was being taken to hospital before . . .

I wrapped the supper in cling film and settled back down with the children. Claire knew something was up and demanded to know what had happened.

'Daddy's had a little accident but he's all right,' I said.

But it didn't satisfy her and every five minutes she came up with another piping query as to Daddy's whereabouts. I found myself going over the phone call in my mind. I wondered why Peter rather than Frank had rung me. Where had Frank been while Peter was speaking to me on the car phone? If they were taking him to hospital surely he would have been in the car as well? And if he was as unhurt as Peter implied, why hadn't he just said hello? Maybe he hadn't been in the car. In which case where was he? In an ambulance? Was Peter keeping something back from me? Had there been a note of unease in his voice?

I felt my composure wavering. After half-an-hour with no more news I decided to ring Sheridan Thynne, Williams sponsorship director and an old friend, to see if he had any information. His wife Eve said that Sheridan was in the bath and asked if Frank and I would like to come out for dinner the next Wednesday night. Obviously she hadn't heard anything and my anxiety was allayed a little. Poor Sheridan was dragged out of the bath and I inquired if he knew anything about Frank having an accident.

Sheridan's familiar unruffled slow tones helped restore my equilibrium. 'I haven't heard anything Ginny, so I wouldn't think it will be serious. I'll make some inquiries and get back to you in five minutes.'

I told the children to get ready for their baths and tried not to let my imagination run away with me. Frank's policy in life had always been to refuse to worry about things that were out of his control and I endeavoured to follow his example. Nevertheless when the phone rang again I jumped to pick up the receiver.

It was Patrick Head. Little alarm bells began to ring in my head, there was something wrong here, this was out of sequence. Why hadn't Sheridan rung back?

'Ginny? You've heard from France haven't you?'

'Yes, about an hour ago.'

'Is there anybody with you in the house?'

At his words I felt cold fear. For the first time in my life I knew what the expression meant. The hairs on my arms literally seemed to stand up with fright. My insides felt as if they were physically dissolving.

I must have stammered out an answer. Patrick carried on speaking. 'Look I know that Frank's been involved in an accident, but I haven't got all the details. I think the best thing is if I come down to Boxford as you're by yourself, and we can wait for news together.'

I waited in sheer terror while Patrick drove those twenty or so miles from his home in Aston Tirrold. I was sure he was coming to tell me that Frank was dead. I would not be able to cope with the news. If it were true I knew I would die myself.

As I stood by the phone in a stupor my mind flashed back two days to the last time I had seen my friend Susie. We had been standing in the sunlight by the river in Hungerford after a lovely day spent gossiping and exchanging news. Out of the blue, I had remarked to Susie, 'My God, if anything happened to Frank, I just don't know what I'd do.' There hadn't been any reason to say it. Had I had a premonition that day?

I didn't know what to do with myself. The children's insistent little questioning voices – 'Who was that Mummy?' 'What did he say?' 'When's Daddy coming home?' – were driving me frantic. I tried my best to reassure them as I dialled the number of Sarah, our nanny, who lived in Newbury.

Her father promised to locate Sarah and ask her to come over. She arrived within twenty minutes, tactfully avoided asking questions, and whisked the children off for their suppers and baths. I tried to compose myself before Patrick's arrival.

By the time the doorbell rang I thought I had myself back under control but my face must have given me away. As I opened the door Patrick reached out and laid a reassuring hand on my arm.

14

'Frank is not dead Ginny.' He emphasized each word. During the drive down it must have occurred to him that I might misinterpret his journey and think he was the bearer of bad tidings. Weak with relief I led him into the kitchen, plying him with questions.

'Where is he Patrick? What condition is he in?'

Patrick made me sit down and seated himself opposite me at the kitchen table before he started to tell me the story, as he knew it, of what had happened. Most of the details had come from Peter Windsor who had rung him, as he had me, on Nelson's car phone.

The accident had taken place about three miles away from the Paul Ricard circuit. No other car had been involved and the road was clear when Frank's car left the road at high speed and landed on its roof in a field. Frank had hit his head in the accident and although he was conscious and lucid he had been taken to the Timone Hospital in Marseille so that his head injuries could be assessed.

That was the latest information Patrick had. It was not much more than I already knew. Patrick had arranged that any news from the hospital would be passed on to us via Bernie Ecclestone, head of FOCA, the Formula One Constructors' Association. All calls to Patrick's home were being diverted to my number. We settled down to wait. Sarah had put the children to bed and the house seemed suddenly quiet. I offered Patrick a glass of wine and decided to have one myself. It seemed important to try and retain a semblance of normality by keeping to the conventions of social behaviour.

Sarah had fed Claire and Jaime but the pasta lay untouched under the cling-film. I warmed it up in the microwave and divided it between us though I had no appetite. While we ate we discussed the accident and what might have caused it. I think both of us in our hearts knew it was due to Frank's wild driving. I don't think Patrick was too surprised by what had happened since he drove in similar fashion to Frank. Both of them loved speed and both frequently came off the road. Patrick was always ending up in the back of horseboxes or in hedge bottoms. I wondered aloud why so many men involved in motor racing behaved like frustrated racing drivers, but Patrick did not supply me with an answer. At around ten o'clock I jumped as the phone rang again.

It was Bernie Ecclestone, a longtime friend, and by virtue of his position, probably the most powerful man in Formula One. His manner as he spoke to me was friendly and lighthearted.

'Don't worry about your old man. We're looking after him,' he said. 'There might be something a bit wrong with his back and they want to operate to sort it out, so I've sent Prof. Watkins down in my plane tonight to assist with surgery.'

At the mention of the word 'back' a fleeting image crossed my mind of Clay Regazzoni, confined to a wheelchair since a back injury had paralysed his legs and ended his driving career but I dismissed the thought instantly. Bernie Ecclestone's tone was comforting and cheerful. And I felt comforted. I wanted to believe him.

'Try not to worry,' he continued. 'Prof. Watkins will sort things out. I'm sure he'll be okay. You know Frank . . . '

Bernie must have guessed that the involvement of Prof. Watkins would reassure me. 'The Prof.' as he is known, is employed by FOCA specifically to deal with racing injuries. He attends each Grand Prix and his role in the event of an accident is to accompany injured drivers and arrange for the best doctors or surgeons to attend them wherever they happen to be in the world. Frank could not be in better hands.

Having laid my fears to rest Bernie said he didn't think there was any point in our going down to France that night. Why didn't we wait and see what the news was in the morning? I interpreted this to mean that Frank might be fit enough to fly back in the morning and I passed the receiver over to Patrick feeling almost embarrassed for getting myself into such a state unnecessarily.

Patrick's face, normally very mobile and expressive, told me nothing as he spoke to Bernie. I assumed he was just hearing a repeat of what I had been told. Finally he hung up. 'Bernie will ring at eight a.m. to let us know how the operation went,' he said. 'I think it's best if you pack something ready to fly down in the morning, just in case.' I didn't press him for more details. At around midnight I showed Patrick into the guestroom for the night and went to my bedroom.

Alone in the quiet and dark my fears rose up again, I hardly slept at all. Frank's side of the bed seemed horribly empty. I spent most of the night padding restlessly up and downstairs making myself one cup of tea after another and gathering together a haphazard collection of clothes to throw into my overnight bag. I said a few prayers and longed for daylight to cast sanity onto my night time imaginings. In my mind eight a.m. became a goal I was struggling to reach. If I could only get through the night without giving way to my fears I felt everything might start to improve. Perhaps by the morning Frank would be well enough to speak to me on the telephone. That was what I wanted above all else. I'd had enough of other people's reassurances. I didn't want to speak to third parties any more. I needed to hear Frank's own amused voice telling me impatiently, 'Of course I'm all right. Don't be so stupid. Relax.'

As dawn arrived I found myself staring at the collection of photographs of Frank which I kept propped above the bedroom fireplace. My confidence grew at the sight of his familiar face. I had enormous faith in him. He was very fit, very strong, and I couldn't live without him. He knew that, he wouldn't let me down. And I wasn't going to let *him* down. He certainly would not be impressed to know I'd been worrying myself sick.

The phone rang precisely at eight o'clock as promised. Bernie Ecclestone greeted me in what I thought was a rather wary manner compared with his warmth of the previous evening. He asked to speak to Patrick and I passed over the receiver. As he listened silently to Bernie, Patrick started to turn slowly away from me. He reminded me of my son Jonathan when he was being introduced to someone and felt shy. By the end of the call he had completely turned his back to me. Whatever it was Bernie Ecclestone was telling him, he didn't want me to see his reaction.

All my alarm bells started jangling again.

'What *is* it?' I demanded, as he put the phone down. Patrick swallowed, obviously struggling for words.

'It could be bad,' he said. 'Bernie says we should get ready to go down to Marseille.'

All my good intentions flew out of the window. I lost control and heard myself screaming. Screaming at Patrick to tell me what had happened. Screaming at Sarah to get the children, who had followed me downstairs, out of the kitchen. Screaming silently to Frank, 'Do not die.'

Two hours later we were on board a scheduled flight from Heathrow to Marseille, leaving Sarah to organize the household and children. Patrick still insisted that Bernie had given him no details. He said the doctors would tell me everything when we arrived at the Timone Hospital.

At Marseille airport we were met at midday by Nelson Piquet and by Frank Dernie, Williams research and development engineer. To my bewilderment they were both smiling and cheerful. Frank Dernie was catching the next flight home so stayed at the airport while Nelson's chauffeur drove the rest of us to the hospital. During the journey, Nelson and Patrick kept up a steady stream of cheerful banter and enthusiastically discussed the previous day's testing programme, adding to my confusion. I didn't know what to think. My emotions had seesawed up and down so much in the past few hours I felt I was losing my grip on reality. It didn't make sense. Earlier I had felt that Patrick had been preparing me for widowhood. Now the two of them were behaving as if nothing was wrong. I had yet to learn that people cope with difficult situations in different ways.

The Timone is a huge 1,000-bed hospital in the centre of Marseille. To me, all hospitals look threatening but the Timone seemed particularly so as I stood at the bottom of the huge flight of steps which led up to a mausoleum-like entrance hall. A reception committee of four was waiting for us just inside the hospital. Nigel Mansell and Peter Windsor greeted me and a distinguished looking man, his hair greying at the temples stepped forward and offered his hand.

'Mrs Williams? I'm Professor Watkins.' He gestured to the fourth person in the group, 'May I introduce Professor Vincintelli?'

I shook hands with a swarthy Gallic-looking man.

'Professor Vincintelli is head of neurosurgery here at the Timone,' Prof. Watkins continued. 'He is the surgeon who operated on Frank last night. I think it would be a good idea if we take you up to his office now and fill you in on what's happened before you see Frank.'

My spirits lifted at the news that Frank was at least well enough to see visitors. But I seemed to be alone in my reaction. Everyone looked very sombre. A complete contrast to the jovial mood in the car. Both Nigel and Peter appeared tired and strained. I learned later they had spent the night along with Nelson and Frank Dernie in the corridor outside the operating theatre, waiting for news. Nigel had to catch the same plane as Frank Dernie but he said a few encouraging words to me before rushing off to the airport.

I was led towards the lifts and we were all propelled up to the fifth floor and into Professor Vincintelli's office. During those few minutes, when no one spoke, I was very aware of being the only woman in the group and conscious that all attention seemed to be focused on me. I felt small and cold, and a little like Alice in Wonderland, as though I were shrinking in the presence of these important men. I would have liked to disappear altogether and felt a desperate need for support.

In his office Professor Vincintelli, dressed in an immaculately cut suit, and not looking in the least as if he had just spent all night in an operating theatre, indicated a chair in front of his desk. I sat down and he seated himself solemnly at the other side. Prof. Watkins, Patrick, and Peter Windsor remained standing on my left. Behind me, Nelson, unintimidated by the formal atmosphere, perched himself on top of a filing cabinet.

In the brief moments before anyone spoke I got the impression that I was being assessed by the doctors. In particular I sensed Prof. Watkins eyes on me and felt that he was trying to work me out; examining me for clues as to how I would cope with whatever it was they had to tell me. I could feel my heart thudding in my chest. Prof. Watkins asked me if I would understand if Professor Vincintelli spoke in French. I had become reasonably fluent during my schooldays and agreed to try.

Professor Vincintelli cleared his throat. In an impersonal manner he started to describe the details of the operation he had conducted on Frank during the night. There had been various minor injuries to be attended to, he said, and he outlined what they were while I struggled to comprehend the French medical jargon.

Then his voice seemed to take on a different intonation. It had, he informed me, been a very long operation. There was a reason for that, which I ought to know. It had been necessary to remove part of Frank's hip-bone in order to fuse broken vertebrae in his neck. Professor Vincintelli gestured with a little chopping motion to his neck in case I had misunderstood and looked me straight in the eye.

'*Vous avez compris?*'

I stared at him in disbelief, certain that my schoolgirl French, previously put to the test only on shopping expeditions with girlfriends, had let me down. I must have got it wrong. Not his neck! Not in my worst imaginings during the last few hours had I considered a broken neck.

I looked around the room for reassurance and my eyes met those of Nelson seated on the filing cabinet. And I saw that Nelson, twice the World Champion driver, always in command of the situation, always bubbly and cheerful and ready with a joke, had tears streaming unheeded down his cheeks. Nobody spoke.

I heard a terrible strangled noise and realized with surprise that it must have come from me. The professors looked uncomfortable. Prof. Watkins had his eyes fixed on my face and I felt he was challenging me to be controlled. Eventually when no one else moved, Peter came over and put his arm around me. I was immensely grateful. But there was no escaping the question I had to ask. I took a deep breath.

'Is he paralysed?'

Professor Vincintelli nodded silently. I wanted to cry loudly and violently but the presence of those five men in the room prevented me. A couple of tears did escape and ran down my face and Professor Vincintelli looked disapproving. Sternly he said that I had to show courage in order not to distress Frank. My husband was going to need a lot of support, not more stress than he already had. When my silent tears continued to flow he leaned forward and said in an exasperated voice that unless I was able to pull myself together he would not allow me to see Frank. The shock of his words and the lack of sympathy behind them jolted me back into control. Perhaps that was his intention.

I was conscious of a sudden raging headache. Apart from that I felt numb. I was only vaguely aware of being led out of the office, back down to the ground floor and towards the intensive care unit. Patrick followed me. A nurse took me into a small side room and gowned me up. I stood unprotestingly as my hair was tucked into a plastic hat, my feet were encased in rubber boots, my hands were gloved and my whole body covered from head to toe in a sort of white shroud. Only then was I permitted to walk through two sets of doors into Frank's ward.

It was stiflingly hot. The side ward I was directed to had three beds. Each contained a still silent body surrounded by batteries of hi-tech equipment. I felt sick with fear. I had no idea which patient was Frank and I turned to the nurse at the central station for help and recoiled. The nurse's face was terribly burnt – so badly scarred and mutilated that it was impossible to tell if it was a man or a woman. I felt as though I was living through a nightmare. Following the direction of the nurse's gesture I walked towards the bed in the corner. I was unprepared for what I saw.

Frank lay motionless on the bed, covered from the waist down by a thin white sheet, a human clearing in a forest of machinery. Behind him monitor screens bleeped and flashed, recording every conceivable bodily function. Four or five drips and bottles of blood on stands were attached by tubes to his limbs. More tubes drained from his body into ominous looking bags filled with dark fluids slung under the bed. His hair was matted with dried blood, the inside of his ears and nostrils encrusted with it. Even his fingernails were black with blood. Overriding all my other reactions I felt an irrelevant sense of outrage that no one had even bothered to wash him.

Frank, the man I had lived with for fourteen years, was almost unrecognizable. His face was bruised, cut, and horribly swollen, his forehead covered in stitches. His body, which only yesterday had been so fit and lean, was distended to horrendous proportions. At every rasping breath his lower abdomen heaved up and down with effort. A long, livid, freshly-stitched incision ran across the front of his neck. His eyes were closed. I wanted to speak to him but found that I was unable to open my mouth. It was as though I were paralysed myself. Behind me, I was aware of Patrick staring down in shocked silence.

I don't know how long I stood there. It could have been a few minutes or as long as half-an-hour. Then, gradually, I became aware of a slight pressure against my stomach and when I glanced up I saw that Frank was looking at me – his eyes bloodshot and unfamiliar but the gaze as piercing as ever. Somehow he had forced his arm towards me. He was trying to say something, but his voice was little more than a whisper and I bent over him to catch his words.

'Did my arm move?' he asked slowly.

I nodded, speechless.

'What have they told you Ginny?'

I was unable to answer him. Patiently he rephrased the question, struggling to articulate each word.

'Have they told you that I'm paralysed from the neck down?'

Haltingly, I told him that I thought they had said it was a possibility. There was a long silence. Hot tears streamed down my face.

Frank watched me, dry-eyed. He was so much braver than I was. As I fought to control my sobs he spoke to me again very clearly.

'Ginny, as I see it, I have had forty fantastic years of one sort of life.' He paused and stared at me unblinking. Then he said very slowly and deliberately. 'Now I shall have another forty years of a different kind of life . . .'

BOOK
1

CHAPTER 1

*T*he first time I saw Frank Williams I fell in love with him. Totally. Utterly. Hopelessly. I knew instantly that I wanted him to be the man in my life. Since I was already engaged to be married this was rather inconvenient.

It was 1967 and I was twenty-one years old. My fiancé Charles, who was trying to make it as a racing driver, had taken me to look at his new 'toy', a Formula Three Titan which was being stabled at a garage in Bath Road, Cippenham near Slough. I didn't know much about racing cars. My interest in them had only been kindled since I'd met Charles but I was learning slowly. In the past few months I'd started to spend weekends at race meetings watching him practise on Saturdays and compete on Sundays. I quite enjoyed the atmosphere; the crescendos of noise, and the smell of fumes from burning fuel and hot tyres. But I was no fanatic. Any romantic illusions about motor sport hadn't lasted long. There wasn't much glamour about freezing in the paddock car park all day at Thruxton while a swarm of Formula Threes charged round and round the track.

However when Charles wanted to show me his purchase I put on an interested look and went along. It was while we were driving down to the garage at Slough that I first heard the name Frank Williams. Charles told me that this man from 'up north' had just set himself up in the workshop and garage at Bath Road. He called his company Frank Williams (Racing Cars) Ltd and he planned to enter his own team in Formula Two the following year with Piers Courage driving.

I might not have heard of Frank Williams but I had heard of Piers Courage. He was an old Etonian son of the Courage brewing family and one of the last of the breed of private 'gentleman' racing drivers: good-looking, high-living and already quite successful.

It was to help finance his Formula Two venture that Frank Williams was looking after other people's cars. He had recently started operating a 'stable' for Formula Three drivers like Charles. For a fee he would provide mechanics for races and in-between race maintenance. I was mildly interested by the Piers Courage connection but far from enthralled. Frank Williams sounded like just another racing car addict. I certainly was not expecting to be swept off my feet when I visited the Bath Road workshop that day.

But that's what happened. As we walked into the garage a smartly dressed, dark-haired man in his early twenties appeared from behind a car and walked over to us. He introduced himself as Frank Williams and, as he greeted Charles, he flashed me a private, meaningful, and very wicked smile. I felt a blush creeping across my cheeks.

For the next five minutes while he discussed the Titan with Charles, Frank flirted surreptitiously with me. Every time I looked up I found myself gazing into a pair of piercing greeny-brown eyes. I stared back like a mouse looking at a snake. He smiled again, revealing gleaming white teeth. The effect his smile had on me was extraordinary. I became as embarrassed and tongue-tied as a schoolgirl. Unable to think of anything intelligent to say, I shadowed Charles silently as he toured the workshop, feeling like the original dumb blonde.

I was pretending to examine the Titan when I suddenly found myself thinking, 'I want this man.' As a well-brought-up, rather conventional young woman, I was taken aback by my reaction. Frank, I'm certain, was fully conscious of the impact he was having on me and appeared highly amused. His eyes continued to tease me as I shuffled uncomfortably next to Charles.

I still find it hard to understand why I fell so instantaneously for Frank. He was not tall, dark and handsome. He stood only five foot, eight inches high and even in 1967 his hairline was receding rapidly. There was no obvious reason for me to go weak at the knees which only made it more disturbing. If I'd been looking at Steve McQueen it would have been understandable. I felt very confused and it was a great relief to leave.

I couldn't get him out of my mind. He obsessed my thoughts. As the days towards my wedding ticked off, my main occupation became looking for Frank. Like a teenager with a crush, I spent days compulsively driving around Slough in my Mini in the hope of seeing him. What I would have done or said if I had bumped into him I have no idea. The only time I did see him again during the next few weeks was at a Formula Three meeting at Thruxton where he was keeping a friendly eye on some of his 'livery stable'.

I was sitting with Charles in his E-type in the car park after a race when Frank suddenly appeared. He squatted down, not at Charles' side of the car, but at mine. I wound down the window and Frank chatted away to Charles across me, his face only inches from my own. My mouth dried up. Again I found myself completely unable to speak. I could feel his eyes sending me wicked messages, and understanding all too well what they were saying, had to look the other way. Strange things were happening to my stomach. Any hopes that my first reaction had been a transitory madness were dashed. I was still hooked.

I spent the next two months desperately trying to wriggle out of marrying Charles. I failed. I didn't have the self-confidence to face the confrontations involved. It felt as though I were being swept along by a tide of events and I wasn't certain enough of what I really wanted to make much of a protest. If Frank had declared undying love for me there would have been no problem but I was bright enough to realize that the infatuation was probably entirely one-sided. I might have thought, 'Wow! This is my destiny' but there was nothing to indicate that he had. His flirting had a well-practised air about it.

Charles and I had never been a love-match but, at least, with him I knew where I stood. We had met two years earlier and as 'good friends' we had gone through a hectic period of partying. It was the height of the swinging sixties and life was wonderful. I had moved into a flat with my girlfriend Susie, thrown out my twinsets, and joined the queue outside Biba every Friday night to buy the latest clothes. I earned £18 a week as a receptionist but I was always turning up late for work after nightclubbing and getting the sack. My father was rather indulgent and I had the security of knowing that he would pay the bills when necessary, which was probably very bad for me. Life was one long party, with Charles conveniently around to act as my escort.

Then Susie got married, which meant I had to look for somewhere new to live. When Charles asked me to marry him I rather passively went along with the idea. Coming as I did from a protected and privileged background, I was very immature for my age. I quite liked the prospect of having a house of my own and the idea of giving dinner parties for my other newly-married friends.

At first my parents had been opposed to my engagement. I had received an expensive public school education, after which I had been 'finished' in Switzerland and Monte Carlo where I had been well grounded in French conversation, skiing, tennis, *cordon bleu* cooking and flower arranging. To my parents' way of thinking, the whole point of acquiring these skills was to equip me for marriage to someone like a lawyer or stockbroker.

Because I had been forced to work so hard to get them to accept Charles, I found it hard to change my tack now. With the peculiar logic of a twenty-one-year-old I felt that it would be somehow disloyal to him to tell my parents, 'You were right after all – he's not the one for me.' I did tell Charles that I didn't want to marry him, though not the reason for it. He was completely unaware of the consequences of my encounter with Frank at Bath Road. He refused to take my rejection seriously, attributing it to 'pre-wedding nerves'.

By now we were deep into the fittings for my Nina Ricci wedding dress. Presents were arriving daily. The flowers were ordered from Constance Spry. It would have taken a lot of nerve to call it off and I didn't have it.

The wedding took place three days before Christmas and I cried all the way up the aisle. My father looked rather taken aback at this development and said in a reverberating whisper as I clung tearfully to his arm, 'You don't have to go through with this if you don't want to, you know.'

I looked up the aisle at the mass of smiling expectant faces under a sea of hats and thought despairingly, 'It's a bit bloody late now.' Half-an-hour later the deed was done. After the ceremony Charles and I set up home in a lovely three-storeyed house, bought for us by my father, in Easthampstead in Berkshire. For a while I did try to make a go of it. I had given up my job and I quite liked living in the country playing at being a housewife, choosing colour schemes and furnishings for all the rooms.

But my mind was still preoccupied by Frank. I made a point of going to the race track with Charles whenever I thought Frank might be there keeping an eye on 'his' drivers. I was usually disappointed. Frank had achieved his ambition and he was running a Brabham in Formula Two that year with Piers Courage driving. They were racing up to three times a month and flying to meetings all over Europe. By keeping my ears open I learned that they were achieving modest success.

Every now and then, my vigils at the Formula Three meetings paid off and I would spot Frank's lean figure striding through the pits. I would at once extract myself from the crowd and put myself in a prominent position where he could see me and, hopefully, speak to me. I was so anxious to be more than just a pretty face to him that I used to rehearse intelligent things to say, but I never used any of my sparkling opening lines. Once his eyes met mine I was invariably dumbstruck. He probably thought I was half-witted but the idea failed to deter me. I just wanted to be near him.

I discovered something rather unwelcome while standing at the track discreetly observing my hero – Frank was a terrible flirt. On several occasions I saw him make eye contact with a new female who walked into his group in just the same devastating way he had with me that day at Bath Road. But at least I was still included on his list of flirting partners. My being married didn't inhibit him at all. Whenever he saw me he would fix me with that dreadful intimate stare or worse, give me a meaningful wink. Subconsciously, I accepted that my days as Charles' wife were numbered. But I did stay faithful to him for quite a decent interval – a whole year – before fate presented me with a golden opportunity.

Charles was trying to sell the Titan and Frank, who was looking for potential buyers for it, rang up one day a month before Christmas. I answered the phone, stammered a few inanities, and then, struggling to find something to say, asked, 'What are you doing for Christmas?' 'Nothing,' said Frank instantly. Before I could think twice, I said, 'Why don't you spend it here with us?' Frank accepted on the spot. I put the phone down thinking, 'Wow, Ginny. What have you done?'

Charles and I were invited to a lot of parties that Christmas and I wangled invitations for Frank as well. On Boxing Day we all went to Susie's house for a lunchtime party. Everyone was in festive mood, though I noticed that Frank drank only mineral water. Charles on the other hand had drunk several glasses of wine, when Frank challenged him to run a couple of miles with him. Charles accepted the challenge but said he wanted time to recover from the lunch and wine first. 'Okay. Fine,' said Frank, 'I'll go back to my flat and fetch my running gear. Want to come for the drive Ginny?' I froze, then nodded.

As I slipped into the passenger seat of Frank's Granada I was uncomfortably aware that one or two nudges and winks had followed our exit together. I sat clutching the seat nervously all the way to Slough, due partly to my first experience of Frank's driving and partly to my suspicion of what was about to happen. To this day I'm not sure if the whole thing was a carefully engineered-plan on Frank's part, or simply an enterprising grasping of opportunity. Suffice it to say that in the process of looking for Frank's running clothes at Bath Road, our relationship moved several steps beyond eye contact . . .

If I had imagined myself in love with Frank before, what I experienced now was on a completely different level. I had never felt this way about a man in my life. I was crazy about him. I came to a decision that Boxing Day. It might take time, but somehow I was going to get him.

It took several years. Perhaps Frank sensed a net closing around him. Perhaps, though somehow I doubt it, he felt bad about Charles, but our relationship smouldered rather than flamed for quite a time. Probably the main reason was that Frank was becoming more involved in running his racing team. 1969 was even busier for him than the previous year. He and Piers Courage had ventured into Formula One, the pinnacle of motor racing, for the first time. They were running a Brabham, purchased with other people's money and they spent the year chasing all over Europe and America, competing in both F1 and F2 races. My study of the sports pages revealed that the season was reasonably successful, with two second places achieved in Monaco and the United States at Watkins Glen.

It wasn't long before I was inviting Frank to stay at the house regularly, thinking up all sorts of contrived reasons for him to visit. I decided there was no point in playing hard to get on these occasions and really behaved very badly, waiting for Charles to go to sleep then sneaking down the corridor and up the stairs to Frank's bedroom. In the morning, dutifully reinstated next to Charles, I would get up and rush down to prepare breakfast to deliver to Frank in bed. Then with Charles hopefully in the shower I would spend a few more precious minutes in bed with Frank.

I was living dangerously, but I couldn't help myself. I found our relationship so intoxicating I was prepared to take any risk. For me it wasn't just about sex. I found that being with Frank made me feel alive in a way I'd never experienced before. He was so vital, never still for more than a few minutes at a time. He radiated so much energy that it was almost visible – and somehow this energy was infectious. When I was with him it transferred itself to me, when he left I felt as though I had been switched off like a light.

I did feel guilty about Charles but, by this time, he was being unfaithful to me – going off with girls because of what he saw as my 'coldness' – which helped ease my conscience.

Frank was quite intrigued to have this recently married woman throwing herself at him at every opportunity. The danger of being caught just added to the excitement. He thought it was magic. But he was also wary of letting the relationship get too serious. To Frank, I knew, I was no more than an enjoyable diversion. While he was always affectionate and we had a lot of fun together he made it plain that he was far too wrapped up in his business to consider 'getting involved'. I realised even then that, for him, women would always take second place to cars.

Conveniently, the ever-increasing activities of Frank Williams (Racing Cars) Ltd gave him a perfect excuse for disappearing for months at a time and letting our affair cool off. By 1970 Frank's involvement in Formula One racing completely dominated his life. He could happily talk about it for hours. He never discussed his feelings or emotions at all. But I didn't complain, I was perfectly willing to listen to him expounding on his obsession. It saved me having to think of things to say to him, which I still found inexplicably difficult.

At this stage it was not Frank's ambition to become a constructor, and I'm quite certain he never visualized himself as one of the world's leading constructors. He motivation was simply his love for Formula One racing. He was addicted, no lesser word will do, to all aspects of the Grand Prix circus. He didn't really mind whether he was on the trapeze or cleaning out the cages so long as he was there.

Then on 21 June 1970 at the Dutch Grand Prix at Zandvoort, disaster struck. Piers Courage driving an Italian deTomaso car for Frank's team, crashed into the fences and banks on the back-stretch and was killed. I saw the news on television and was devastated for Frank. I had only once met Piers but I knew their relationship had been much more than driver and employer. In their early twenties they had shared a flat in Harrow on the Hill and I had heard of some of their escapades. Once, Piers and another driver, Jonathan Williams, had persuaded Frank to strip off and run down to the railway line at the end of the garden for a bet. When he was safely outside they had locked the door so he was trapped stark naked as a tube train passed by full of gaping commuters.

At one time Piers and Frank had both been struggling to make a name as racing drivers, dining together on five shilling suppers in a café on the Pimlico Road. As finances improved they had gone nightclubbing together. Piers was probably the closest friend Frank had ever had.

The newspapers had a field day. Piers had led such a high profile life and his family connections through birth and marriage – he had married Lady Sarah Curzon – were so illustrious, that it kept the papers going with stories for days.

I wondered what Frank would do. I suspected it would be a moment of truth. He could either drop out of Formula One racing for good or bite the bullet and carry on. I soon knew which option he had chosen. Just four weeks after the accident I read in the papers that another driver, Brian Redman, was representing Frank in the British Grand Prix at Brands Hatch. It was several months before I saw Frank again and when I did, he never mentioned Piers' death. I sensed it was something he did not wish to discuss and I never brought the subject up. In the end, the tragedy seemed to inspire him to go for it with even more determination. He was committed now to Formula One, come what may.

With every one of our subsequent meetings I learned a little more about Frank. But only a little. Our relationship was still depressingly one-sided. I never knew when I would see him again. He never said he loved me or asked me to leave Charles, but the more he played hard to get, the more I wanted him. Before I got married most of the men in my life had been available – perhaps too available. Frank was a challenge to me and the fact that I didn't really understand him only made him more interesting. After two years of our on-off affair I still knew very little about what made the guy tick and most of what I knew was up front, what he chose to reveal about himself. I sensed there was a lot more beneath the surface. I did pick up some information by discreetly questioning people who knew him.

I learned that Frank Williams had been fanatical about fast cars since he was a boy of ten, when he used to hitch-hike with a friend to Brands Hatch. His childhood had been rather austere, far removed from the comfortable happy family life that I had experienced growing up in the Surrey stockbroker belt. His father had walked out on Frank's mother before he was born in South Shields in 1942. She had worked as a residential teacher in schools for the handicapped and Frank had been educated in Catholic boarding schools, first in Liverpool and then in Scotland, since the age of three. Due to his mother's work commitments he had sometimes spent part of his holidays at boarding school as well, where for weeks, he would be the only child in a community of monks. It must have been a strange, institutionalized upbringing and it seemed as though he had closed a door in his mind on that part of his life. However hard I tried he would not be drawn into discussing either his mother or his childhood.

By the time he was twenty-one, Frank was completely bitten by the motor racing bug. Although he had a shoestring budget, funded by a job as a travelling grocery salesman, most weekends found him competing in saloon car races at tracks around the country. It was there he had met Piers Courage and Jonathan Williams and, in 1963, he moved south to share a flat with them and Charlie Crichton-Stuart in Pinner Road, Harrow. He was virtually penniless, at least compared with this Old Etonian motor racing set that he had taken up with. He used to pay to rent a sofa because he couldn't afford a bedroom, and when he fell behind with the rent on the sofa he would move out and sleep in the back of a van parked outside. He got his first toe-hold in single-seater racing by becoming a mechanic for Jonathan Williams and travelling round Europe with him while he competed in Formula Junior races.

Frank did some Formula Three racing himself, but without much success. He soon discovered that his real forte was in wheeling and dealing. By 1967 he was doing well enough selling spare parts and second hand cars to contacts made in his racing days, to be able to rent the premises in Bath Road, Slough and go into business as a registered company.

Of the present day Frank Williams I knew rather more than I did of his background, even though much of that knowledge consisted of trivial details. I knew that he liked nightclubbing, Porsches, tailor-made suits and travelling by air. That he had a weakness for freshly squeezed orange juice. That his taste in music ranged from classical to the Moody Blues. And that thanks to the monks' education and his travels with Jonathan Williams, he spoke French and Italian fluently. Although he enjoyed many of the luxuries and finer things in life there was a self-disciplined, almost spartan side to his nature which intrigued me. Perhaps it was a result of his monastic upbringing. He was very keen on exercise and on keeping himself fit, and although he enjoyed good food he never over-indulged or put on an ounce of spare flesh. Nor did he smoke or drink alcohol, which was almost unique among the people I knew.

Frank *was* different in many ways from most of the people I knew. He was much more pushing and aggressive in his drive to do things. He worked seven days a week, every week, which I found astonishing. He was also a perfectionist. Whether he was dealing with cars, drivers or nuts and bolts he was reluctant to settle for second best. The cost of his choice and his ability to pay for it were minor considerations. Since there was a strong perfectionist streak in my own personality I could identify with that.

But what I loved most about Frank was his wicked sense of humour. It wasn't the sort of humour I'd been a party to before. In my circle of friends the men tended to be rather conventional and serious. In contrast Frank had a schoolboy naughtiness about him which came from an utter lack of respect for authority. He was always teasing people and winking at unsuitable moments; he didn't take the same things seriously that most people did. He was anti-establishment, anti-respectability, anti-responsibility. I found this outlook on life slightly scandalous and at the same time very exciting.

Frank's humour was a vital part of his charisma, which was not only exerted on women. It also came in useful when he was looking for sponsorship. Funding the team was a continual headache, but PR was one of Frank's greatest talents. When he was appealing for money he was able to charm the birds out of the trees.

When Frank paid his, by now, annual visit to our house in Easthampstead for Christmas 1970 he told me that he had been able to attract enough funding from various companies to run two March Formula One, and three Formula Two cars for the coming season. It was an ambitious venture since he at that time only employed ten people. Everyone was stretched to the limit and Frank often needed to be in half-a-dozen places at once.

Early in 1971 in one hectic week he flew with the team to Colombia for an F2 series, only for a part of the chassis on both cars to split open during the first race. The next race was just seven days away. Frank had both cars stripped down overnight, removed the chassis from each, flew back to London – virtually a 24-hour trip – carrying them as hand-baggage and took them to March's headquarters at Bicester. There the March mechanics worked non-stop to repair and reinforce each chassis and Frank was able to accompany them back to Bogota in time for the team to practise on the two days left before the second race.

It was this single-mindedness, this sense of purpose, that kept my interest burning. I admired the way he never got disheartened by failure, though as far as I could see, he rarely encountered anything else.

For the past year Frank had been jetting off all around the world, his racing no longer confined to Europe, and since he was always extremely cagy about revealing his plans and never liked to be tied down by making arrangements for future meetings I rarely knew when I would see him next. I would hover by the phone, sometimes for weeks on end, knowing that sooner or later the call would come.

'Hello. I'm back,' the teasing voice would announce. 'Are you alone? How about coming over to see me?' And within minutes I'd be driving off to the flat above the garage in Bath Road.

Charles and I were watching television one night when the phone rang. Suspecting who it might be, I sprinted upstairs to answer it. I told Frank that I couldn't come over and when Charles asked who had rung said it had been a wrong number. I sat in front of the television fuming with frustration. What I needed as an excuse to get out of the house was a full-scale row. Charles was watching one of his favourite programmes. Without a word I walked over and changed channels. Not surprisingly this triggered a violent reaction and verbal abuse hurtled through the air. Seconds later I had stormed out of the house and was heading towards Slough.

I was driving along feeling improperly pleased with myself when it occurred to me that Frank would by now have had time to pick up the phone and invite someone else over. I had no illusions that I was the only woman in his life. I had to ring him again urgently. Unfortunately there was a GPO strike and all coin telephone boxes were out of use. I stopped at the first pub I saw and pushed my way to the bar through a crowd of rather inebriated men who watched my solo progress with interest. Uncomfortably aware that my mini-skirt was only about four inches long, I asked to use a phone. The publican produced his private telephone which he plonked down on the bar. I dialled the number and a fascinated hush descended in the pub as I informed Frank that I had been able to get away after all and would be over at his place in twenty minutes. I scuttled out of the bar amid cackles of ribald laughter and shouts of, 'Have a nice time. Enjoy it!'

My marriage was approaching its end. One day shortly after that episode I woke up realizing that I couldn't live with the deceit and guilt any longer. Frank was my entire motivation, he occupied my thoughts every hour of every day. And Charles was completely unaware of it. I owed it to him to stop the charade. I didn't have the nerve to tell him my real reason for leaving. Instead I engineered another row (they were becoming regular events by now) and in the middle of it I said, 'Right. I'm off,' and just walked out. I felt so guilty I hardly took any of my possessions with me – it was a real red-spotted hankie exit. I had prudently arranged to rent a girlfriend's flat, and with relief already helping to soothe away my guilt, I climbed into my Ford Capri and headed towards Chelsea.

CHAPTER 2

My immediate problem, having settled myself in a rather dreary flat in a mansion block off the Kings Road, was how to break the news to Frank that I had left Charles. I knew I must behave as if I regarded our affair as lightly as he did if I were to avoid him haring off in fright. During my first week in London I considered endless approaches before a solution came to me. Whenever Frank paid a visit to our house in Easthampsted I had squeezed oranges to make juice for his breakfast. After much pen-sucking I wrote Frank what I thought was a suitably casual postcard: 'If you fancy some fresh orange juice, it's now being served at Flat 30, Brittain House, SW3, Love, Ginny.' I added a kiss at the bottom.

Once I'd posted it, I waited in fear and trepidation thinking, 'Oh God, how corny!' and wishing I hadn't sent it. But it worked. A week later, unable to resist seeing where I'd installed myself Frank rang the doorbell and our affair resumed on a new footing. We never discussed the reasons for my marriage break-up, as it was important to keep up the pretence that it had nothing to do with Frank. For the next two years I handled our relationship with as delicate a touch as I could muster, desperate not to frighten him away. Even as a child I had never given up easily when I wanted something.

1971 and 1972 were disastrous racing seasons for Frank. It looked as though he might have had his heyday with Piers in the Brabham. When Piers was driving he had been able to raise money without much difficulty, now, with every new season, it was becoming more of a struggle. He had embarked on 1971 with far too little sponsorship to run five cars and, as usual, when companies are underfunded and overspending, the firm lurched from one crisis to the next.

People say that there is no such thing as good or bad luck in motor racing. You get the results you deserve. Frank had nothing right in those days, so perhaps his lack of success was predictable, he never had good engineering and he could rarely afford top drivers. F1, meanwhile, was getting more competitive every year. Frank admits that he had no idea how to handle his limited finances in those early years. He always wanted to spend money on more modifications. Better this and better that, but it didn't work. He didn't get the results, and not getting the results meant that the next season he didn't get the sponsorship. The situation was in danger of spiralling out of control.

I had unswerving faith in Frank. It never occurred to me that he would go under. Some day I was convinced he would come good. But my view of the future was very vague, I could not visualize exactly what 'coming good' would entail. I just believed that one day he would find it easier to keep going.

For some time Frank had been living with his old friend Charlie Crichton-Stuart and his girlfriend Jenny whenever he was in England. He enjoyed city life and would have liked a place of his own. But he certainly wasn't going to put his head in a noose by moving in with me and I knew better than to suggest it.

After I left Charles, I had been interrogated by my father as to my reasons, which had been a bit of an ordeal. I had shrunk from bringing up the subject of Frank and had led him to believe that the break-up was due to incompatibility. Somehow he restrained himself from saying 'I told you so'. Instead he gave me the verbal equivalent of a smack on the wrist for being a silly girl, and loaned me the money to buy myself somewhere to live. I found a maisonette in Rawlings Street behind Harrods and to help pay the bills took a job as a Girl Friday with a firm of interior designers.

Now that we both lived in London Frank spent more time with me, but his visits were still erratic and unpredictable. I grew accustomed to hearing his code of three rings on the doorbell at two a.m. and to watching him depart again at six or seven a.m. I was pretty certain that there were other women in Frank's life. I was not particularly outraged by the idea. It was pretty standard behaviour in those 'liberated' days in London, but not knowing what competition I was up against made me nervous. My feelings for him had never wavered but his for me seemed as mercurial as ever.

There came a point after a few months when I thought, 'There has got to be a different way of going about this.' I decided to offer something that 'the others' didn't. I would look after his comforts. If I offered to wash his knickers and his socks, cook him some nice meals, and lend him a fiver now and again then perhaps I would be in with a chance. He seemed to like it. He liked it possibly better than he felt was healthy for his preferred single status and it made him itchy. He would stay regularly for a few nights, then suddenly I could sense him thinking, 'Hang on a minute – she's getting her claws in' and he would disappear for three weeks. But slowly I made progress. He started to leave his sponge bag and a few clothes around the flat. I surveyed them like trophies, pondering my next move.

My girlfriends thought I was mad and put it down to masochism. 'It's no use talking to Ginny. She likes being kicked in the teeth,' was a comment I heard more than once. It wasn't true, but I was determined. I wanted Frank, and if that meant making myself useful to him then so be it. I cooked him meals at all hours of the night. I would spend my last pound on fillet steak and rush home from work to make his favourite banana *brûlée* only to have him not turn up. I would lend him my car – his own had long since been sold to pay company debts – and when he returned it empty of petrol three days later I would smile sweetly and never dream of asking where he had been. The more he pushed off, the more I wanted him. The more casually he treated our relationship, the more I fought to keep his interest.

Looking back now I am amazed how I stuck with it when there was so little comeback. I was as dogged in my pursuit of Frank as he was in his quest for Grand Prix success. Perhaps it was because up until then I had been rather spoiled and was used to getting what I wanted. I don't think I would have the same tenacity or tolerance of Frank's antics today.

It helped that Frank's charm was as strong as ever. Whenever I felt a little peeved he would smile and put his arm around me and sweet-talk me out of my suspicions. His gift of the gab was always his strongest weapon, in business and with me. He was brilliant at confusing the issue. I'd mention a rumour I'd heard about some woman and he would simply confound me with words. I couldn't counter his arguments at all. But it was a game we were playing. From Frank's point of view what we had was not a friendship. It was strictly a man-woman affair. I sometimes wondered whether being brought up in a totally male environment made it difficult for Frank to relate to women as human beings. He certainly liked their company, but he also seemed terrified of the power they wielded and of the way they could tie a man down and clip his wings, as was happening to most of his bachelor friends.

By the 1972 season Frank had abandoned his F2 ambitions and was concentrating entirely on F1, running two Marches with Henri Pescarolo and Carlos Pace as the team drivers. The disasters continued unabated: barely a race seemed to go by without an accident or an engine blowing up. Henri Pescarolo in particular seemed jinxed that season, crashing time after time and failing to score a single world championship point. Miraculously Frank managed to talk enough money out of different companies to struggle on.

He had decided in 1971 that if he was to have any future in F1 he would have to start constructing his own cars. In this venture he was offered sponsorship from Politoys, the model car firm, and with that finalized he started looking for premises with the room and facilities for manufacture. In February 1972 he moved out of Bath Road into a new industrial unit in Bennet Road, Reading. Building it took months longer than it should have done but by July 1972 the first Williams-constructed F1 car, to be known as the Politoys FX3 was ready. It made its entrance – and exit – in the British Grand Prix at Brands Hatch. Henri Pescarolo crashed the car in the opening laps – completely destroying it. It was the first time I saw Frank come back looking physically grey after a race.

Frank's financial troubles in 1972 coincided with a boom in the property market. Out of curiosity I had my maisonette valued one day and discovered that in nine months it had doubled in value to around £23,000. I realized that if I sold it I would be able to buy myself another cheaper flat in a less smart area of London and use some of the profit to boost Frank's income with a loan. I wasn't being entirely altruistic. I reckoned it would do my prospects with Frank no harm at all to push a few thousand quid his way in his hour of need.

Within weeks I had acted on my impulse and the maisonette in Rawlings Street was sold. Initially I loaned Frank £4,000 which I borrowed from the bank against the security of the sale contract. I thought it would help tide him over until he got more sponsorship. Practically all his own possessions had been sacrificed in the same cause – his watch, his car, his stereo system, even most of the furnishings in his flat. If he had no money he had on occasion paid his mechanics with watches and clothes. My £4,000 was gratefully accepted. Over the next few weeks as crisis followed crisis yet more of my profit was diverted to Frank.

With the date for my departure from Rawlings Street approaching, I realized with alarm that when I had paid back the bank loans I would have only £11,000 left. It looked as though a move from SW3 to SW10 was in prospect. Frank too was about to become homeless since Charlie and Jenny Crichton-Stuart were moving house. In a weak moment one night he suggested that we should look for somewhere to rent jointly. I leapt at the idea. It was what I had been hoping for all along but I would never have had the nerve to propose it myself. I was so lacking in self-confidence in my relationship with Frank that I had never even offered him a key to my flat. I felt it would have seemed presumptuous on my part.

I acted quickly before he could have second thoughts and at the end of 1972 we moved into a cottage at Old Windsor which we rented from Gordon Spice, the saloon car driver. I hardly dared believe it. At last I was officially living with Frank.

I did not stay thrilled for long. At times the arrangement scarcely merited the description of living together. Frank was an intermittent lodger. During 1973 he had a new sponsorship from the Marlboro cigarette company who adopted us as their junior team and the Italian Iso car manufacturers. The Iso-Marlboro was Frank's second attempt at being a constructor but it was not much more successful than the first. Despite a new engineer and two new drivers, Howden Ganley, and 'Nanni' Galli, the Iso-Marlboro ran into constant problems. First 'Nanni' Galli's promised sponsorship didn't materialize, then Iso turned out to be in financial difficulty and were not making their sponsorship payments on time. Then the mechanics wanted paying and there was nothing to pay them with . . . Fortunately, Marlboro supported Frank well beyond the call of their contract and he saw out the season by the skin of his teeth.

Trying to keep everything afloat took up not only all Frank's mental energy but most of his waking hours. With a Grand Prix every two or three weeks he was rarely at the cottage for longer than two days at a time.

I had left my job when we moved and spent my new-found free time trying to create as nice a home for Frank as I could on the limited funds available. At least when he did appear I hoped he might be able to relax and unwind in comfortable surroundings. It was a mistake; after a while I sensed that Frank was finding all this domesticity claustrophobic. While one part of him liked having his laundry done and his meals cooked and the bath cleaned out after him, another part found it terrifying. He felt tied down and restricted.

It came to a head several weeks after we had moved in when a friend informed me that she had seen Frank eating in a London restaurant with a pretty girl. I challenged him, feeling by this time that I had established some sort of rights. Frank denied the whole thing but I could tell he was brooding about it, and he became very withdrawn. One morning, a day or two later, he came out of the bathroom after he had finished shaving. 'Ginny I just don't fancy this,' he said, and walked out of the house.

When, after a few days he had still not returned I was devastated. Slowly however my unhappiness changed to anger and my anger to fury. I had been used. How dare he treat me like this? All the time we'd been together he'd had it all his own way. I had done everything in my power to please him while he had made no concessions at all. I paced around the house, my mind in turmoil. The wardrobe door was open and a couple of his expensive white shirts – lovingly ironed by me – caught my eye. I fetched a large pair of scissors from the kitchen and attacked the shirts, cutting out the arms with angry sweeping cuts. Then I did the same with one of his best suits. I didn't pause to examine my motives but steadily continued until I had amputated the limbs of every one of his garments. Then very coolly I folded everything back together so that my sabotage didn't show, packed all his clothes into a large box and posted them to his factory in Reading.

I felt that I had come to the end of my tolerance. No one can go on banging their head on a brick wall for ever. After posting the parcel I changed all the locks on the doors and set about planning a new life for myself. I would go back to London, perhaps get another job in interior design and turn my back for ever on being Frank Williams doormat.

I was still in this frame of mind when, early one evening, I became aware of the sound of music outside the cottage. Or rather the sound of unmelodious caterwauling. Looking out of the window I was confronted by Frank and Howden Ganley, his new driver, arm in arm on the lawn, serenading me with stupid songs and generally playing the fool. It was typical of Frank to bring someone along for moral support. He probably thought I wouldn't create a scene if Howden was there. I unlocked the door and let them in as it seemed the only way to stop the music hall performance. Frank was obviously trying not to laugh but I stayed very icy and asked him what he wanted. He said he had come around to see if there was anything left for him to collect. He wandered casually around the house, and seemed in no hurry to go even when he discovered his wardrobe was empty. After a while Howden became fidgety and embarrassed, which was hardly surprising. 'Howden, you can get going now. I'll see you tomorrow,' Frank said with a grin. Poor Howden didn't need telling twice.

Frank sat down as though he'd never been away and said nonchalantly, 'What's for supper gal?'

I could hardly believe my ears. I had known other people who evaded reality, but never anyone to match Frank.

'I haven't made any supper,' I said frostily.

Frank leaned back on the sofa and surveyed me thoughtfully. 'What are you planning to do?'

'I'm going back to live in London,' I was desperately trying not to meet his eyes in case my resolve weakened.

'Oh,' said Frank. 'Well. It'll be okay if I stay here in the meantime won't it?'

Frank obviously felt he was reinstated at the cottage and I was powerless to do much about it. I didn't like emotional scenes and I did not want a blazing row with him but I was determined that our relationship was not just going to resume in the same old rut as before. For the next few days I steadfastly resisted all his efforts to charm his way back into my affections.

A week later Frank came back from the office early one evening. 'Um. Ginny?' he said hesitantly, 'I've been thinking. Why don't you look for a house a bit nearer to the new factory at Reading for us.'

He caught me by surprise. I looked at him startled and was lost.

'That's a good idea,' I said, and we both smiled rather sheepishly. I felt that some sort of breakthrough had been made. From now on we would view each other a little differently.

I wasted no time in picking up the latest copy of *Country Life* to look at the property ads. Despite our lack of income, I had quite grand ideas, and among the classified ads at the back I saw just what we wanted. 'To Let – Drake House. A furnished detached property in a small village five miles south of Reading.'

Life is really extraordinary. At a time when rentals in that area were very rare, here was this house, just a short drive from Frank's new factory, staring me in the face like a gift from the gods. We went over to Mortimer, the village in question to inspect it and found it perfect for our needs. No furniture to buy, plenty of quiet countryside for Frank to do his running, and a rental I could just about afford. At the end of 1973 we moved in.

I think of that move as a milestone in our life together. In Mortimer, Frank started to spend much more time at home. If he wasn't away racing we would spend our evenings curled up close together in a comfortable muddle on the sofa, reading, watching the telly, or listening to music.

I'm sure Frank did not consider for a moment that he had succumbed to domesticity. It was against his nature to do anything so conventional. Perhaps, for his own benefit, or perhaps for the outside world, he liked to keep up the illusion that he was answerable to no one and had no responsibilities. He had enjoyed being a fancy-free bachelor for too long to change overnight. He still played his cards close to his chest, hating me to know his whereabouts. He would seldom warn me that he was going away till the day he was due to leave and would make endless excuses as to why he couldn't leave a telephone number, so I was very far from feeling secure.

But for the first time he started to tell me that he loved me. And he never left home again.

CHAPTER 3

I was still at finishing school in Monte Carlo when I saw my first Formula One race. The headmistress called us together one morning and announced, 'You are all going to the Monaco Grand Prix.' It was supposed to be one of the highlights of our year abroad. We bought our tickets and trooped down to the circuit – a lot of giggly sixteen-year-olds looking for excitement and glamour. But we were terribly disappointed. We weren't in a grandstand but down in the crowd and all we saw were the tops of people's heads and all we heard was the roar of the engines as invisible cars flashed past. It poured with rain the whole time. I learned afterwards, with complete indifference, that Graham Hill had won and as we made our way back to the school, soaked to the skin I thought, 'My God. How boring.'

I did not see another Formula One race until March 1973 when Frank decided to bring me out of the closet and take me along to the Race of Champions at Brands Hatch. I soon discovered that being on the pit wall was a much better deal than being squashed in among the throng. This time I saw it all; the cars coming in for wheelchanges, all the mechanics frantically buzzing about and other team-members doing the time-keeping. I was right there among the action. It was the day I glimpsed for the first time what it was that inspired Frank about motor racing. I watched him during the race as he sat, his ears masked by protectors, intently filling in his lapcharts, noting down the relative positions of the cars every time they passed the pits in a screaming blur of noise. Over all the years that I was to watch him at Grand Prix races, his face, as he concentrated on these lapcharts, never betrayed any emotion. You would never know from his expression whether his cars were running first and second or were on fire in the pits.

On this occasion Howden Ganley retired with wheel failure but Tony Trimmer in the second Iso-Marlboro wended his way through the field to finish fourth. I had never seen anyone so engrossed as Frank that afternoon. I'm sure if I had approached him during the race he would not have recognized me. Only after Tony had taken the chequered flag did he allow his face to break up into a big beam. That fourth was one of his better results.

The tension he felt during racing was so great that Frank never ate on race and practice days. Not a thing passed his lips, not even a cup of tea, until the action had finished. Perhaps an obsession as strong as Frank's is infectious. Whatever the reason, I was bitten by the F1 bug that day. The excitement, the buzz held me enthralled and has done ever since.

Despite Howden Ganley's retirement, the Williams cars performed well enough in the Race of Champions to make me think that perhaps Frank was on the verge of making a breakthrough. But I was over-optimistic. Tony Trimmer's fourth place was to be the best result the team had all season.

I was by now aware that Frank's vocabulary did not include the word budget. He loved motor racing to the extent of taking desperate and often unthought-out measures to keep the team running to the next race. What ready money he did have was always spent on the most immediate requirement with no thought to the huge mounting debt. This resulted in our being hounded by many creditors, among them our unfortunate landlord.

When we moved to Mortimer, I had been confident that I could take care of paying the rent. I was fortunate in having as my grandfather a clever man called Herbert Berry who had invented the first imitation coal effect fire, 'The Magicoal'. His grandchildren had all benefited financially from this invention and since the age of sixteen I had received an allowance from the Berry Trust which was administered by my father. It was not a regular or predictable income but I used to get fairly substantial share bonuses and, about twice a year, a nice little cheque for five hundred or a thousand pounds would land on my doorstep. I had thought this would easily cover the rental of £120 a month for Drake House. What I had not bargained on was my father's reaction to the news that I was living with the infamous Frank Williams.

I had avoided telling my parents about Frank for as long as I could but decided to come clean when we moved to Mortimer. They were dismayed. In their eyes Frank seemed an even less suitable match than Charles.

Frank had no intention of presenting himself for inspection to my parents. On several weekends when I was living in London he had turned up at Rawlings Street to find that I was planning to go to my parents' house for Sunday lunch. He always saw this as an opportunity to borrow my car and used to suggest that he drop me off at Wentworth and return to collect me later in the afternoon. Frank's habit of leaving me on my parents' doorstep, speeding back up the drive in a flurry of gravel, only to return several hours later and hoot the horn outside the front door did nothing to endear him to them. My mother would have appreciated a modicum of polite social behaviour. I made endless lame excuses on Frank's behalf.

But it was realizing what I had done with the profits from the Rawlings Street maisonette that really infuriated my father. Although I had repaid the original loan of £11,000 to the Berry Trust he soon put two and two together and realized where the profit had gone. It only took a small leap of imagination for him to realize that if the Rawlings Street money had gone Frank's way then my Berry Trust income was probably being channelled in that direction as well. He never discussed it with me. It had always been an unwritten rule when I was growing up that you didn't talk about money – it was socially unacceptable. So he didn't say, 'Well you won't be getting any more money to give to that man!' but from the moment he discovered my misdemeanour, the well dried up. That was how members of our family knew they were out of favour with the Berry Trust. You didn't hear anything official. You just suddenly didn't get any cheques.

I did have a personal allowance of about £30 a week which continued to be paid but that was it. We had no other income – it never occurred to Frank to draw a salary. The weekly rental was £30 so if I was rash enough to buy food there wasn't enough left for the rent. I did pay whenever I could but it was an erratic 'whenever,' and it wasn't long before our landlord joined the queue of people hammering at our door. When I spotted his car approaching I would rush to lock the door and hide upstairs until he gave up and drove away.

The telephone was always being cut off at the factory and often it was disconnected at Drake House too. For months on end Frank's 'office' was the telephone box down the street from the factory. On it he set up new sponsorship deals, interviewed potential staff and assured creditors that their cheques were in the post. It was hard luck on any locals who wanted to make a call. I didn't dare tell my parents that the phones were cut off. It was outside the realms of their experience. My mother would complain that she hadn't been able to get through to me and I would say in an exasperated voice, 'Oh not again. I don't know what's the matter with our line. I keep reporting it and they just don't seem able to trace the fault!'

People who were owed small amounts often had less patience than the big creditors and soon county court judgements started to be taken out against the company. One day I went round to the factory and discovered that the bailiffs had been in and taken all the desks and chairs out of the office against an outstanding bill. I was horrified but Frank was quite offhand about it. 'It's no big deal,' he insisted, amused at my sense of disgrace. Over the next couple of years, I was to become as blasé as he was about the confiscations.

How Frank paid his mechanics during this period I never understood. They were amazingly loyal in the face of adversity. Sometimes it would be weeks between their pay cheques, though £20 or £30 would always be rustled up in the event of anyone threatening to leave. Why they showed such fortitude was a mystery to me. Like Frank they all seemed to regard the company as their baby and felt that they had to stick with it, but the supermarket bill still had to be paid every Friday night and those with families to feed must have found it a struggle. Sometimes the pressure from their wives, who didn't hold Frank Williams (Racing Cars) in the same affection as they did, caused them to make a stand.

Whenever the situation looked truly desperate and Frank feared he was about to lose his entire workforce he would clown about on the factory floor, teasing everybody. On one occasion, learning that a protest was imminent, he stripped off until he was wearing only a smile and a peaked cap and walked into the workshop demanding to know what was going on. The impromptu cabaret took the tension out of the air and when he announced that everything was being done to make sure that the wages would be paid as soon as possible, they went back to work. It was very hard not to forgive Frank.

He always seemed confident that fate would look after him and usually she did. He had long ago cashed in his last road car and he was dependent on sponsors loaning him cars. This year no such benefactor was forthcoming. Frank was on the verge of finding himself without any personal transport when the company was loaned some Fiats by Enzo Ferrari, head of the mighty Ferrari company. He had taken a liking to Frank and must have been aware of the difficulties he was in. He was able to keep the cars running thanks to a fuel company with whom he had a sponsorship agreement.

In the middle of all this financial chaos, at a time when the telephones had been disconnected at the factory for two months and we were hanging onto our line at Mortimer by the skin of our teeth, Frank told me that he thought he needed a secretary. I could hardly believe my ears. Two days later I found myself opening the door to innocent interviewees obviously unaware of the company policy of not paying its employees.

Among the applicants was a tall blonde lady with startling blue eyes and an infectious giggle. I liked her immediately. Her name was Alison Morris and she had recently moved to Mortimer with her husband. She didn't have children and wanted something to fill in her time. Frank appointed her on the spot. Since the office at Bennet Road was currently without furniture or a telephone he diplomatically suggested that she work from our house 'while the office is being redecorated'. It wasn't until her first morning, as we sat chatting over a cup of coffee, that we learned that her husband was a high-powered executive with British Leyland. I was very embarrassed, knowing it was highly unlikely that she would be paid. I dreaded to think what her reaction would be when she discovered our world of disconnection and bailiffs.

I needn't have worried. When, a few weeks later, she moved into the office at Bennet Road she summed up the situation at once and metaphorically rolled up her sleeves to do something about it. Within a short time Alison was one of Williams most ardent supporters. There was very little that defeated her. Her sense of humour and her natural air of authority were soon persuading hard-bitten bank managers into parting with the money to pay our most pressing bills. She would sit it out for hours at the bank in order to borrow £10 or £15 for a consignment of nuts and bolts. If it prevented another visit from the bailiffs then, to Alison, it was worth it. She wasn't always able to forestall their arrival but in confrontations she proved more than a match for them. One day, when they arrived for the fourth time to impound the office furniture, she refused to get off her chair. 'I think it's most ungentlemanly of you to expect me to work on the floor,' she said. Defeated, they left her the chair.

Alison was not paid for some time but I never heard her complain. Instead, she used to invite Frank and me for three-course dinners at her house with her husband Bobby. They were most welcome. By this time even feeding ourselves was becoming a test of my ingenuity. If I had paid the rent we couldn't eat and if we ate I couldn't pay the rent. One day, when I had simply exhausted every other possibility, I went into the Mortimer village shop and asked if I could open an account. I don't know how I had the nerve. I was so overwhelmed when they said yes that I blindly grabbed the nearest items in the freezer which turned out to be three enormous packets of frozen beans. We ate them for dinner for the rest of the week.

Our constant financial embarrassment meant I was never able to return Alison's hospitality but she didn't seem to mind. During those weekly evening chats over dinner Frank and Bobby developed a friendship which was to bear unexpected fruit years later when the truck and bus division of British Leyland sponsored the team in 1980.

The debts and the seemingly endless line of irate creditors weighed more heavily on my conscience than they did on Frank's. If things got too bad Frank would simply take off for a run. He was increasing his mileage steadily and tried to run at least six miles a day now. It was during our time at Mortimer that his running turned from an occasional pastime into a serious hobby. The countryside around the village was lovely – true rural Berkshire with pretty red-brick Georgian farmhouses set among gentle rolling hills. The roads had little traffic and most evenings as soon as he arrived home Frank would don his tracksuit and trainers and set off down the lane with Sam our new black labrador puppy running alongside him keeping him company. While he relaxed after his run Frank would often talk over business problems with me. Many an evening was spent cuddled up together on the sofa discussing the latest company crisis. Afterwards, I would lie awake in bed worrying myself sick. Frank, in contrast, had the ability to get into bed, close his eyes, and go straight off to sleep. He almost seemed to thrive on catastrophes, while they felt to me like the end of the world.

There could hardly have been a more inopportune time for me to become pregnant. But fate dictated otherwise. Maybe my subconscious also played a role. I was twenty-seven years old. My friends were all having babies and in my insecure moments I had sometimes wondered if a baby might not put a seal on our relationship. I broke the news to Frank at the end of 1973.

He was silent for a while but his expression as the news sank in spoke louder than words. I could almost hear him thinking, 'My God she's pulled that old trick on me. I wouldn't have expected her to do that.'

He wasn't pleased, but he wasn't particularly displeased either. There was no big scene. For the first couple of months he adopted an ostrich-like policy towards my pregnancy. It was the way he always dealt with situations he couldn't alter. But in the New Year, as I started to get bigger he would give me gentle pats on the stomach and say with a grin, 'I could get used to this idea.' I was getting used to it myself. We started to talk about boys' names. There was no question in Frank's mind of it being a girl.

Then one day early in 1974 when I was four-and-a-half months pregnant the dream collapsed. Frank was away and I was sitting watching television when a violent pain seized me. I knew at once it was something to do with the baby and struggled to the phone only to realize we had just been cut off again for non-payment. Somehow I staggered down the road to some neighbours. They took one look at me and decided not to wait for an ambulance, I was loaded into the back seat of their car and they drove me to the hospital. It was a painful and interminable night and at some stage during it I lost the baby.

I discharged myself the next morning. I hated the hospital atmosphere and wanted to get home. Frank came in to collect me, seeming at a loss for words. I was very upset and Frank has always found it difficult to cope with emotions, whether they are other people's or his own. This time he was faced with both at the same time. I wanted him to say something to help me, but I didn't know what. Because he hadn't particularly wanted the baby, I suspected that he might be pleased that it was gone. But I couldn't bring myself to ask him if it was so. We travelled home in miserable silence.

Years later Frank told me that although he had been terribly sorry for me he had no idea how he could help console me. He said he decided that morning that the best contribution he could make to my welfare would be to ensure I became pregnant again as quickly as possible!

I think Frank was surprised at his own disappointment over the miscarriage and the realization that now he would have no son. He had just been getting used to the idea and from that time on we both accepted that having children was to be a part of our life together.

My mother came over to see me when she heard the news. She told Frank disapprovingly, 'I don't know how you can expect her to hold onto a baby when you're not married.'

Flawed though her logic was, I understood her despair at my way of life. She could not possibly feel happy about the fact that her eldest daughter was living in sin, in some rented house with the telephone cut off, and the landlord banging on the door for his money. There was nothing that could make her look kindly on a man who had inflicted this upon her daughter!

It took me quite a long time to get over the miscarriage. I felt a need to mourn and there was nothing to help me. No grave, nothing to remember the baby by. I went for long walks and dug up clumps of snowdrops and replanted them in the garden at Drake House, making little floral memorials. I seemed to cry incessantly. I tried to keep my depression from Frank fearing, perhaps unfairly, that he would interpret it as weakness. He was away a lot anyway now that the new season had started. Instead, I leaned on Alison and Susie.

In some ways my life and Susie's continued to mirror each other. She had divorced and remarried and was living with her new husband Hilary at Windsor but in much more established fashion than me. I sensed that she was as appalled as my mother by my lifestyle, but tactfully she kept her opinions to herself.

Gradually the pain retreated and when four months later I found I was pregnant again I started once more to look to the future. Frank's obvious pleasure at my news was an unexpected bonus.

On 15 August 1975 Frank was leaving for the Austrian Grand Prix and I came out of the kitchen into the hall to kiss him goodbye. I always hated him going away and usually burst into tears, which he found hugely funny. I put my face up for a kiss, but he put his arms on my shoulders and held me away from him. He said slowly, 'I think it would be a good idea if we got married. What do you think?'

I cannot believe that Frank ever had any doubts about what I would think. I was ecstatic. I flung my arms around him and jumped up and down with joy. Since my divorce from Charles had come through after two years of separation I had hoped at the back of my mind that it might one day come to this but it had always been rather a forlorn hope. Most people's assessment of Frank was that he was not the marrying kind and I understood their point of view.

He hugged me goodbye. I disentangled myself from around his neck and allowed him to pick up his briefcase. 'You'd better organize it,' he said, opening the front door. 'Fix a date. You can tell me the arrangements when I get back.'

I wanted it done as soon as was humanly possible. I wasn't going to give him a chance to change his mind. I enlisted the help of Dave Brodie, always known as Brode, one of Frank's oldest friends.

'Could you help me fix it for Tuesday?' I asked.

'Is that possible?' he said doubtfully.

I had done my research. 'Yes, but you need a special licence and it costs £8. Could you lend us the money?'

'Yes of course,' Brode grinned. 'As long as we're invited.'

I hugged him gratefully. I had nothing in the bank and all the cash in the house added up to only £30. I knew because I had earmarked it for our landlord. Now I decided to spend it instead on the wedding ring. Even if I had to get married in jeans I did not want a cheap ring. The possibility that I might want to replace it one day if we hit better times appalled me. I thought, 'To hell with it, I am going to go up to London and buy the ring that I will wear for the rest of my life.' As for the rent, I would adopt Frank's policy and worry about that after the wedding.

I chose a narrow ring of three entwined 18-carat gold strands. On the same day Brode returned with the news that the registry office in Reading was booked for two p.m. on Tuesday 20 August.

Late on Sunday night Frank returned from the Austrian Grand Prix full of news of the race. Merzario had retired with fuel pressure trouble and our new driver, Jacques Laffite, although his car was still running, had not completed enough laps at the finish to be classified. Having informed me of all this Frank helped himself to a bowl of cereal. It seemed to have slipped his mind that he had asked me to arrange our wedding.

Tentatively while he was still eating I broached the subject, 'Um, Brode's booked the registry office.'

Frank looked up blankly. Then the penny dropped. 'Oh. When?'

'In two days. Tuesday. Is that all right?'

'Yes, fine,' Frank nodded vaguely and returned his concentration to his cornflakes, apparently unperturbed that he had just two nights left as a free man.

I let my mother know about the wedding the day before the ceremony. Her reaction was immediate, 'You must be pregnant.'

'No, certainly not,' I lied, indignant at her assumption that Frank could have no other possible motive for marrying me.

I planned a lunch for us and the Brodies on Tuesday at 12.30 following which we would go down to the registry office. Brode and his wife Kath were to be our witnesses. For the lunch I had decided that everything should be white. On the centre of the kitchen table (we didn't possess a dining table) there was a big arrangement of white flowers sent by Susie. The tablecloth was white, as were the napkins and candles. I even carried the theme through to the main course, chicken in cream sauce.

Kath and Brode arrived early and we sat down to wait for Frank. At one o'clock just as we were all shifting nervously in our chairs, thinking that the groom had done a bunk, the phone rang.

'Ginny? *What* time are we meeting at the registry office?'

'Two o'clock Frank. Aren't you coming for lunch?'

'No. I'm sorry. I'll have to leave it. I'm running late at the factory. I'll see you there.'

It was typical.

I wasn't upset so much as worried. I prayed this wasn't a sign of cold feet. I really didn't care about the lunch as long as Frank turned up for the wedding.

He did. We were married at ten minutes past two with Kath and Brode as the only guests. It wasn't done in quite the style of my first wedding. Instead of a Nina Ricci dress I wore a cream silk shift to disguise my four month pregnancy. And there were no Constance Spry flowers. They had asked at the registry office if we wanted fresh flowers but I said no we couldn't afford it. As a substitute they supplied a dusty plastic arrangement. It drooped wanly in front of us as the registrar, a disapproving looking man with awful thyroid eyes, glumly intoned the words of the wedding ceremony. I wasn't sure if I wanted to laugh or cry but Frank seemed unaffected by the bizarre surroundings. He repeated his vows clearly and solemnly with his eyes fixed on mine and I thought, 'He means it!'

It was all over in minutes. Frank likes to say that he left the factory for the registry office at five minutes to two and was back at the factory at two-thirty. It could well be true. He looked very subdued when we came out. He gave me a brief kiss, glanced at his watch and said, 'Okay. I'm off back to the office. I'll see you later.'

Kath and Brode looked incredulous. Being unconventional was all very well but I think they felt that a groom who didn't appear for the wedding lunch and then disappeared before the reception was carrying it a bit far. We all looked uncertainly at each other for a moment and then burst out laughing. I genuinely thought it was funny. I knew I couldn't ever complain about such behaviour because when it came down to it, this was what drew me to Frank. What other people saw as his faults were, for me, part of his attraction. I thrived on the way that he kept me on my toes, on the knowledge that I could never, ever be sure of him. If he had been the archetypal perfect lover, solicitous, unselfish and at my beck and call, I would have felt suffocated. I knew myself well enough by now to realize that what I sought in my relationships was uncertainty and excitement rather than contentment. That was my perverse quirk. Being unpredictable was Frank's. As quirks go they were pretty compatible.

After Frank's departure Kath took me out for tea in Henley as a substitute for a wedding reception. I spent an hour happily chatting with her and reflecting on my new name. I felt absurdly pleased with myself. Mrs Williams. I liked the sound of it.

Nothing much changed in our lifestyle with marriage. I had not expected it to. The one noticeable difference was that Frank was terribly quiet for several days after the ceremony. There was much less wise-cracking, fewer tales of the happenings at work. One evening, worried that some new calamity might have occurred at the factory that he was keeping from me I asked him if anything was the matter. He looked at me with a schoolboy grin, and shook his head.

'It's just that I'm bloody terrified of being married,' he said. 'I've never been as scared of anything in my whole life!'

I enjoyed the rest of my now legitimate pregnancy. The only sour note came from our landlord who had taken to making frequent tours of inspection of his house. He made no attempt to disguise his dislike of us. His disapproval had been initiated by our tardiness with the rent – at times we had been four or five months behind – but it was compounded by my pregnancies and by his discovery of Sam, the labrador. Since under the terms of the tenancy we were supposed to have neither dogs nor children he became very irate. It was obvious that he wanted us out. I had some sympathy with his viewpoint but his way of going about it made life very unpleasant.

In February 1975 just four weeks before the baby was due, an eviction notice dropped through the letterbox. We had six weeks' notice to find somewhere new to live. I was terribly upset (it occurred to me at times that I had spent a large part of my life since I'd met Frank being terribly upset), but Frank took it all very lightly. I negotiated a six week extension to our notice and over the next few days I settled down, taking my cue from him. Something, I felt sure, would turn up.

On 22 February, the day Frank was due to leave for the South African Grand Prix, our first baby was born. Frank was terribly squeamish about anything connected with 'female plumbing' and I had no more desire for him to be with me during labour than he had. He would have been a liability in a delivery room. I was also extremely anxious to find out what sex our baby was before Frank did. He was absolutely set on the idea of having a son. I don't think he had ever considered that any other sort of baby was possible. I went through labour in absolute dread that I might do the unthinkable and present him with a daughter. The wives of Henry VIII must have felt much the same way during their labours. I had confided the pressure I was under to my obstetrician and I think he was nearly as pleased as me when at 3.30 in the afternoon he held up a squalling bundle and announced, 'It's a boy.'

I thought 'Thank God for that' and sank back in relief onto my pillow. I would not have to put it out on the hillside after all.

Frank had arranged to dash in to see us before he left for Kyalami and I was on tenterhooks waiting for him to arrive. I felt so proud of myself. They had taken the baby down to the nursery while I rested and the nurses said they would take Frank in to see his son before he came up to me. I sat up in bed, a big smile on my face, feeling terribly clever as I waited for him. At six o'clock the door opened and an ashen-faced Frank stumbled in. He grabbed the nearest chair, sat down and put his head between his legs. I was quite concerned.

'Frank, what on earth's the matter?'

'Oh I've seen him,' he said. 'I feel sick.'

I stared at him askance.

He squinted up at me, his face somewhere below the bed level. 'You look all right,' he conceded. Then he groaned again. 'God, I feel so ill. Oh it's revolting.'

It turned out the nurse who had taken Frank to see the baby had proudly opened the blanket so he could see every tiny inch of his offspring. It was a mistake. If she had allowed Frank only a glimpse of his little screwed up face he might have come through the ordeal but to have to witness the baby's bright pink wrinkled body with its tied-off stump of umbilical cord had finished him off. I have never understood why so many men are squeamish. Although Frank could be spellbound by the mechanism of some car engine he had an absolute phobia of confronting the internal workings of the human body.

He spent most of his allotted half hour with me with his head cradled between his knees, trying to fend off his nausea. He was so obviously relieved when it was time for him to buzz off to South Africa that I almost felt sorry for him. Almost but not quite. I was still pretty aggrieved on behalf of my poor baby.

Fortunately his looks improved rapidly over the next few days and by the time Frank returned to take me home from hospital a week and a half later they had both recovered from the shock of the birth sufficiently to make a fresh start to their relationship.

Frank drove us home from the hospital in Ferrari's loaned Fiat at 120 m.p.h. 'To give him a taste for speed,' as he put it. I didn't mind, I was a fast driver myself, and it felt appropriate. As if he'd been blooded.

I had wanted Frank to choose the baby's name and on the way home to Mortimer he announced his decision. He had always looked back on his own racing days as some of the happiest in his life and the friends he made then as the best he was ever likely to have. The baby would be christened in honour of two of those friends. His first name was to be Jonathan, after Jonathan Williams, who by employing Frank as his mechanic had helped him put his foot on the first rung of the motor racing ladder.

Our son's second name, said Frank, knowing that he did not need to explain, was to be Piers.

CHAPTER 4

*F*rank was quite taken with being a dad. The moment he arrived home in the evening he would tiptoe in to see Jonathan in his cot and make fond goo-goo noises at him. Not that he would ever have changed a nappy or fed him but he was terribly proud of this small person he had helped produce.

Thanks to the eviction notice I returned home from the maternity hospital with the baby knowing that we had only six weeks to find somewhere to live. I turned again to my old standby *Country Life*. Despite our dire financial straits I never considered that we might have to look for a semi-detached or a council house. What I fancied was a country residence, and once more my delusions of grandeur paid off.

In the March edition I spotted an advertisement for a house with a full-repairing lease near Basingstoke. It was rather far away from the factory – a good thirty minute drive – but it sounded lovely; an old Laundry House on the estate of Sir Michael and Lady Colman, of Colman mustard fame. I drove over to the offices of Knight, Frank and Rutley, the estate agents handling the property. They told me that about £8,000 worth of renovations were needed to make the house habitable and that the tenants would be expected to undertake the improvements and in return would only have to pay a peppercorn rent — about twelve pounds a week – for a seven-year lease.

I said, 'Oh perfect. We'll have that.'

The man behind the desk explained with an indulgent smile that it wasn't that simple.

'If you are interested we will arrange to interview you first on behalf of the owners. We, as their agents, will then make a short list of prospective tenants and *if* you are on that . . .' he managed to make it sound unlikely, 'then you may be called for interview by Sir Michael and Lady Colman.'

Suitably chastened I asked if I might go and see the Laundry House. It was an enchanting Victorian house built of red brick with mullioned gable windows. It stood on Malshangar Green in a tiny hamlet in the heart of the estate. Looking around I could see that a lot of work was needed and it was equally obvious that there was no way we could afford the £8,000 required to restore it. But I wanted it and Frank, trusting my judgement, put up no argument against it. He may have been swayed by the fact that it was situated near lovely landscaped parkland and approached by quiet twisty Hampshire lanes so once again it promised to be a wonderful place to run.

Somehow we bluffed our way through the selection interview and found ourselves with an appointment to meet Sir Michael and Lady Colman. Uncertain as to what reaction I would get, I had not admitted to having a baby so Jonathan was left at home with Alison while we were ushered in to the Colman's country house to be assessed.

Sir Michael and Lady Colman were installed in their drawing room wearing brave faces at the prospect of giving up their Saturday to cope with an invasion of would-be tenants. They had already interviewed several couples. Both of them were quite young – in their mid-thirties – and very pleasant but I felt uncomfortable as I answered their questions knowing we were there under false pretences. What they were looking for was a credit-worthy couple who would honour their contract to improve the house. What would they say if they knew that Frank didn't even have a personal bank account?

They asked Frank about his background and occupation and Frank said he ran a Formula One team. I could see from Sir Michael's face that he was completely confused. The Colmans were hunting, shooting and fishing people. He didn't have a clue what Formula One was.

'You won't be driving them around the estate will you?' he asked when he found out Frank was talking about racing cars. Frank said soberly, 'No, Sir Michael. I won't.' Then he added, 'I'd also better tell you that at the moment I don't have any money but I have every hope that that's going to change by the end of this year.' I squirmed with embarrassment, convinced that Frank had wrecked our chances.

As we were leaving, a very respectable and well-heeled looking couple turned up for their interview. I felt dreadful gloom and despair. 'Why on earth did you tell them we were connected with motor racing?' I asked Frank plaintively. I was convinced we had blown it. But we hadn't. Frank, as usual when he was trying to influence people, had known exactly the right thing to say. We learned later that the Colmans were won over not by Frank's racing involvement but by his honest approach. That evening the estate agents rang to say that Sir Michael and Lady Colman would be very pleased if we would come and live at the Laundry House.

I took Alison down to see our new home the next day terribly pleased with myself. I thought she would die laughing when she learned that we had undertaken to spend £8,000 on renovations. 'And it's just taken me half a day to get twenty pounds out of your bank manager,' she gasped. 'How are you going to do it?'

I had no idea how we were going to do it. We were supposed to put a kitchen in, and two bathrooms. Structurally, the Laundry House was reasonably sound but the walls and plaster required attention and it needed completely redecorating. Optimistically we got the builders in before we moved but they left after two weeks when they had not been paid. When Frank managed to come up with some money for them, they came back for a while. Then left again. Our relationship with them was to continue in this vein all year.

Our priority was to get a kitchen installed. Somehow we had to afford that. But the rest of the improvements would have to wait. We moved in during April and lived there in bleak conditions while the builders worked around us. I had no washing machine and had to take all the clothes to the laundrette in Reading, which with baby laundry meant a daily journey. I didn't mind, but when my parents found out they were horrified. My father insisted on presenting us with a washing machine. The idea of his daughter traipsing through the town with a bag of dirty nappies was just too 'Coronation Street' for him!

For a year we had no carpets. Although I was soon on first name terms with Judith, Lady Colman I could never bring myself to confess the real reason for our bare floorboards. I saw her looking at them in some surprise when she paid us a visit about six months after we moved in. On the spur of the moment I said in disgruntled tones:

'Do you know I ordered the carpet for this room four months ago. I'm having it dyed specially and it STILL hasn't come!'

I doubt she was fooled but she played along with it. We were to become good friends. In later years the Colmans became very interested in motor racing and in the eighties their son Joe came to work for Williams for two years.

Judith was the person who introduced me to the pleasures of gardening. She had a wonderful garden and passed me cuttings to put in our own garden at the Laundry House. In return I resurrected my flower arranging skills and helped her when she had a party or function at the house. Many aspects of living on the estate were wonderful and I look back on those times with some nostalgia. But there were sides to our life at the Laundry House that were not so agreeable, not least the fact that for a whole year we had virtually no furniture. Drake House had been let furnished, so all we had to bring with us were two sofas, which had come from my flat in Rawlings Street, our double bed, and some rather horrible cane and glass coffee tables, also from Rawlings Street, which stood next to the bed. I even had to borrow a cot for Jonathan. I tried not to let our spartan lifestyle get me down but occasionally the combination of broken nights with the baby and the constant worries over money got too much.

One morning I put a cup of tea down on one of the glass coffee tables. It was already loaded with a table lamp and a couple of books and the extra weight was just too much. The glass shattered and I burst into tears. Frank looked at me in amazement.

'There's no need to cry about it! It's only a piece of glass. We can replace a bit of glass.'

'No we can't,' I wailed. 'You always find some money to replace engines but you'll never ever replace a glass coffee table.'

It was true. At this stage it would have been the last thing Frank would have spent twenty quid on. When the funds were being distributed, Williams the company came first and Frank Williams the man (and his family) last. There just never seemed to be anything left over for us. Sometimes I felt there was never going to be any light at the end of the tunnel. Every time a little glimmer showed itself it was snuffed out.

At one time 1975 had looked as though it might be a turning point for the team, as unusually and almost by chance we had found ourselves with two very quick drivers. Frank had come home to Drake House one day shortly after we were married and announced that

Jacques Laffite was coming for an interview. Would I lay on a meal for him and his wife?

Business entertaining was always done at home in those days for the good reason that it was cheaper. I enjoyed it. It kept me involved in the company and meant I could offer an opinion about people Frank was considering employing, whether they were drivers, engineers or secretaries. Frank has always believed that women are good judges of character and would usually take note of my comments.

Jacques Laffite had quite a reputation – he had just won the European Formula Two championship. I had seen his wife Bernadette at race meetings. She was typically French, very pretty, chic and sophisticated. I worried what a well-off successful young couple like them would make of our rented, rather neglected accommodation. Drake House had looked increasingly shabby towards the end of our stay. Even with the landlord's furniture we hardly had enough chairs to seat four people. The garden was an utter wilderness. I had the lawn cut the day before the Laffites' visit, but it only seemed to emphasize the untidiness of the flowerbeds . . .

My anxiety was unnecessary. Both Jacques and Bernadette had a lively sense of humour and I quickly relaxed in their company. When Frank and Jacques disappeared to discuss business I dusted off my schoolgirl French and Bernadette and I talked happily until they returned.

I formed opinions of people quite quickly and usually categorized any potential employee as light, medium or heavyweight. Jacques Laffite was smaller than most drivers but I sensed at once he was a heavyweight.

I used to enjoy meeting racing drivers. They are a special breed. There is a magnetism and a vitality about them. They have the same kind of mystique as the matadors like El Cordobes had, which comes from flirting with death. These days, top drivers have achieved superstar status, and don't spend as much time around the company premises but in the mid-seventies I got to know most of our drivers and their wives socially, and several, like the Laffites became good friends.

Our other driver for 1975 was Arturo Merzario, a very good Italian driver – a lovely man, who used to walk around wearing a big cowboy hat. Like Jacques and most of the best racing drivers he was small, but as an employee he was another heavyweight. We were lucky to get such good drivers with our record of retirements and engine failures in the previous two seasons, but there weren't many seats available at the end of 1974 and we reaped the benefit. In most years drivers of their calibre could have gone somewhere better, but for 1975 they ended up with Frank.

By the end of the year I suspect both of them regretted it. There was no disputing that the Williams cars let them down. By 1975 Marlboro had pulled out of their sponsorship and Iso had gone bankrupt, so for the first time the car was known simply as the Williams. During the previous winter Frank had flown around looking for sponsorship for the team and for a new car, the FW04, and had managed to fund it with a lot of small deals. One of his backers was an Italian baby group Chicco which proved very fortunate for me as, in return for displaying their logo on the side of the car, we were partially paid in nappies and carrycots.

The funding was still insufficient to iron out the problems with the cars. Nothing went right. Time after time engine problems put paid to our chances. For the first time Frank started to show the strain, he would come back after some races looking drawn and grey after yet another engine had blown up. Every time it happened it meant a four figure bill. When he set off for a race I used to pray that the car might finish because if you finished, even if you were in twentieth position, you won a few pounds. More importantly it meant the engine was still running.

By now Frank's attempts to put together a car were becoming a bit of a joke in motor racing circles. Keith Botsford looking back on this period in his biography of Alan Jones describes Frank as, 'One of the game's all-time least successful constructors'. It was a saying amongst some of our previous drivers that one of the quickest ways to wreck your career was to drive for Williams. In spite of this, everyone in the game seemed very fond of Frank. As he walked into the pits at the British Grand Prix at Brands Hatch or Silverstone he was starting to get a cheer from the crowd. It was obvious they were longing to see him do well; he was everybody's favourite underdog. Even the other constructors were friendly towards him, probably because they didn't see him as a threat. If Frank had blown up two engines in practice someone like Ken Tyrrell would usually send one over and lend it to him for the race. Today, when constructors have contracts with the major engine manufacturers this would not be possible, but even if it were I don't think it would happen. The atmosphere in Formula One at that time was more friendly and less aggressive than it is now.

I was determined to watch the cars make their British debut under the Williams name in the Race of Champions at Brands Hatch.

Jonathan was only three weeks old but I discovered that the Norland nursery at Hungerford offered a babysitting service. For £4 a day they took Jonathan for the apprentice Norland nannies to practise on.

The Race of Champions took place only a week after the South African Grand Prix, which for us had resulted in Merzario retiring and Jacques finishing too far behind to be classified, so no one was too optimistic. But unexpectedly at Brands Hatch Merzario managed to finish seventh. It seemed a promising if modest achievement. I thoroughly enjoyed my day out, unaware that the storm clouds were closing in. Frank however was very conscious that the debts were now mounting beyond the stage where a call from the bailiffs was the worst threat we faced. It was starting to look as though the next visitor might be the Official Receiver unless there was a huge injection of funds from somewhere. Knowing the effect money worries had on me Frank tried to avoid revealing the scale of the problem until he could come up with a solution.

Then luck lent a hand. An Italian contact of Frank's, an engineer with Lamborghini, met a Canadian called Walter Wolf who expressed an interest in Formula One. The engineer suggested that Frank get in touch with him. He said there was a rumour that Mr Wolf had made a lot of money in North Sea Oil and was looking for somewhere to spend it. Ever the opportunist, Frank immediately sent Walter Wolf a couple of tickets for the International Trophy meeting at Silverstone in April and his gesture paid off when Walter turned up at the Williams pit with his wife. I had left Jonathan at the Norland nursery again – he was becoming quite a favourite there – and found myself being introduced to Walter and Barbara. Although I knew that they were potential sponsors I did not really appreciate the significance of their presence or know how much Frank was depending on being able to attract their backing.

I liked them. Walter was a very big heavy muscled, larger than life sort of man. He had a strong Austrian accent – the result of a European childhood. The main thing that struck me about his attractive wife was that she was rather too well-dressed for a Grand Prix meeting. She wore an elegant navy short-skirted suit and very high heels – she looked as though she was more accustomed to going to horse races than to motor racing circuits where most women dress casually. She told me that this was indeed her first ever visit to a Grand Prix. She realized her mistake and at later races she always wore immaculate jeans.

It was not the best meeting Frank could have chosen to impress a possible sponsor. Both the Cosworth engines blew up in practice and consequently in the race itself the FW03 was unable to start. I felt terribly embarrassed on Frank's behalf. How could you possibly ask people to back you when you couldn't even get your car onto the grid?

But something must have made an impression on Walter. He offered to pay for the engines to be rebuilt, and he and 'Barb', as he called his wife, continued to come to races through the year. Williams did have one brief moment of glory at the German Grand Prix in August when Jacques finished second behind Carlos Reutemann's Brabham. It was a bit of a fluke result. Most of the other cars had retired with punctures caused by the sharp stones used to construct the verges. But it was significant. It meant that we won about £5,500 and more importantly, we guaranteed our membership of FOCA for the following year. This ensured we would get team expenses paid for competing, a very significant benefit.

The team jubilation was short-lived. After Germany it was back to the old routine of 'retired' and 'also ran'. Disillusioned, Merzario left the team in June and the second car was rented to one driver after another. Despite our poor performances I still did not truly appreciate what desperate straits we were in, or how much Frank was pinning his hopes on Walter offering to fund him for the following year.

Motherhood was demanding most of my attention. Before the year ended I was pregnant again, and between my duties at home and the fact that we now lived over thirty miles from the factory I spent much less time at Bennet Road than before so was unaware of the sheer volume of the debts which were piling up.

Encouraged by Bernadette I made plans to attend the American Grand Prix at Watkins Glen in October. Bernadette was a practised international traveller. She informed me that America was *the* place to buy baby things – all the drivers' wives bought their children's clothes as well as their sheets and linen there. Somehow I talked Frank into letting me go. Maybe he felt that with what we already owed, what I could spend would be neither here nor there. The Norland nannies were delighted by the prospect of getting Jonathan for a whole week.

The Grand Prix was on the fifth of October. In the days leading up to it Bernadette and I shopped till we dropped. A little money from the Berry Trust had started trickling through again since Jonathan's birth. It meant I was able to buy some nice linen and watch and learn from Bernadette as she spent money with practised skill.

Watkins Glen is close to the Finger Lakes in Upper New York State – peaceful stretches of deep blue water where well-off city people take their weekend breaks. There are dozens of lakes, all lined with trees. Dotted around between the trees are wooden cabins, some of them built out on struts over the water. In the fall with all the maples around the lakes turning wonderful shades of red and gold it was breathtaking.

All the drivers and team managers stayed at a motel on one of the lakes called the Glen Motor Inn, which, although not luxurious, had a wonderful atmosphere. There was always someone around to talk to or have a coffee with. It was like a big informal social club for the Grand Prix circus. For four days I had a lovely time, happily unaware of the crisis about to happen at the track.

Bernadette and I arrived at the circuit on the morning of the Grand Prix in high spirits and went straight to the pits. We were met by sombre faces. Lella Lombardi, an Italian woman driver had rented the second car for this race, paying us a much needed £10,000. During practice that morning she had hit a crash barrier, breaking a valve spring in the process. Apparently not noticing the changed engine note she had blithely carried on driving until eventually the engine just fell apart. The whole thing was destroyed. The estimated cost of the rebuild was over £9,000.

Our smiles disappeared and Bernadette walked over to say a few words to Jacques who was cleaning his visor before going out for his warm-up lap. He asked her to spray some Optrex in his eyes. Most of the drivers used it to help keep their vision clear during a race. Neither of them noticed that by mistake she picked up the bottle of visor cleaning fluid instead of the Optrex. Seconds after she sprayed the stuff in his eyes Jacques doubled up in agony clutching his hands to his face. They rushed him off in an ambulance and Bernadette had hysterics, convinced, fortunately wrongly, that she'd blinded her husband for life.

It was especially ironic because Jacques had qualified quite well and had won what for us was an unusually good position on the grid. Frank's last straw-clutching idea was that Lella Lombardi could take over Jacques' car but it was not to be. Jacques looked more like a jockey than a racing driver. He took a smaller size in jeans than even Bernadette (which was a constant source of annoyance to her) and Lella was nowhere near as petite as Bernadette. Embarrassingly for her she totally failed to fit into Jacques' car and once again the dread initials DNS for 'did not start' appeared beside our name on the results sheet.

I knew that Walter had been helping to fund the team to some extent that year. It was only after America that I learned that a completely different proposition was up for consideration. It was an open secret now that Williams was in deep debt. Frank admitted later that the company liabilities stood at around £140,000. Not surprisingly Walter was not prepared to put in substantial funding only to see it swallowed to pay off existing creditors. He wanted to see his money working to improve the level of competitiveness of the car, not paying for other people's past mistakes. The deal he was offering Frank was radical. He would take over the liabilities in return for sixty per cent of the company.

After Watkins Glen, Frank put me in the picture and asked me what I thought of the idea. I didn't like it one bit. I bristled at the news that Walter planned to change the name of the team to Wolf-Williams. I felt I had a stake in Frank Williams (Racing Cars) myself by now. We spent hours discussing it.

After ten years Frank had no wish to give up control of his own company but he was a realist and, by the end of 1975 he knew that if Williams was to survive in any form he did not have much choice. Possibly the swaying factor was Walter's announcement that he had agreed to purchase all the cars and equipment from Lord Hesketh's team which had recently been wound up. The almost new Hesketh 308C car would form the basis of the FW05. It was a tempting carrot; a promising new car and funds to allow freedom of driver choice. It would mean an end to the rent-a-drive deals with no-hopers which had characterized too many of our races in the past.

One night at the end of November Frank went off on a long solitary walk around the lanes of Malshanger. Shortly after he returned home he telephoned Walter and agreed to sign. Frank Williams (Racing Cars) Ltd ceased to exist. In its place the Wolf-Williams team was born. One of the immediate casualties of the decision was a young man whom Frank had interviewed only weeks before and had just signed up to be Williams new chief engineer. His name was Patrick Head.

Due to the austerity of the decor at the Laundry House, Frank had taken to interviewing people at the Carlton Towers Hotel in London. It set a tone of luxury and wealth which he thought gave people a good impression – albeit the wrong one!

Patrick was one of several who succumbed to the Carlton Towers treatment and agreed to work for us. He was a well-qualified engineer with racing experience already, which had not always been the case with his predecessors. Frank had been quite hopeful that he might be the one to sort out our fuel system problems but now he had to tell him it was not to be. Walter planned to bring in a man called Harvey Postlethwaite from Hesketh as chief engineer. Harvey had designed the car which had launched James Hunt's career. Frank could only offer Patrick the choice of moving on or staying as Harvey's underling. Patrick chose the second option, a decision whose significance no one could have predicted at the time.

The immediate consequences of Walter's intervention in our lives were quite dramatic as far as I was concerned. There was an immediate and most welcome perk when I was invited to accompany the team to South Africa in March for the Grand Prix at Kyalami. Then, too, there was real money. For the first time since I'd met him, Frank was on a payroll and had a monthly pay cheque. All at once he was giving me money to go out and do the shopping and the word 'housekeeping' was added to my vocabulary. Frank's salary was around £25,000 a year which seemed like a fortune.

As soon as the first pay cheque was safely in the bank I rushed out to Conran and spent £50 on a kitchen table. We wouldn't have to eat off plates on our knees for one day longer. On the strength of that same pay cheque I also ordered the carpets I had told Judith I was waiting for. Not long afterwards the alterations and decorations were completed. The phone was reconnected. We got a second television. And at long last I put new glass in the coffee table.

Despite my unwillingness to let go of the company it did feel as though an enormous burden of worry had been lifted off our shoulders.

One of my extra luxuries was to arrange for a daily nanny to come in three days a week to help me with Jonathan as my second pregnancy approached its end. The summer of 1976 was scorchingly hot and, at times, I felt as though I had a huge internal blow heater running at full blast. I spent hours lying gasping in cold baths trying to cool down while the nanny, Frances, played outside in the sunshine with Jonathan. She was a sweet girl. I don't know how I would have managed without her. The Norland nursery was out of bounds to me now since Frank had bounced a cheque for £12 on them at the end of 1975.

I was of course hoping for another boy. Frank had left me in no doubt about his views on daughters. The previous year when my friend Susie was expecting a baby she had come to visit us and told us she was absolutely longing for a little girl. Frank had looked at her incredulously, 'I can't *imagine* anyone wanting a girl,' he'd exclaimed. So I knew what was expected of me.

On 22 July, one of the hottest days of the year, with the temperature in the nineties I went into labour and a few hours later gave birth to our second child. The doctor, knowing we already had a son, informed me with a big smile that we had a daughter. He was taken aback by my reaction.

'Oh no,' I wailed. 'Oh my God, what am I going to do?'

Poor Claire. I don't think she has suffered as a result of her less than enthusiastic welcome, but I still feel guilty about it sometimes. At that period of my life, in my blind devotion to Frank, I saw everything through his eyes and her arrival felt like a disaster to me too. Frank, as I had expected, was terribly disappointed. He thought it was the end of the world. She was not a contented baby and her constant crying did nothing to warm him to her. For a while, overwhelmed by the effects of childbirth and broken nights, I felt I had wrecked our family.

Then one day she started to smile at him. The effect on Frank was instantaneous. I was stunned at the swiftness of his change of heart. From that moment he was won over and she has been the apple of his eye ever since. Claire was a very pretty baby with blonde hair and very dark eyebrows and lashes and fabulous dark eyes – Frank's eyes. Now predictably Frank spoils her. He says to her, 'I didn't like you when you were a baby, Claire, but I'll make it up to you now – because you're so special.' She, like most daughters, worships her father and thinks he can do no wrong.

Once again I wanted Frank to name her, but he had only prepared boys' names and it was some time before he announced that he thought it would be nice to call her Claire after his mother. I was delighted. Not only did I like the name but it marked the healing of a rift which had existed between Frank and his mother for too many years. In our early years together I could never get him to talk about his mother. He had had very little contact with her since he had come down to London. I sensed there had been some big showdown with her at that stage.

After Jonathan's birth I had taken it on myself to make contact with her. I wanted my son to know his grandmother and I wanted her to meet her first grandchild. Frank had resisted my impulse, saying darkly that I was opening up a can of worms, but for once

I had not let myself be overruled. His mother had come down and stayed with us at the Laundry House and she and Frank started communicating again. It was an achievement I felt quite proud of.

It had been strange meeting her that first time. She travelled down by train from the north-east where she still lived and it was obvious to me from the first hour we met that she and Frank had absolutely nothing in common apart from a keen intelligence. She is quite different from him in looks, opinions and temperament. She told me what a difficult child Frank had been and how from the age of three he used to walk out of the house and disappear, and how the police once brought him back from miles away. She told me of his childhood obsession with cars. From his earliest days, his heroes, she said, were drivers – people who could make wheeled machines do as they wanted.

'I took him on a bus one day Ginny,' she said. 'He can't have been more than five years old and he just sat there staring at the bus driver as though he was looking at a ghost, his mouth open. When I asked him what the matter was, he looked at me and said, as though he was watching a *miracle*, "That man can *drive* this big bus Mum!"'

Frank's mother had got married again since she had last seen Frank – to another teacher. She had become a headmistress by the time of her retirement a few years previously. As I chatted to her about Frank and parenthood, I started to understand her motivation for sending Frank away. She had been determined that Frank should have the one thing that, in her eyes, could help him get his head above the crowd, a good education. The only way she could pay for it had been to work as a residential teacher, which meant Frank had to go to boarding school. She had found herself in the cleft stick of many single parent families and had struggled to do what she thought best in difficult circumstances.

I had uncharitably assumed that Frank's institutionalized childhood had been due to his mother not caring about him. Now I realized that she had cared, perhaps more than many mothers did, in her own way. She had certainly made sacrifices to bring him up as she thought best.

Years later, as she sat with Jonathan on her knee, looking at the bare floorboards in the Laundry House, I sensed her trying to comprehend Frank's chosen life of racing cars and comfortless homes. I doubted whether at that moment she felt her fight to educate him had been

70

worthwhile. Later we met her new husband, Uncle Tom, as he became known to us, and I think Frank was pleased that contact had been restored. Maybe understanding some of his mother's motives in sending him away helped him view her in a different light. To name his daughter after her conveyed his change of heart better than anything else could.

I found myself even less involved with the racing scene in 1976, partly because it was now mainly Walter's concern and partly because the two babies occupied most of my waking hours. But by the middle of the year I knew that all was not well in the Wolf-Williams camp. The new team was very far from covering itself in glory.

The team's driver was Jacky Ickx, Jacques Laffite having moved rapidly on to greener pastures when his potential was recognized by the up-and-coming French Ligier team. We parted on good terms. Before he left he gave Frank a photograph of himself inscribed *'Ton courage et ta détermination te conduiront aux plus grands succès'* (Your courage and determination will bring a lot of success for you). I felt he was being rather optimistic.

Jacky Ickx was the nicest, most charming of men, extremely good-looking and charismatic. He reminded me of Warren Beatty. The trouble was he no longer seemed hungry enough to make any impact in a less than competitive car.

Jacky's performances were not the sole cause of dissension in the camp but he was the first one to suffer its consequences. After he failed to qualify for the British Grand Prix in July, Walter stood him down – something quite unusual for a driver midway through the season.

In October it was the American Grand Prix again. I had decided on my first trip that Watkins Glen was my favourite place in the world and was determined to go again, so I wangled a ticket. It was on that trip that I became aware that the writing was on the wall for Frank too. I would have had to be nearly blind not to read it.

Patrick Head came with us. It was his first trip to Watkins Glen and we had all planned to stay, as we had the previous year, at the Glen Motor Inn with all the other teams. But Walter had other plans for us. We were informed bluntly on our arrival that we were to give up our rooms for some of Walter's entourage and move elsewhere.

We found ourselves miles from anywhere in quite the worst hotel I have ever stayed in.

Worse was to come. Since the departure of Jacky Ickx, Wolf-Williams had not had a steady driver. Merzario had returned for a few races but finding someone for the second car was a constant headache in mid-season when everyone reputable was signed up. Finally after a succession of back-outs by prospective drivers Frank ended up with an American driver, Warwick Brown.

Warwick Brown eagerly agreed to drive. I think he couldn't believe his luck. He'd never driven in a Grand Prix before. Patrick was assigned the double duty of collecting him from Rochester airport and buying in grocery supplies so we could feed ourselves in the hotel. On the way back from the supermarket Warwick took the wheel of the hire car, obviously eager to demonstrate his capabilities to Patrick. The hotel was situated up a fairly arduous track which was axle-deep in mud after the storm the previous night. At a critical moment Warwick lost control and the car plunged a hundred feet into trees and undergrowth before finally coming to rest. Mercifully neither Patrick nor Warwick was hurt, despite being hit by flying groceries, and they were able to crawl out of the wreck and struggle back to the hotel. The memory of them both standing at the door of our hotel room covered from head to foot in mud, milk and jam is one that will remain with me always.

On the race day itself the foul weather continued. The Glen was like a swamp. Merzario crashed, while miraculously Warwick managed a fourteenth position.

By now Frank was running seriously over budget – his financial management had not improved – and rumours were rife that heads were about to roll in the new company. Walter had expected more immediate results from his investment, he had been a big wheel in the oil industry and had commanded respect. He was finding it hard to take the indignity of this very visible failure of his new venture. It was obvious to outsiders that scapegoats would have to be found and that Frank was in the firing line. But Frank seemed blind to the threat. He couldn't imagine that anyone would expect instant success with a new team and a new car in such a competitive business. He viewed this first year as a time to lay the foundations of the team and he had no idea that Walter saw things so differently.

The moment of truth came in November shortly after Frank's return from the Japanese Grand Prix where both cars retired ignominiously. Walter summoned Frank to his office and informed him that he was calling in Peter Warr from Lotus to take over the running of the company. Walter had always been fair and straightforward in his dealings and I don't think he liked hurting people. He attempted to soften the blow by offering Frank double his salary and making him personally responsible for seeking sponsorship. Although officially he was being moved sideways Frank knew that in effect he was sacked and the Press knew it too. They made a meal of it. It was a very public humiliation and Frank, who for ten years had been boss of his own team, found it difficult to swallow. It did not help when he arrived at the office one day and found all his personal things, his framed photos of Piers Courage, the contents of his desk, in a pile on the forecourt of Bennet Road. They had been moved out of his office so that Peter Warr could move in. From now on Frank was expected to work from home.

Within weeks he was being treated as a sort of odd job man by the Wolfs. True they were glamorous odd jobs; picking up Walter's personal Mercedes from Stuttgart; driving his Lamborghini to Paris, but nevertheless it stung Frank's pride. At the age of thirty-five and with a decade of running his own company behind him, he saw himself as something more than a high-class personal chauffeur. I felt equally humiliated. For me the final straw came when Barbara Wolf telephoned and asked Frank to advertise for and select a married couple to live in one of their many houses.

I took over that job myself. I was livid. How dare Barbara suggest that Frank – *my* Frank – become an interviewer for her domestic staff!

In February Frank was left behind when 'his' team set off for the first Grand Prix of the new season in Argentina. Walter's new driver, Jody Schechter, drove the Wolf-Williams to a startling victory – the team's first. It must have seemed to many that Walter's reshuffling had justified itself. The fact that Frank had been head of the team which had worked on the car for the previous eight months and that this victory was the culmination of all that preparatory work went unacknowledged.

That galling victory of Wolf Racing in his absence was the deciding moment for Frank. No matter how comfortable it might be to have a big salary and a nice standard of living it couldn't make up for not being directly involved in Formula One. He felt that he was branded a failure, a Jonah, after his sacking. He had something to prove now. He had to show the world that he could make it in Formula One without Walter Wolf.

CHAPTER 5

A surprising number of bookmakers seem to be called Williams and some are even called Frank Williams. This fact came to light when we tried to register a name for Frank's proposed new company. Although Walter was not using the name Williams on his cars any more, he still owned the title Frank Williams Racing Cars which meant we had to think of something different. It proved more difficult than we had expected. Each combination of Williams and Racing that we submitted to Company House turned out to have already been registered by some obscure turf accountant.

It was at about the tenth attempt that Frank and Patrick came up with Williams Grand Prix Engineering, which was accepted. Nobody liked it much. At the time it seemed far too much of a mouthful.

Patrick, who had agreed to leave Wolf to be the new company's engineer, was also to be a director of WGPE as was Brode. I don't think it was a difficult decision for Patrick. Frank had invited him to lunch with us at the Laundry House soon after the Argentinian race and it was obvious then that he wouldn't take much persuading. Patrick had never liked Walter. They were poles apart both in their personalities and in their approach to motor racing. Patrick was a true English gentleman and did not appreciate Walter with his go-getting Canadian brashness and big leather jacket and sparkling gold Rolex. Walter's ego and his transparent desire to win races to feed that ego made Patrick wince.

There was still a strong loyalty to Frank within the old team and he and Patrick were fairly confident that they could lure a few more of Wolf's personnel away to the new company. They started to make secret overtures to the people they wanted. When Walter was alerted to Patrick's defection he panicked, called Frank to his office and offered him a great deal of money to stay out of motor racing.

I'm sure it wasn't the prospect of losing Patrick that prompted his offer – Walter did not rate Patrick very highly as a designer – but he obviously feared that other employees of Wolf Racing might follow him and break up his own team.

We considered Walter's offer a joke. It wasn't something we ever sat down and seriously discussed. Now that Frank had the bit between his teeth nothing would have made him change direction. By March 1977 five key people had agreed to leave Wolf for Williams Grand Prix Engineering. Frank would have liked a couple more but by now the game was up. Realizing what was happening Peter Warr had quickly increased salaries to prevent any more lemmings jumping over the cliff – for I am sure that is how he and Walter viewed the departures.

Once they had taken the decision to 'go for it' Frank and Patrick put the wheels in motion very quickly. A week after the Brazilian Grand Prix I went with Frank to look at two possible factory sites at Thatcham and Didcot. There were pluses and minuses about each of them but the vote was cast in favour of Didcot since it was better situated for attracting a labour force. It was a small site: an old carpet warehouse of only six thousand square feet. But a short term lease was available which meant that the only investment required was the 'key money' of about £1,500. After raiding the coffers to pay this the new company had virtually no capital, but compared with the position less than eighteen months earlier, when Frank's business had owed £140,000, it was a clean slate. Everyone was optimistic.

I was no exception. The fact that my housekeeping allowance was likely to dry up again did nothing to dampen my enthusiasm. I had hated knowing that the Frank Williams car was out there racing and that it was now called a Wolf. That name had been with us for eleven years and I felt very possessive about it. More possessive than Frank did I think. But we have never got annoyed about the same things. I felt more bitter towards the people whom I felt had treated Frank badly than he did himself. Frank would go up to the Wolfs not long afterwards and slap Walter on the back and give Barbara a big kiss. He never holds grudges.

I, on the other hand, had for some time been walking around with a black cloud over my head smarting at the injustice of what had happened. It might be a gamble to start again but as far as I was concerned it would be worth it. How we funded it was a minor consideration. I had faith the money would turn up. Positive thinking must work because one after another, sources of income appeared, sometimes after a great deal of hard groundwork by Frank, and sometimes out of the blue.

A benefactor of the latter kind arrived in the form of John Makepeace, the manager of Barclays Bank at Didcot. Frank had always been allergic to bank managers and his secretaries were instructed that no bank manager of any description was ever to be shown into the office without prior clearance to decide if Frank was 'in' or not.

Over the years he had acquired a terrible reputation with banks and in the pre-Wolf days had always been 'taking his overdraft elsewhere'. He had spent ten years bouncing cheques on people. He had even bounced them on me, which meant that mine in turn had bounced. Towards the end of the pre-Wolf year I had stopped opening the threatening letters from bank managers. I hid them away in the backs of drawers, afraid my hair would turn white overnight if I read any more. It was during those years that I developed a morbid fear of banks which I have never been able to shake off. Even now when I put my cheque card in the cash machine I'm half-afraid it's going to say, 'NO! Go away Mrs Williams. Insufficient funds.'

Frank did not suffer from my paranoia but he certainly regarded bank managers as *persona non grata*. So when, shortly after Frank had moved into the factory at Didcot, Mr Makepeace walked in and divulged his identity, Alison went into the standard routine and said, 'Oh no! no! no! I'm afraid Mr Williams isn't here.'

'Oh? What a pity. Never mind. I just thought I'd see if there was anything I could do to help,' said Mr Makepeace.

Alison, backtracking swiftly said, 'Well I'll just check to make absolutely sure,' and beetled off to Frank's office.

At the news of his uninvited visitor she swears that Frank dived under his desk and it was much against his better judgement that he was persuaded to let her show John Makepeace in. But for once his better judgement was wrong.

John was a keen motor racing fan. He was also a shrewd and ambitious bank manager. He had just been transferred from the north-east and was making it his policy to visit every potential business customer of Barclays in his area. Within five minutes of meeting Frank he had heard enough to convince him that Williams Grand Prix Engineering was worth backing.

'It looks good,' he said. 'How much do you want?' Frank came home that evening with the news that he now had an overdraft facility of £30,000.

'Oh sugar, this is going to be the kiss of death,' I thought. If we started off owing money I feared the whole thing might escalate and, before we knew it, we'd be up to £140,000 like before. But I was wrong. John was one of the main people responsible for putting WGPE on its feet. Years later he told me that he rated Frank from that first encounter, claiming that he was very impressed by his drive and energy. He was the first bank manager ever to experience such a reaction!

Very quickly more funding came from other sources. Brode proved an invaluable ally as he was regarded as respectable by people who wouldn't have considered doing a deal directly with Frank. He introduced Frank to a finance company called First Fortune who came up with a loan to buy a transporter and the machine tooling needed to construct a car. An old friend and supporter, Ted Williams of Ward, donated a brand new capstan lathe. And very early on – though we didn't fully appreciate its significance at the time – the most important support of all materialized.

Frank had a good friend called Tony Harris in a London advertising agency. Whenever he was in London Frank would go in and do a dance of death in the reception area of the advertising company and say to any clients present, 'Come on. Won't you put your name on our car? How about sponsoring us?' Almost invariably they'd look aghast and say, 'No thank you.' But in 1977 Tony was approached by someone from the Saudi Arabia Airline, Saudia. They were looking for something interesting and out of the ordinary to sponsor. Tony suggested a Formula One car. More precisely, Frank's Formula One car. Shortly afterwards Frank found himself being introduced to a Mr Al Fawzan of Saudi Arabian Airlines. The sponsorship was agreed in time for the Saudia logo to adorn the rear wing of the Williams entry in its first race in 1976. For the privilege the airline paid WGPE more than £100,000 which was a small fortune in those days. The money had an immediate effect in making the team breathe more easily but that first Arab sponsorship was also to have much wider repercussions.

This was the time when the Arabs were spending substantial sums of money in London and a lot of Arab companies were looking for investment opportunities in Britain. Saudia was owned by the Saudi Royal family which seemed to give us instant credibility in the eyes of many of the other Arab investors around. Over the next two years, thanks to the Saudia link, Frank was able to attract several more Arab sponsors, though he often had to use considerable ingenuity.

On one occasion, hearing that an Arab prince was staying at the Dorchester in London, he arranged to have the prince's company logo painted on the nose cone of one of the current F1 cars. As soon as the paint was dry he had it loaded onto a trailer and driven from Didcot up to London and straight down Park Lane where it drew up in front of the Dorchester in the middle of the rush hour. The Arab prince emerged rather reluctantly in response to Frank's bowings and scrapings in the lobby but, once he saw the car, he was instantly taken with the idea. He insisted that Frank unload it from the trailer, oblivious to the chaos it created in the rush hour traffic. The prince walked around it thoughtfully a couple of times, liked the effect of his company's name in conjunction with Saudia, and agreed a deal on the spot.

Over the next two years the Saudis came to regard the Williams as 'their' car and it was even taken to Riyadh to be put on public display. Arab sponsorship made an enormous difference to us financially, though not all the companies were good payers. Their intentions I'm sure were fine, but all too often Frank would turn up to collect the money only to find his benefactors elsewhere. Frank's response was simply to turn up again the next day, and the next. He spent a lot of time in Riyadh waiting to see people about money that year. I spent a great deal of time alone.

There was insufficient time for the new company to construct a car to race in 1976 and as a stop-gap solution they bought a March. The driver was to be Patrick Neve who brought with him £100,000 worth of sponsorship from the Belgian Belle-Vue lager company. Together with the Saudia money it helped get them through that year while Patrick worked at Didcot designing what was to be known as the FW06. His brief: simply to produce a neat light little car that would do the job. Nothing revolutionary or over ambitious.

1976 was a lean year. Neve's performances in the March were professional but lacklustre. Later, when they could afford to smile about it, Patrick and Frank would joke about their attempts to debrief Neve after a race.

'How did it go Patrick? How is it handling?' they'd ask eagerly.

Neve would look at them sourly. 'My bum, it hurts,' he'd say, and walk away. The March 761 was nobody's favourite car, least of all the drivers, but it fulfilled its purpose that year, enabling us to compete and maintain our vital membership of FOCA.

There was only one major drawback to being based at Didcot; it was even further away from the Laundry House than the Bennet Road factory had been. The round trip was now eighty miles which meant Frank was no longer able to pop home for a run around the lanes at Malshangar whenever he felt like it. This had become a regular habit of his in the last couple of years and he missed doing it.

The drive to Didcot took him via the A34, which was a terribly dangerous three lane road. At night Frank would come in and say, 'Thirty-three-and-a-half minutes tonight Ginny. I'm going to kill myself on that road if I'm not careful.'

'If you kill yourself I'm not coming to your funeral.' I would reply, sweating at the thought. On those roads Frank was a suicide lane driver, never anywhere but in the middle. It was a mutual decision to move nearer to the factory.

Around the middle of the year I noticed an auction advertisement for an old rectory in Aston Tirrold which was just a few miles from Didcot. Now that Frank was once more without a salary, viewing it was only an exercise. What we required was another tenancy, but I couldn't resist having a look. I loved it. It was pure Regency, a Grade II Listed house, though quite small and in dreadful condition. Most of its land had been sold off for development in order to keep an incumbent rector in funds so it was hemmed in by new property. I let a glimmer of hope flicker. Maybe these drawbacks might bring it within our scope if I could persuade my father to lend us a deposit.

The auctioneers told me they expected it to fetch about £30,000. Even that would be too much. However my father did agree to lend us £10,000 and Frank reckoned we could get a mortgage or scrape for a loan of £15,000. It wasn't enough. But there was always a chance that the auctioneers had overvalued it. It seemed worth going to the auction just in case and Frank arranged to join me there. Brode came along for the ride. We agreed in advance that £30,000 was to be our absolute ceiling although God knows how we would raise it.

The first bid was £15,000. I could feel my heart thudding. Frank was sitting beside me but as far as I could see he didn't even get in a nod before the bidding had escalated out of our reach to £40,000. Even at that price there still seemed to be several people competing and it was a couple more minutes before the hammer finally dropped at £52,000. That was the end of that particular dream I thought ruefully. I sat downcast while the auctioneer, looking around to identify the last bidder, focused on a person to my right and said, 'Mr Williams isn't it?'

Incredulous, I stared at Frank, who gave me one of his wicked grins. He was so pleased with himself.

I don't think I have ever been angrier with him. How could he have done anything so stupid? Now I knew why we had suffered so much financial aggravation over the years. The man was utterly irresponsible. I couldn't believe that the bank would even meet the deposit cheque of £5,500 which Frank was now making out with gay abandon. Even if it did, how on earth were we going to raise another £47,000 in 28 days – the terms of the sale? I was terrified of the consequences. I could imagine nothing worse than the shame of not being able to complete on the purchase, but there was nothing I could do about it. I had always unquestioningly allowed him to run our financial affairs, however haphazardly. I knew he would be furious if I were to query this extraordinary transaction.

Having completed the formalities Frank turned to me and said cheerfully, 'Brode and I are going back to work. Are you going over to look at your new house?'

'No. I certainly am not,' I said through gritted teeth and drove back to Basingstoke under a fresh black cloud.

I might have known that Frank would come up with the money. It was always the same. While I used to sweat and worry Frank would sleep like a log, confident that everything would be 'all right on the night' and as usual it was. My father had to part with his promised £10,000 rather prematurely and various other sources had to be tapped but somehow it was done.

Once the finance had been sorted out I forgave Frank rapidly. It was after all the first home we had ever owned and it was exceedingly pretty. We moved in quite quickly and Frank was once more able to nip home for a run when the mood took him, and drive to and from work without brushing shoulders with death.

There were no profits at the end of the first season's racing but we did manage to break even. Knowing that the FW06 would be ready to race at the start of 1978 Frank started to look around for drivers for his new car. He and Patrick drew up a list of possibilities. Patrick

Neve had been a 'rent-a-drive'; a last-minute choice. What they wanted now was a top-class driver.

The trouble was, Williams Grand Prix Engineering was far from being considered a top-class constructor. They ran through their list of desirables very quickly indeed. Hans Stuck, six foot tall, and a good middle running driver looked straight over Frank's head and laughed when it was suggested he drive the FW06. 'You must be joking,' he said and walked off.

Undeterred, they pressed on.

Jochen Mass, whom I favoured for all the wrong reasons (primarily because he was so good-looking) didn't bother to return Frank's phone call. Neither did Ricardo Patrese. Gunner Nilsson, the Swedish driver had become a good friend of Frank's and did discuss coming but, in the end, went to Arrows. Tragically he was in the early stages of cancer and was to die the following year never having driven for his new team.

Frank had just about exhausted his list of 'possibles' when during the last meeting of 1977 at Watkins Glen he approached Alan Jones. Alan was an Australian driver who had been making his mark in Formula Two and had driven an F1 Shadow the previous season in which he finished seventh in the driver's championship. He was hardly the high-flyer Frank had set his sights on but compromise was clearly called for, at least initially.

I had wangled my usual trip to the States and Canada and we were coming out of the hotel at Toronto when I noticed a dark broad-shouldered man walking towards us with a pretty blonde woman. Frank nudged me.

'That's Alan Jones and his wife Beverley.'

I was introduced and we chatted briefly. Drivers still under contract did not like to be seen in public talking to constructors even in those days. Even less so today when any deals are usually done surreptitiously in hotel rooms after racing. I took an instant liking to Jonesy, the name by which he was generally known. He was very funny, his conversation peppered with wisecracks. I was not so sure about Beverley. Her glamour rather intimidated me. She seemed so sophisticated. They had the aura of a real superstar couple.

Although I enjoyed socializing, I still lacked confidence when confronted by the high-flyers of the motor racing world. I felt we didn't belong in their company. The big names had nothing to do with us underdogs. If Carlos Reutemann or any of the Brabham hierarchy walked past the pits I made way for them. To a certain extent I think the whole Williams team made way for them and the stars seemed to accept it as their right. Alan was down on the same rung of the motor racing ladder as us, but I had an intuitive feeling that he and Beverley would make way for no one. I was right about Alan but, underneath the polished veneer, Beverley had a much softer centre than I imagined.

During the Toronto meeting Frank invited Alan to come down to Didcot and have a look at the new car. A couple of weeks later he turned up and spent a few hours talking to Patrick. Before he left the factory he had agreed to drive the FW06 in 1978. Charlie Crichton-Stuart, who had been one of Frank's flatmates in the old Piers Courage days, had joined the Williams team earlier that year to co-ordinate sponsorship deals. He was at that first meeting where Alan gave him the impression of being 'a very shrewd guy'. Alan seemed equally impressed with Patrick. 'Switched on bloke' he had confided to Charlie. He liked the look of the car so that was it. Alan was not one for agonizing over a decision.

Some people say that it was the alliance of Frank, Alan and Patrick which brought 'overnight success' to the Williams team. I disagree. To attribute what followed Alan's signing to some magic interaction between those three is to discount the previous twelve years of hard slog. There was nothing 'overnight' about it. But certainly from the moment Alan came onto the scene there was a change in our fortunes.

It first became obvious in the run up to the second race of 1978 in Brazil. Up till now we had always run about twentieth in practice which meant we got the worst of everything. We always got the worst tyres because we weren't worth giving the special qualifiers to. They were reserved for the elite up on the first half of the grid. Then out of the blue, on re-scrubs that had belonged to someone else, Alan completed the eighth fastest lap. Although he had to retire during the race he also clocked up the second fastest race-lap. The Williams pits were buzzing with excitement.

In the 1982 book *Racers* Frank told Doug Nye, 'It was a completely new world to me. I had difficulty coping with the sudden enormity of it. Alan was among the quick boys . . . For years I had become accustomed to just hanging in there hoping to qualify, and now we were showing real signs of becoming truly competitive . . .'

Describing the next race in South Africa two weeks later, where Alan started eighteenth on the grid Frank told Doug, 'Alan began simply ripping through the field, passing car after car. He was twelfth ending lap five and fought his way through the pack to seventh as the race progressed. It was fantastically exciting. It really stirred me and I remember calling to Patrick, "You know even if we don't finish, this will be my best race. If it doesn't come round next lap I will still be happy." It was like one of Piers' drives. It took me some time to appreciate fully that Alan was really that quick. It was as if I had been in prison for ten or twenty years of a thirty-year sentence and somebody had suddenly come up with the key and set me free. My initial reaction was "Bloody hell, I'm not sure I can cope with this. Help! Please let me back inside . . ." '

Frank's reaction confirms my belief that he was never really driven by the urge to win as much as most people assume. He just wanted to compete. To be there. He was genuinely, completely unprepared for success. It all came as a big surprise to him. Having said that, he adapted pretty quickly.

Charlie Crichton-Stuart always says that it was Alan's next race at Long Beach that convinced him we were heading for the big time.

Alan was running second to Carlos Reutemann and he was literally right up there behind him, for lap after lap until the front wing collapsed. But he still kept going. In the end he got a misfire and fell back to seventh but Charlie remembers saying to Frank, 'The guy's a world champion.'

Charlie made sure in his capacity as sponsorship liaison officer that the people who counted knew of Alan's potential. Shortly afterwards, at the Monaco Grand Prix where Alan ran sixth for several laps and the Saudi sponsors were beside themselves with excitement, a young Arab/French businessman called Mansour Ojjeh arrived as a guest. Charlie accompanied him around and from that day on Mansour was absolutely hooked on F1. His father's company was TAG who were to become one of our most important sponsors.

Alan went on to complete the season with eleven world championship points. More significantly he ran second on six occasions. Frustratingly he only actually finished second once that year. Every other time something fell off the car. Usually the failures were due to lack of quality control on small but vital components. We had to have better organization and reliability if the team was to take advantage of Alan's ability.

No one knew that better than Alan himself but fortunately he now had faith in Williams. He agreed to stay with them for the next season despite several approaches from top teams; these approaches must have been in his mind at Long Beach, the third race of 1978 when he finished third. Afterwards, all hyped-up because he knew he could have won, Alan went over to Frank and said, 'Your new car had better be f—ing good!'

It was good. Patrick and the team had been working frantically in preparation for the 1979 season but the 07 was not ready until the Spanish Grand Prix at the end of April. Everyone in the team knew that it was something special soon after it made its debut. It was a ground effect car, with the controversial skirts–which were later banned–which utilized aerodynamic effects to increase traction during cornering and braking. What it boiled down to was that the car could take bends considerably quicker.

Frank had committed himself to running a two-car team in 1979 and had signed up the experienced Swiss driver, Clay Regazzoni who got on well with Alan and was a reliable finisher. Both drivers found the ground effect car strange to drive at first. Alan said it felt like being on rails but by the Belgian Grand Prix in May he had got the hang of it. Starting from third position on the grid he was leading by lap twenty-four. It was the first time Frank had ever had a car he'd constructed running first in a Grand Prix. Although the euphoria in the pits didn't last (Alan retired with electrical failure with just a few laps to go) the possibility of winning was now on everybody's mind. When Clay finished second at Monaco it was obvious the 07 had what it took. The question now was not if, but where and when, the dream was going to come true.

The answer for an anglophile like Frank could hardly have been more appropriate. The British Grand Prix that year was at Silverstone. During testing Patrick and Frank Dernie had fitted one more streamlining refinement, developed as a result of wind-tunnel tests. Whether it was that, or Alan's determination to prove himself to 'the Poms' or a combination of the two, no one knew but Alan's qualifying lap was six seconds faster than the lap record. He found himself in pole position, the privileged leading place on the grid that goes to the fastest qualifier in practice. Neither Alan nor Williams had ever been there before. The honour brought with it a dozen bottles of Moët & Chandon champagne – completely wasted on teetotal Frank but much appreciated in other quarters.

I always attended the British Grand Prix. This year, my two young children had prevented me travelling abroad so it was the first race I had been able to go to. Beverley was terribly nervous before the start. We positioned ourselves out of everyone's way on some Goodyear tyres at the back of the pits and prepared to close our eyes for the first lap. Clay was far from eclipsed by Alan and had qualified fourth fastest. Their cars were split on the grid by a Renault and a Brabham. 'Help,' I thought. It was a quite different feeling to being on the back of the grid. Much more frightening to be up with the superstars.

Seventeen laps later we were in front of the superstars. Williams cars were leading one and two for the first time ever. I picked at my nails and wondered if my heart would hold out. Beside me Beverley was stiff with tension. I glanced over at Frank who was sitting on the pit wall. His eyes were rivetted grimly to the lapcharts in front of him as if his life depended on it.

Alan and Clay led that race for twenty-two glorious laps. It was unbelievable. I stood beside Beverley, neither of us speaking or moving in case we broke the spell. Then disaster struck. Alan came into the pits in front of us and failed to go out again. A water pump had cracked. His race was run. Beverley was in tears, desperately upset. She had been all set up for a fairytale ending to the race and once again for her, it had been for nothing. I took her behind the pits and we walked back from the garages towards the rented motorhome we used as the team base.

I felt torn. I had been longing for Alan to win too but I knew that Williams were still in the lead and I couldn't help keeping half an ear on the commentary even while I struggled to console Beverley. After a few minutes she was back in control and recognized my dilemma. 'Look,' she said, 'you're still winning. You've got to go back.' I hesitated. She smiled and gave me a push and I went gratefully. I couldn't miss this whatever happened. Beverley went off to find Alan and they left together, unable to face seeing the end of the race.

Back at the pits there were five laps still to go and the journalists and TV crews had started to gather. In the second half of a race the press always gravitate towards the pits of the leading team. They had never gathered in the Williams pit before and the atmosphere was electric. For the first time ever during a race Frank found the television cameras focusing on him and reporters with microphones and notebooks surrounding him. I could see him sitting there in the middle of them all, concentrating on the track, the usual deadpan expression fixed on his face.

Those last five laps were the longest I had ever lived through. They just seemed to go on and on. Finally, as the end of the last lap approached a Union Jack went up opposite the grandstand and with it the Saudi flag. Frank had arranged it beforehand 'just in case'. As

Clay came over the line and took the chequered flag, pandemonium broke out and the crowd went wild. Williams had always been thought of as a staunchly British team and the British public always loves an underdog. Clay with his cheerful personality was very popular too. Everything was right as far as the crowd was concerned. Every single person out there seemed to be cheering for Frank and for the team, the noise was deafening.

I had always known that if victory ever came there would be no chance of me getting near Frank. He was besieged. I watched it all from the fringe of the crowd. The press, the men from Williams, and sponsors, including Prince Mohammed of Albilad, all crowded around him. At least half of the people in the pit were in tears. It was an emotional moment for all Frank's loyal workers after those long years of struggle. Frank seemed both exhausted and elated. I have a wonderful photograph of him taken after the race in which he looks like an Olympic athlete who has just taken the gold medal.

Even in victory he thought of his sponsorship and his future. He sent a message up to the podium that Clay wasn't to drink the traditional champagne in deference to Prince Mohammed's Muslim faith. Clay sprayed orange juice while the drivers who were second and third drenched the crowd with champagne. It made it an even bigger story for the press the following day.

I watched Clay being presented with his trophy before, floating on air, I started to make my way back towards the motorhome. I had just reached the back of the garages when I saw Clay heading in the same direction. He'd collected his prize and now, for some reason, he was alone, a small figure looking rather sad and lonely, walking across the grass. He'd obviously sneaked away from the interviews and attention. I went up and congratulated him. I felt I knew exactly how he must feel. He'd just driven his heart out and given Williams their first ever success and yet there was no escaping the knowledge that most people in Williams were slightly disappointed that it wasn't Alan who had won. He gave me a hug and a smile and we walked together the last few yards to the motorhome.

It was already surrounded by reporters, friends, and sponsors. Champagne was being opened for the non-Muslim sponsors. Soon Frank arrived with Prince Mohammed and they and Clay gave one interview after another. It was past nine o'clock and starting to grow dark before the party broke up.

Outside the motorhome, Silverstone grew quiet again. There was just the odd person kicking round the paddock. Frank didn't want to leave any more than I did. We sat snuggled inside on the bench seat, our arms around each other looking out of the window at the deserted circuit. We didn't speak. We didn't need to say anything. We just sat there thinking about it. Contemplating. I felt exultant. Frank deserved it. God he deserved it after working so hard. He had spent half his life struggling to stay in the game. No one had returned to 'go' more often than Frank. He had never relaxed the pressure: no holidays, no days off. Just utter total commitment for seven days a week, fifty-two weeks a year.

People have said to me that what happened that day must have made all that went before worthwhile. But I think that's the wrong way of looking at it. Not for one single moment had I ever thought that it wasn't worthwhile. Just as failure had never made him think of doing something else, so it had never occurred to me to wish that Frank would go out and do a different job, or be like other men. Even if this day had never happened it would still have been worthwhile because he was doing what he loved doing.

But undeniably victory was sweet. Frank had made it. All those people who ran him down and wrote him off as a joke, from drivers to the other team bosses, from my family to Walter Wolf, had been proved wrong. It was a very nice feeling to know that from now on we would be able to hold our heads up in any motor racing company. There had been no fluke about Clay's win. We were also-rans no more. I felt I could stay at Silverstone sitting in the motorhome with Frank's arm around me, for the rest of my life. Every so often the door would open and someone would stick their head in and smile and say, 'I just wanted to say congratulations,' and shut the door again and Frank would acknowledge the greeting with a wave and a grin.

Eventually at midnight, reluctantly, we left, wandering back slowly to the car across the moonlit track.

Even now, many successes later, I think we both look back on that first ever victory at Silverstone as the highlight of Frank's career. It was marvellous to win your first Grand Prix in your own country and to hear the roars from your own British crowd willing you to win . . . Drivers Championships and Constructors Championships were to follow but nothing, nothing at all, would ever compete with that day.

CHAPTER 6

*T*he win at Silverstone marked the start of a spectacular change of fortunes for Williams. Alan compensated for his retirement in the British race by winning the next three Grand Prix in a row, and, as often as not, Clay was running only a place or two behind him. The new car had come too late for Alan to get closer than third in the Drivers Championship in 1979 but the prize was now in our sights and so was its twin, the Constructors Championship.

By the end of the season, the top drivers were queueing to join Williams for 1980 – a sharp contrast to the situation twelve months earlier. Clay's contract had only been for one year and though his results had far exceeded expectations Frank now wanted another number one driver. After much deliberation he offered the second seat to Carlos Reutemann, the tall good-looking Argentinian who had been driving very successfully for Lotus in 1979. After the American Grand Prix and following one of the most unusual job interviews Carlos can ever have attended, he accepted the job.

Frank had been for a run and was taking a shower when Carlos knocked on the door of our room at the newly built Corning Hilton. (To my regret we no longer stayed at the Glen Motor Inn after the Hilton was built.) I answered the door and nervously invited in this world-famous racing driver. A year earlier I would hardly have dared say hello to him. He had just sat down when Frank walked out of the shower, sat on the bed and proceeded to conduct the interview stark naked. I was hideously embarrassed. I sensed that Carlos thought it was a little odd as well. It would have been all right if there had just been the two of them but my presence somehow made the whole thing different. Eventually I couldn't stand it any longer and disappeared into the bathroom where I stayed until Carlos had left. Frank was amazed when I protested later. Typically he couldn't see anything amiss with his behaviour at all. Carlos couldn't have been too put off because he agreed to come and drive for us as joint number one driver with Alan for 1980.

It was a magical season in which everything came together. Perhaps the most emotional moment for the team was at the British Grand Prix, held that year at Brands Hatch, where Alan avenged the previous year's disappointment and easily took the race. Carlos was third.

At this stage of the season Williams Grand Prix Engineering was already the leading constructor by eighteen points and Alan was heading the Drivers Championship by six points. By Montreal, the penultimate race of the series, Williams still led the constructor's table but Nelson Piquet was leading Alan by just one point. After the qualifying laps they stood in the one and two positions on the grid. Alan and Nelson were not what you'd call good friends. The atmosphere in the pit lane was electric before the warm-up lap. Everyone knew there was no chance whatsoever of either of them giving up the first corner. The pile-up when it came seemed inevitable. Nelson and Alan collided, Nelson smashed into the guard rail and behind them car after car crashed in their wake. Undeterred, Alan, who was the least scathed, charged around the first lap, ignoring the red flag and was finally forced to halt in front of his pit. He jumped out of his car absolutely furious, shouting to Frank, 'Why the f— have the w—s stopped the bloody race?'

The entire pit crew burst into laughter. Alan had lost a front wing, the whole side of the monocoque was smashed in and more importantly there was no one else left in the race. Those few cars that had escaped being smashed into were parked up on the side of the track behind the carnage that Nelson and Alan had started.

Alan, when driving, was a man possessed, which while it occasionally made his behaviour extreme, also made him nearly unbeatable if the car held up. Winning was all that counted. Second was not good enough for him. When the race was restarted with Nelson in the practice car the dual was resumed but it came to an end when Nelson's engine blew up and Alan went on to win. Carlos came second and on top of that, both World Championship titles were clinched. It was the climax of an incredible year.

Frank and I returned to our hotel in the centre of Montreal. The Ojjeh family of TAG had put on a party for the team and it was the early hours before we retired to bed. Neither of us felt in the least sleepy and we lay staring at the ceiling drinking in the implications of what had happened. Frank shook his head slowly from side to side. 'Wow! Ginny, do you realize we have just won THE WORLD CHAMPIONSHIP? Wow!' He clutched his hand to his forehead in disbelief.

We had just a couple of minutes to try and come to terms with our new status before the ring of the telephone jolted us back to the present. It was Alan, his timing perfect as always.

'Hey Frank, you ought to know that I have just been offered an enormous sum of money to drive for Ferrari next year.'

All the wind was taken out of Frank's sails. But there was little time to brood about it. Watkins Glen was coming up in a week's time and though there was nothing left to prove, the team was determined to underline its superiority. They did it in style with Alan and Carlos finishing first and second once more. Shortly afterwards, to Frank's relief, Alan signed for Williams for another year. Charlie always says that Alan never had the slightest intention of going to Ferrari and that his phone call that night was a typical Jonesy prank, aimed at winding Frank up.

But the offer was real enough. Alan was now hot property and I believe he wanted to make sure that Frank appreciated it, and realized that he would have to pay more for Alan's services the following season.

Frank did appreciate it, though that did not stop him negotiating hard. That last win at Watkins Glen had been the high spot, setting the seal on the world championship title. It signified for us that the years of struggling just to stay in the lower levels of motor racing were behind us. Having arrived at the summit Frank definitely liked the view and from now on the target was to stay there.

It would be silly to pretend that success did not bring with it a change in our lifestyle. But that change consisted more of a gradual relaxation of the domestic pursestrings than in an explosion of big spending. There were no purchases of helicopters or swimming pools or trips to the Caribbean. Sadly I was not presented with diamonds. Frank had no intention of dissipating his hard earned capital on frivolity. If more money was available, then first and foremost it had to be used to consolidate the position of Williams Grand Prix

Engineering. It was not going to be siphoned off and used to buy executive toys or to pay lavish expenses bills.

There were times when I felt he carried this policy a little too far. Both Frank and his employees were granted a subsistence allowance during race meetings. The mechanics were allowed six dollars for their evening meal and Frank refused to pay himself any more. At the American Grand Prix meeting for the two years after we won the championship he would drag me out of the hotel restaurant where all the mechanics were dining, to a big hamburger joint called the Red Barn 200 yards down the highway, where the menu stated that you could eat all you wanted for one dollar fifty. Since I was not a bona fide employee of Williams he did not think it right that he should claim expenses for me and this way he didn't need to. He could feed us both adequately on half his allowance.

Frank was never terribly keen on my attending Grand Prix anyway, claiming it was distracting for him and unprofessional.

'It's like a doctor taking his wife with him on his rounds,' he would complain. So it's just possible that eating at the Red Barn was a ruse to get me to stay at home next time!

His frugality became a bit of a joke among the racing fraternity and people would often kid him about it but only Jacques Laffite ever managed to get him stirred up. We were in Canada one year and Bernadette wanted to buy a mink coat. Jacques came along with us to the shops – unlike most men he never minded shopping – and while Bernadette was standing in front of the mirrors for three hours trying to decide, I passed the time by trying on a mink coat myself. Bernadette suddenly saw me and exclaimed, 'Oh that is lovely Ginny. You must have that one. We will ask Frank tonight, yes?'

So at dinner that night Bernadette said, 'Oh Frank. Ginny tried on this mink coat today. It's lovely. It's really nice.'

Frank's eyebrows shot up about three inches. 'You must be joking,' he said and went back to eating his dinner.

'*Quelle vache!*' said Jacques. 'You mean you are not going to buy your wife a fur coat? Oh you are mean! Oh you pig! You are not serious?'

Frank just grinned and ignored him.

The next day we went to the shop to collect Bernadette's mink coat and Jacques pointed, 'And can we have that one too please for Madame Williams?'

'Oh no Jacques. Absolutely not.' I was horrified.

'Yes, yes, yes,' they insisted.

At dinner that night Jacques announced casually, 'I bought Ginny a mink coat today Frank.'

Frank nearly choked on his food. He was utterly speechless.

Jacques laughed, 'It's all right Frank. You can pay me every week ten pounds. You pay me for ten years. I don't mind.'

There are not many racing drivers like Jacques. But I don't think Frank ever did pay him.

Frank was capable of spending money – if he felt it helped the image of the company. In some ways, even when we were on our uppers, he had behaved as if we were millionaires. There were very few concessions to poverty and he had always worn tailor-made suits to conduct his interviews at the Carlton Tower. He never considered himself poor, despite the bailiffs, the eviction notices and the cut-off phone. Or if he did, he saw it as a transient state and refused to let it cramp his style. But he was always critical of what he saw as 'indulgence'. Purchases had to be justified.

I found restraint much harder than he did. I began to enjoy shopping with a credit card. Since I was a teenager I had practically lived in jeans and tee-shirts, but now I started to buy these items from much more expensive shops, contriving to look like a 'designer' bag lady. I was subject to monthly blastings when the bills came in and very often I would have to hide them between the pages of cookery books and wait until Williams had won a race and Frank came home in a good mood before handing them over.

I got myself into serious trouble over one excess in America. The facilities at most circuits were very basic and Watkins Glen was worse than most. The lavatories were terrible. Beverley and I decided on race day that we couldn't suffer them. We had arrived by helicopter which was running a continual shuttle service back and forth from the hotel. Frank was busy when I asked him if he would mind if Beverley and I took the helicopter back for half-an-hour. He wasn't listening or interested and dismissed us with what we chose to assume was an affirmative grunt. We giggled our way back in the helicopter, used the hotel loo and were back at the track before our absence had been noticed. Later Frank was absolutely furious, 'Do you have any idea at all what you've done Ginny? Do you realize that you have just cost me 300 dollars to have a pee!'

I should have liked to take the children on holiday with Frank now that times were not so hard but that was not to be. Frank was not a holiday person. To him they were a waste of precious time. He couldn't see the point. No amount of persuading would drag him away from Williams to sit on a beach with his wife and kids so we took off to Marbella without him. I consoled myself with the thought that he would be a complete nightmare on holiday anyway. He would be so fretful at being away from work that no one would be able to relax at all.

The main indulgence that we both enjoyed as our funds increased was furnishing and restoring our homes. In 1980 I got itchy feet once more and we moved to Battle House, Goring-on-Thames, a lovely large nineteenth century house of grey brick which stood in six acres of gardens. It provided me with the perfect excuse to go antique hunting. I had always been keen on antiques and even when money was scarce I had been an avid window-shopper, I had never been able to pass Sotheby's in Bond Street or Christie's in South Kensington without going in for a browse around. I like to think that I had developed a good eye and now I started spending time at antique fairs, this time with a cheque book!

I was keen on most antiques but porcelain was my big weakness. I quickly became a porcelain junkie. My mother had always been a great collector and started to come with me to fairs but since we had a very similar taste this presented us with a new problem as we would often select the same things. We nearly came to blows over a mutually desired item on a few occasions! But they were friendly blows. Happily my parents' attitude to my marriage to Frank had altered and they were now proud of the association.

I bought most of my furniture at private sales, regarding it as a challenge to find a bargain and we started to accumulate a collection. Frank too began to take an interest and would occasionally come to auctions with me. He had always staunchly resisted having hobbies other than running but if life had taken a different course he might have become quite an expert on antiques. He liked the house to look nice. He would suddenly say, 'I think you should buy something for that corner Ginny. Pull your finger out and go and find a piece of furniture for it.' I found to my astonishment that I was actually being encouraged to spend money, as long as it was a quality antique. That was crucial. He wouldn't have liked me to come home with a plate and tell him, 'It's got a crack, but it is eighteenth century.' That wasn't for him. It was perfection or nothing.

Battle House had the space to accommodate my purchases and was the ideal setting to show them off. I worked hard for a year at Battle, lovingly restoring it as I felt it should be done. It was built in 1830 and I kept strictly to the style of the period in decorating and furnishing it. I had wonderful curtains made and put hours of thought into choosing and positioning each item of furniture. When at last it was finished I was really pleased with it.

I remember vividly the first day Alan and Beverley came down to see us at Battle. Beverley followed me around, her eyes getting wider with every room she visited. To many Australians I think 'antique' translates as second hand and I could read the thoughts going through Beverley's head. I'm sure she thought I hadn't started on the place yet. At the end of the tour when we were sitting in the drawing room having a cup of tea she turned to me and asked thoughtfully, 'Do you want to borrow any magazines with up-to-date ideas, Ginny?'

Tastes in decor apart, Beverley and I had a lot in common and we became close friends during those years. She had a sharp Australian wit which I enjoyed. We spent hours browsing in garden centres together picking shrubs and flowers for our new homes. Bev was very homesick and wherever she lived she tried to create a little bit of Australia. The garden of the Jones' house in Ealing was full of eucalyptus and other Australian vegetation. She was not at all the sophisticated socialite I had imagined but a real home-girl. She and Alan were unable to have children and her overriding obsession was their imminent adoption of a baby.

Beverley hated watching Alan racing. I think she felt as strongly about Alan as I did about Frank. She absolutely worshipped the ground he walked on and she just couldn't cope with the first laps when they were jockeying for position. Neither could she bear to be on her own on a race day, she would come down to Battle House and we would walk around the garden. I usually arranged for someone to be in the house and come out and give us a signal that the race was under way and Alan had made a clean start. Only then would we go in and watch it on television.

For drivers' wives, more probably than for the drivers themselves, the fear of death is ever present. Even though cars are now built much more with driver safety in mind and there are fewer fires, you cannot ignore the possibility that a crash at over 150 miles an hour is potentially lethal. They don't talk about it but the wives support each other. Whenever someone goes off the track the driver's wife concerned finds herself surrounded by a knot of other wives and girlfriends waiting with her to hear the outcome.

I was more nervous myself now, not just because of the risk of accident but because of the possibility of victory. In the old days, even when a Grand Prix race was on TV you never saw our car, and I never looked in the papers to see if we'd qualified because they only reported the first ten and we were never among them. So I had not experienced motor racing tension before Jonesy came along. When you are twentieth on the grid and you might finish eighteenth there is no tension. But now, with Jonesy, Frank would phone up and say, 'We're fourth on the grid,' and I'd think, 'Oh my God,' and start picking my nails. Frank felt it too. There was no talking to him for three days prior to a race meeting.

Our relationship with Alan and Bev was much closer than it has ever been with drivers and their wives since. Perhaps it was because Alan was driving with us through the formative years and we made the breakthrough together. Alan spent nearly as long at the track as Frank, turning up at eight in the morning and staying until they locked up at night. He, Frank and Charlie Crichton-Stuart became an intimate little clique. Whenever they were together there was a non-stop stream of wisecracks and blue jokes, most of them emanating from Alan.

The three men would regularly take 'the wives' up to London for dinner. On non-racing weekends a Sunday rarely went by without Alan and Beverley's Mercedes turning into the drive at Battle House. Charlie and Jenny would come over with Patrick and we'd all spend hours playing tennis. Frank distanced himself from the fun on these occasions; running was the only sport that interested him. He would bring his portable phone with him out of the house and his relief if it rang was so obvious that we joked that he had instructed someone to call just so he could get off the court.

Frank and Alan had a lot of respect for each other. Although Alan was more of a socializer than Frank, they shared certain characteristics. Both of them were egotistical and self-confident, and while in some men those traits are unbearable, it was redeemed in their cases by a roguish charm which made people forgive them almost anything.

I had always loved entertaining, even when we hadn't two pennies to rub together. I try very hard and everything has to be spot on. When we lived at Drake House 'entertaining' had meant the odd driver eating lunch in the kitchen but I had still kept a record of the menu and the guests. As the eighties progressed and our social circle enlarged we started to give many more dinner parties. Frank enjoyed these occasions with one proviso – the conversation had to revolve around cars. His powers of concentration are notoriously limited. Charlie once observed to me, 'You have to get your message over in two sentences to Frank or you've lost him.' Small talk absolutely bored him rigid. He would be an animated and sparkling host as long as we were discussing engine technicalities or driver technique, but as soon as the conversation switched to politics or summer holidays his eyes would glaze over and he would suddenly get up and announce, 'I'm going to take the dog for a walk now,' or 'I'll just pop upstairs to put on the electric blanket.' The party tended to break up very shortly afterwards.

Charlie said this lack of social chit-chat sometimes led to embarrassing situations at work. Once a year Mansour Ojjeh from TAG, now one of our biggest sponsors, would invite Frank and Charlie over to his Paris office for an informal meeting, at the end of which they were to collect the money. Frank would stand around looking totally bored while Charlie and Mansour and his entourage chattered away about sun and swimming and California. On one occasion Frank had been standing silently looking out of the window of the office at the Eiffel Tower while Mansour conversed with Charlie. There was a lull in the conversation and Charlie suddenly heard Frank say to Mansour with no preliminary social niceties, 'The budget's going up next year. It's got to be 1.3 million.' It was Frank's sole contribution to the conversation during the whole meeting.

Charlie, who believes that sponsors should be wooed, felt he was terribly discourteous. But in other ways Frank was always impeccably polite. His courtesy and charm were what had secured much of his sponsorship in the first place. It was just that Frank was not interested in anything outside motor racing. It was what occupied his mind every waking minute of the day and he saw no point in pretending otherwise. From a sponsor's point of view this dedication was a plus rather than a minus.

One morning in 1981 I found an imposing crested envelope in the mail. Inside, a gilt-edged card commanded Mr and Mrs Frank Williams to attend a state banquet at Buckingham Palace in honour of King Khalid of Saudi Arabia.

I went into a flat spin panic. It seemed no time at all since we had been potential candidates for a debtors' prison. Now we were being invited to dine with the Queen. The transition was too rapid for me. Frank adjusted far better. He felt very gratified, realizing that King Khalid must have put his name forward due to the Saudia connection. In unusually expansive mood he told me I could buy whatever I liked to wear. I chose a black taffeta dress from Belville Sassoon and spent the next three weeks frantically studying Debrett's *Etiquette and Modern Manners* for guidance on how to behave.

At 8.21 precisely, as commanded, we arrived at the palace, with Jamie my brother, determined to get in on the act, masquerading as our chauffeur. An equerry ushered us upstairs to the Long Gallery where we were to wait with the other guests before being presented to the Queen and King Khalid.

I recognized some of the faces around us – they were cabinet members and junior royals. Frank was handed a guest list and scanned through it. He raised his eyebrows at me and whispered, 'Look at this! What are we doing here?' Everybody on the list seemed to be at least a knight or a lady or the Archbishop of Canterbury apart from the lowly little Mr and Mrs F. Williams at the bottom. I felt terribly out of place. Most of the other ladies were wearing tiaras. When I spotted another bare head I breathed a sigh of relief – until I realized it belonged to Mrs Thatcher.

We were waiting in line to curtsey to the Queen when the lady next to me murmured, 'Isn't it a nuisance having to wear gloves?' I looked down at my bare hands and hissed back, 'What do you mean?'

'Oh you have to wear gloves to shake hands with the Queen,' she said, obviously thinking she was being helpful.

I whispered aghast to Frank, 'I haven't got gloves!'

'I'm sure the Queen won't have you beheaded Ginny,' Frank replied unperturbed.

The ladies-in-waiting might have carried a stock, but there was no time to find one. The Queen had appeared and the line was shrinking fast. When I saw that all the ladies in front of us in the line were dropping the most graceful deep curtseys it was the final straw. I had only practised a bob. Debrett's had let me down twice. It had not said anything about either gloves or a full curtsey. I made a mental vow to write and complain if I survived the evening.

My memory of the presentation is a blur. There was a whole line of royals ranging from the Queen and King Khalid down to the minor princes and dukes. I felt as though I was at Madame Tussaud's. For all I can remember of what they said to me they might as well have been a row of waxworks. I was so petrified with fright I do not even remember what sort of curtsey I did except that mercifully I didn't tip over onto my bottom which I fully expected to do. It was one of those experiences that you know you'd enjoy much more a second time but are unlikely to get the chance.

We had an opportunity to meet royalty in a less formal situation that year when the Duke of Kent contacted Frank and asked if he might drive the car. Frank was very honoured. He has always been patriotic and letting English royalty drive your precious Formula One car is about as patriotic as you can get. It was arranged that the Duke come to Silverstone for two testing sessions and have lunch with us at the track motorhome in between his drives. Our previous small rented vehicle had been replaced by a luxurious motorhome now. We laid out the table and I brought all the crystal and the recently purchased grand cutlery and china from home and we had quite a successful lunch. Then in the afternoon the Duke took the car off for another session and to our horror spun off on the far side of the track. Luckily neither Duke nor car suffered any damage but we had an anxious few moments.

The Duke must have spoken to Princess Anne about his exploits because within weeks she was in touch also wanting to have a go. Frank was again delighted to oblige, but my nerve deserted me and this time I called in caterers to supply the royal lunch. The Princess proved to be an excellent driver, very quick, as was Captain Mark Phillips who also tried his hand that season. All in all, it was a royal year which culminated in Frank's being awarded the Queen's Award for Industry as a result of his Saudi sponsorship deals. More limelight – more dressing up, for me more cause for nerves!

But slowly during this period my self-confidence increased. I learned that public figures were human and it was quite possible to have normal conversations with them. I don't think Frank had ever thought otherwise. Although he was respectful when appropriate, he was never overawed.

Around this time we were invited to a sportmen's dinner at Number Ten. Mrs Thatcher seemed to take quite a liking to Frank and she invited us again, this time to Chequers, for a private party being held for Mark Thatcher. I think Frank got an immense kick from mixing with royalty and politicians but he was not sycophantic. He had never been intimidated just because people had a title or lived in a grand house.

We once had an invitation to spend the weekend at a stately home over the British Grand Prix weekend. Our hosts entertained us with wonderful food and fine wines which were completely wasted on Frank and Alan who sat up at night in their four poster beds eating fish and chips from a newspaper.

A year or so later, during the run-up to another British Grand Prix, Frank got one of the biggest surprises of his life when the phone rang and an unfamiliar male voice said hesitantly, 'Hello Frank? I think I'm your dad!'

Frank's father had remarried and was now living in the north-west. He had only seen Frank once, when he was eleven years old, but he had been watching motor racing on the TV one Sunday afternoon when he realized that this might be his son they were talking about. Frank sent him two tickets for Silverstone and he and a friend duly turned up.

Owen Williams was the absolute image of Frank, apart from having more hair. I stared at him fascinated, visualizing Frank in twenty-five years' time. However the resemblance didn't stop at physical characteristics. After that meeting where everyone was laughing and enjoying themselves I went home thinking, 'Oh good, the children have another grandfather.' But that was it. We never saw him again. It seemed as though he was just curious and came to have a look and thought, 'That's nice,' and went away again. Just as Frank would have done, I guessed, in a similar situation. He didn't want any involvement nor to be accused of being a camp-follower so off he went. I admired this in a way – after all he'd made the decision to get out of Frank's life years before for his own reasons. Perhaps he felt it would have been hypocritical to reverse it just because of Frank's success.

Life is never a complete bed of roses and if there was one aspect of our new existence that I did not enjoy it was discovering that Frank had become enormously attractive to women.

I suppose it was inevitable that there would be girls who would try to get him in their clutches. It happens with all sportsmen. Probably cricketers are most notorious in this respect. The combination of success and money is a strong aphrodisiac. Pit-popsies, as they were known, had been around when I first started going to Grand Prix. They are the racing world's equivalent of the music business' groupies. They were very good looking, often well-educated and nicely-spoken girls who followed the Grand Prix circus around from country to country. They would hang around the pits making it obvious that they were available. These days the tightening up on pit passes has curtailed their activities but in the seventies and early eighties they seemed to be everywhere.

Their goal was to bed a driver but if they failed, anyone connected with the team would do. In our struggling days the Williams pits were not a major hunting ground for pit-popsies. But now every man there seemed to be considered fair game. Understandably, some of them were taking full advantage of this perk of success. I didn't approve but I understood. It's difficult for men who find that they are superstars not to succumb to the temptation. When they've been working so hard for years it must seem like part of the spoils of victory. They are flattered by the adulation. I knew Frank was unlikely to be an exception to this reaction. It was my innate insecurity that made me feel threatened. Underneath I knew that Frank was quite happy with the blanket of his family. He loved his kids and he loved his wife and he enjoyed his home set-up, and if he did play away from home then he regarded it as something completely different, a separate sport.

But I didn't like it. So I owe a debt of gratitude to Beverley for coming to my rescue. I was feeling particularly ragged around the edges one day having just discovered yet another incriminating hotel bill for two in Frank's pocket.

Beverley listened to my wailing and said, 'For heaven's sake why don't you come up to London and spend a lot of his money? Cheer yourself up. Buy some frilly knickers on the credit card. Leave the kids with me.' I thought, 'Well that's not such a silly idea.'

I did as Bev suggested, had an extravagant day, and filled the car up with shopping bags. Then, my spirits restored, I picked up Claire and Jonathan from Bev's house in Ealing and drove home.

At six o'clock, exceptionally early for him, Frank came in. He had been quite irritable of late which had added to my conviction that he was misbehaving. But tonight for some reason he was all sweetness and light, jumping about saying, 'How are you? Did you have a nice day?'

Rather taken aback I said, 'Yes lovely thank you.'

'What have you been doing?'

'Just some shopping.'

'Oh. Good. Anything nice?'

I couldn't believe it. Who was this man? For the next week he was transformed. Nothing was too much trouble for him. He was constantly concerned about my welfare. A few days later he came home with a gold Rolex watch which he presented to me sheepishly saying, 'I haven't had time to buy you anything before. This is your Championship present.' I was astounded. Frank had never given me anything in my life before. Present-giving was not a habit he had ever acquired.

We were planning to take the children to the Dutch Grand Prix the following week. Frank still rationed the number of Grand Prix I attended but I was usually granted three or four trips a year.

In Holland, Beverley and I were sitting having a cup of tea when she asked innocently, 'How are things with Frank?'

'Bev, I cannot believe the change in the guy,' I exclaimed. 'He's so nice. It's fantastic.' I flourished my watch at her.

She sat there looking pleased with herself.

'Do you want to know why?'

It turned out that Beverley had used my trip to London to hatch an underhand plot. While I was away shopping Alan had come home and seeing Jonathan and Claire had asked, 'What are Frank's kids doing here. Where's Ginny?'

Beverley shook her head. 'I can't tell you. I know you'll tell Frank.'

'Don't be silly Bev,' Alan protested, 'I'm your husband. You can trust me.'

She hesitated, 'Do you promise? Do you really promise?'

Alan widened his eyes, 'Of course.'

'No, I can't tell you.'

This went on for ten minutes before she relented, 'Okay I'll tell you if you swear to God you won't tell Frank.'

He nodded earnestly.

'Ginny's absolutely had it up to here and she's gone to consult a lawyer. She wants a divorce.'

Alan's eyes rolled into the back of his head. Beverley said she could almost hear him thinking, 'I've got to tell my mate about this. What am I going to do?' She watched him going through agonies. For twenty minutes he was just pacing the house. Then he put his hand to his head as though he'd forgotten something and said, 'Oh. Just remembered. I've got to go and see somebody. Won't be long,' and bolted out of the door and into the car. He was gone for twenty minutes. Bev knew exactly what he was doing – phoning Frank from the nearest public phone box and saying, 'Watch out! Your wife's with a lawyer this afternoon.'

Frank would never have expected anything so devious of me and the fact that I didn't confess it when he asked me what I'd been doing must have made him think I was serious – it wasn't just a gesture to shock him. Bev's plot was brilliant and it worked like a charm. Frank returned to the fold and marital harmony was restored.

'But don't tell him,' she grinned. 'We might need it again one of these days.'

CHAPTER 7

At the end of 1980 Beverley and Alan had adopted a little boy. They were besotted parents. Alan who had originally gone along with the idea of adoption for Beverley's sake became one of the fondest dads I had ever seen.

Perhaps it was the responsibility of becoming a father, as well as Bev's increasing homesickness that prompted Alan's announcement at the end of 1981 that he was retiring from race-driving. It came as a dreadful shock to Frank. We had just won another Constructors Championship and although Nelson Piquet in a Brabham had pipped Alan and Carlos for the drivers title Alan still appeared to be driving as brilliantly as ever. However he stuck by his decision and just before Christmas we saw Beverley, Alan and baby Christian off on their journey home to Australia. Everyone was in tears.

'It's like leaving your family,' Beverley said. Which after those magical four seasons together was exactly the way it felt.

The worst thing about the decision for Frank was its timing. By now Williams was recognized as the best seat going but it was the end of the season and most drivers were signed up. We had to settle for Keke Rosberg as Alan's replacement. After driving in thirty-seven Grand Prix he only had five points to his name but he was the best driver still available to us. It was a worrying time. In 1979 it had seemed to be the charmed combination of Alan, Patrick and Frank that had produced the winning chemistry. Would it be possible to recreate it with different drivers? Especially with one as different as Rosberg?

From anybody's point of view he had an unusual approach to the job. Racing drivers have to be supremely fit to muster the stamina and concentration demanded in a race but Keke was a chain-smoker, enjoyed a drink and appeared to take very little excercise. He was a most unusual choice for someone like Frank, who winced every time he saw him light up a cigarette. But Keke was the exception that proves the rule. By the end of the 1982 season he had won the Drivers Championship for Williams and Frank knew the magic was still there.

In March 1982 I suffered a miscarriage. For the next six months I was plagued with feeling bloated and unwell but I assumed they were all part of the aftermath of losing a baby. In July I was dismayed to find I was developing a bit of a tummy so I put myself on a strict version of the F-plan diet. It was late August before a check-up revealed to my shock that I was approximately five months pregnant. I should have remembered that this had been Frank's way of helping me over my miscarriage the last time . . .

In November our third son, Jaime, was born. He was premature and weighed less than three pounds and for a while it was touch and go but we were lucky. He was a little fighter. After five weeks of being incubated in special care he came home and joined the family.

Jacques Laffite returned to drive for Williams in 1983 and we asked him to be Jaime's godfather which he was delighted to do. Predictably Jacques, ever the joker, completely undermined the solemnity of the occasion. When the priest asked him to 'name this child' Jacques stood at the font and with a perfectly straight face recited: 'Jaime, Sebastian, Francis, Jacques, Clay, Alan, Carlos, James Hunt . . .' The priest did not seem as amused as we were.

Jacques drove Jonathan and Claire back for tea at Battle House in his Mercedes, thrilling them over three miles of country lanes, by driving with both legs out of the window, using one hand to work the foot pedals and the other to control the steering wheel!

Over the next two or three years Frank started at last to delegate, giving himself more time both for his family and for his beloved running. At this stage running was becoming nearly as important to Frank as motor racing. It was almost an addiction. He had started to compete regularly in half-marathons and was obsessed about his diet, wanting to eat only food which would build muscle rather than fat and would provide him with easily available energy during a race. I sometimes wished I had a degree in nutrition. He was regretting now that he had not started competitive running earlier. Since he was over forty he was condemned to run as a veteran but he achieved fast times and regularly won his class. In the early eighties Peter Windsor had introduced Frank to Sebastian Coe and the two became good friends. Motor racing enthralled Seb so with that and running they always had plenty to talk about. Seb was impressed with Frank's half-marathon times which spurred him on to even greater efforts. But despite running's increasing role in Frank's life, racing cars still took precedence – just.

Jacques' return did not bring with it the success we had hoped for and though Keke Rosberg continued to drive well, we managed only fourth and sixth in the Constructors Championships during the two years that Jacques was with us. It was no disgrace. Motor racing has always been cyclical. No team stays at the top consistently and we were not far off the summit but Frank was anxious to get back up there. Since 1983 Williams had been using Honda engines, but, as with every new partnership, the necessary adjustments had taken time. In 1984 the firm had moved out of the old carpet warehouse into a new 60,000 square foot factory on the other side of Didcot with increased development and wind-tunnel facilities. The Williams-Honda combination was now looking good. There was little room for sentiment at this end of the business and Frank felt that sadly we needed to replace Jacques if we were to exploit the full potential of the new car.

The 'silly season' in Formula One starts after the British Grand Prix and is the time when drivers and teams begin to negotiate contracts for the following year. In 1984 when Frank was surveying the talent available for the next season, he took, as he always did, a hard look at the emerging British drivers. The idea of an all British team was one which appealed to him. But only if it was a top-class team. To Frank there was no point in being patriotic if it meant settling for second-best.

Two British drivers were on the possible list this year: Derek Warwick and Nigel Mansell. Frank approached Derek first but he had just started driving for Renault and turned down the offer. Frank moved on to Nigel Mansell without great enthusiasm. Mansell had been driving for Lotus since 1980 but he had met with little success with them and had acquired a reputation, whether deserved or not Frank did not know, for complaining about his lot. So it was with some reservations that Frank asked Nigel if he would be interested in driving for Williams in 1985. Nigel was keen. His contract with Lotus was not going to be renewed. Frank held off for a week or two, uncertain if it was the right move. But the major talent was already placed for the next season, and just before Zandvoort he offered Nigel a two-year contract, with Williams having an option on the second year.

After it was made public the signing was widely criticized. In Zandvoort, after the news broke out people continually came up to me and asked, 'Why on earth has Frank signed up Mansell?' as if I would be able to throw light on the mystery! I wondered why myself. At thirty years old he had yet to win a Grand Prix. He could hardly be considered to be a rising star. Lotus had obviously decided he was not good enough for them and had replaced him with Ayrton Senna. I felt quite embarrassed about it.

Once again, as with Jonesy, subsequent events were to prove the doubters, including me, quite wrong. I don't think at the time of signing even Frank was expecting that Nigel would help put Williams back at the top of the constructors' table but that's what he did. He was brilliant. He proved to be immensely quick, skilful, and best of all, from the crowd's viewpoint, exciting. They loved him. He was aggressive and determined and never gave less than his very best, thrilling the spectators and the watchers in the Williams pits with his performances. By the end of his four years with us the British fans had adopted him as their new hero.

Not at the start of the 1985 season though. Then he still had it all to prove and it was no overnight success story. There were still teething problems with the car and although he consistently qualified well it was September before Nigel's true abilities began to emerge. He finished second at Spa in Belgium and then in the next race, the European championship at Brands Hatch, he set the crowd absolutely alight with a dazzling display of driving which put him into the lead on lap eight and kept him there for the remaining sixty-seven laps. Twenty seconds behind him in second place was Senna, the man who had replaced him at Lotus. In third place, in the other Williams was Rosberg. It was Nigel's first ever Grand Prix win and the first time an English driver had won at Brands Hatch since Jim Clark in 1964.

The bit was between his teeth now. Two weeks later at the South African Grand Prix at Kyalami, starting from pole position Nigel won again. In second place came Keke who, though about to leave to drive for McLaren, had certainly not stopped trying for Williams.

There was just one race left that season: Adelaide. It was a new street circuit, included in the world series for the first time. The

Williams cars again excelled. Nigel started on the front row of the grid next to Ayrton Senna's Lotus on pole. Nigel had taken the lead before the first chicane which to onlookers seemed to provoke Senna. Before the lap was over Senna had knocked Nigel off the track on a left-hand bend. He struggled on for another lap but was forced to retire. Nigel was furious and the Williams pits weren't too pleased. However Keke was still hanging in and by the afternoon's end he had compensated for the first disappointment by once more taking the chequered flag for Williams. It was a magnificent parting gesture.

It really did look as though we had come full circle since 1979 and were again poised at the brink of a triumphant year. Nelson Piquet had signed up to join us in 1986 from Brabham. He already had two world championships to his credit and seemed to be the sort of driver who, if the car was right, could deliver the goods. Nigel, at the end of the season had become a number one driver before our very eyes. The car looked good. The drivers looked good. It seemed that in 1986 the world would be at our feet.

And then, two weeks before the start of the season, at the Paul Ricard circuit in the South of France Frank set off in a hire car to drive to Nice Airport. Minutes later his life and the lives of everyone connected with him were changed for ever.

BOOK
2

CHAPTER 8

We were allowed to spend only ten minutes with Frank on that first visit to the intensive therapy unit at the Timone Hospital. Peter, Patrick and I left the hospital with Graziano, Nelson's driver late on Sunday afternoon. No one said very much. We were all still in a state of shock.

We had not made a hotel booking in Marseille so Graziano took us on a tour of the town to look for somewhere to stay. We found three rooms in a hotel called the Mövenpick, near the centre, and went for a drink in the hotel's coffee shop to plan our next move. We were unanimous in wanting to get Frank back to an English hospital as quickly as possible. I didn't feel it should be too much of a problem as offers of help were already flowing in. Bernie Ecclestone had promised that his private plane was ready to leave whenever we needed it. Peter told us that Mansour Ojjeh of TAG had telephoned to say that his company could convert one of his aircraft to ambulance specifications within twenty-four hours. Yet a third option was to lease a Lear Jet air ambulance from a Swiss aviation company.

Patrick would replace Frank at the helm of Williams for the time being and we decided he should travel back to Didcot the next morning. Meanwhile Peter and I would return to the hospital and consult the doctors before making departure arrangements for Frank. It felt good to be planning something positive. I kept telling myself that if only we could get him home to England everything would be all right.

Peter had not been to bed for thirty-six hours. His clothes were still stained with blood but it was all Frank's – amazingly Peter had not received even a scratch in the accident. It was difficult to comprehend how Frank, sitting only inches away from him in the car could have suffered such a different fate.

Although no one felt very hungry we ordered a snack and were waiting for it to arrive when the hotel's Tannoy system suddenly crackled into life.

'*Madame Williams au téléphone s'il vous plaît . . .*'

I sat rigid in my chair. Graziano had notified the hospital that we were staying at the Mövenpick but we had not had time to tell anybody else. It must be the Timone. Frank's condition must have deteriorated or maybe worse . . . Patrick offered to go for me but if it was bad news I felt they should tell me, not him. Stiff with fear I made my way to reception and picked up the telephone.

It was only a reporter from an Italian newspaper. He must have got the hotel's name from the hospital. 'Would you tell us your husband's condition?' he asked. I muttered something noncommittal and stumbled back to my seat. After that Patrick or Peter took all the calls. I was in no state to speak. There were numerous messages from friends and relatives as well as enquiries from reporters. The Tannoy seemed to be requesting 'Madame Williams' continually.

I took only two calls personally: one from Frank's solicitor John Pickworth, who told me that he was flying down and would like to see me in the morning for an urgent breakfast meeting, and the other from Susie. She had started a holiday in Scotland that day and had been phoned on her arrival by her father who had heard of the accident on the television news. Instantly she had repacked her bags and was ringing to let me know she was on her way down with Hilary, her husband, to hold my hand in Marseille. I protested that there was no need for her to spoil her holiday but she wouldn't listen and I was grateful. Her call reminded me of home. I wondered how Jaime and Claire were and if Jonathan had been told yet. I remembered inconsequentially that it was Mother's Day.

It was nearly midnight before Patrick, Peter and I went off to our rooms. Even then I went reluctantly, knowing there was little chance of me sleeping. My mind was racing with all sorts of disconnected pictures. Against my will I found myself mentally checking through my wardrobe at home for suitable clothes to wear to a funeral. I had nothing appropriate, perhaps Susie would help me buy something. I tried to deflect my thoughts onto another tack but failed. I spent the night picturing Frank's funeral service. I didn't worry about him being paralysed, I had put it firmly out of my mind. He was critically ill, that was all that mattered. My only prayers were to request God to keep him alive. Sometime in the early hours I fell asleep.

As arranged, I met John Pickworth in the coffee shop first thing the following morning. He had the unenviable duty of being legally obliged to protect Williams Grand Prix Engineering and had drawn up a Power of Attorney. I signed it where he indicated. I was now in theory, if not in practice, in control of the company.

Peter met me afterwards in the hotel lobby and Graziano drove us to the hospital. On our arrival at the Timone we were shown to the Intensive Care visitors' room which was bare and comfortless. We were told nothing except that we must wait there until we were called. All around the room the relatives of other patients sat silently huddled in their chairs waiting to be summoned. Nobody looked at anyone else except for the odd furtive glance. There was none of the camaraderie you sometimes get in waiting rooms. Everyone sat isolated in their own private misery.

No nurse came to brief us or say whether we could expect to wait for half-an-hour or for three hours but none of the other relatives demanded to know what was happening. There was a resigned acceptance on the waiting faces. Every now and then an impersonal voice would call out from the Tannoy 'Famille Dupont,' or some other name, and a small gloomy group would be led off for the gowning procedure. After a couple of hours of this I found myself praying hard that I would never be called. Having been given so long to brood about what we were going to be faced with I really did not think I could handle it.

At last it came: 'Famille Williams.' A stony faced nurse appeared and gestured silently to me to follow her. Almost against my will I found myself being led towards Frank's bedside. I had not thought it possible that he could look sicker than when I had first seen him but I was wrong. His bruises were more livid, his colour even worse. I was horrified to see that he was unattended. The nearest nurse was sitting at a desk yards away across the ward. Surely he needed constant monitoring. Wasn't that what intensive care was about?

Frank's eyes were open and although they were swollen and bloodshot I saw them register relief when he saw me. It must have been a long night for him. He was trying to speak, but his voice was very weak. I had to put my ear to his mouth to hear.

'Ginny, get me home.'

I held his hand. It felt icy cold.

'We're going to get you home Frank,' I said.

He seemed to be having even more trouble breathing than the day before. He sounded appalling, like a drowning man gasping for air. His abdomen was still heaving in that awful laboured way and yet his chest stayed unnaturally still. I couldn't understand why he wasn't able to breathe normally.

I sat beside him, my head close to his. He made continual painful efforts to speak. He complained of the cold, though it was stiflingly hot in the intensive care unit and asked me again to take him home. I told him about the various options of aircraft. He seized on the suggestion of a Lear jet. 'Yes. Take me in the Lear,' he whispered. Frank loved flying and had kept an extensive log of all his flights over the past years. Even if he was at death's door he could still summon an interest in his mode of travel. Perhaps it was a good sign.

He was speaking again, 'Are you holding my hand Ginny?'

I nodded.

'I can't feel it.'

'It's all right. Don't worry.'

I couldn't think what else to say.

I wanted to ask lots of questions but bit them back. The effort he had to make to force each word out was painful to watch. I felt Frank needed to concentrate all his energies on breathing.

No one was allowed to spend much time in the Intensive Care Unit. There was vital work to be done and visitors got in the way. Within ten minutes of my arrival the nurse on the central nursing station came across to me and said brusquely, '*Allez-vous-en!*' I inquired when I could visit again and she told me that I could come back at four o'clock if I wanted. I felt very superfluous. Peter had not been allowed in to see Frank. There was no question of anyone but me visiting for the moment. Outside the ward I recounted my impressions to him. I had thought one of Frank's doctors would want to speak to us but the nurse had not mentioned it.

We wandered outside to find a restaurant where we could sit and pass the next few hours. I had not known Peter terribly well up to now but I had always got on with him. He was in his mid-thirties, married, and had started working freelance for Williams in 1978. Since 1984 he had been our full-time publicity manager.

We sat in a café, stirring endless cups of tea as we waited for four o'clock to arrive. We talked about Frank's condition and about the prospects of flying him to England, and finally, unable to avoid it

114

any longer, we talked about the accident itself. Peter said Frank had been driving a rented Ford Sierra. As usual he had been driving fast, though they were in good time to catch their plane. The Sierra had simply failed to take a bend and had left the road, somersaulting several times before finishing upside down in a ploughed field. In the passenger seat, Peter, virtually unhurt, had managed to free himself from the wreckage. He discovered that Frank was conscious but trapped because the roof pillar on his side of the car had collapsed. The fuel tanks had ruptured and were spilling petrol so Peter had found a boulder and broken the rear window with it. Then with the help of a passing motorist he managed to pull Frank across the back seats, out through the window and to safety well away from a potential fire.

Another passerby was dispatched to the circuit to call in help from the test crew who were well equipped and used to handling emergencies. Peter had sat in the field waiting for them, supporting Frank who had several deep cuts on his forehead and scalp.

'The biggest problem was keeping the blood out of his eyes Ginny,' he said. 'I was worried about how much blood he was losing. But he was conscious and he was answering me. I thought perhaps it could all be just superficial damage.'

Within a few minutes Nelson, Nigel and Frank Dernie arrived and they had waited with Frank and Peter until the ambulance came. This took a long three-quarters of an hour by which time Nelson had contacted Prof. Watkins and been told to take Frank to the Timone hospital in Marseille. That did not go down too well with the ambulance drivers. They had come from Toulouse, and they intended, they said, to return to Toulouse. And off they went, hotly pursued by an angry Williams team in Nelson's car. At Toulouse, despite their protests Frank had been removed from the ambulance and stretchered into the hospital. Nigel and Nelson ran after him and created a scene. Only the threat of physical violence from Nelson finally persuaded the ambulance drivers to put Frank back in and drive to Marseille.

Peter was haunted by the worry that in getting Frank out of the car he might have worsened his injury. It was a question that was to play on his mind for months. I did my best to reassure him. I knew as well as he did that in a situation where a car might burst into flames at any minute you have no option but to get someone out. In any case, had Frank been left there upside down with pressure on his head, he might well not have survived until the ambulance arrived.

We discussed paralysis – what it meant and its implications. I was completely ignorant about it. It wasn't a word that had ever meant anything to me. I couldn't take it in. Peter thought I shouldn't attempt to for the moment. 'Try not to worry about it Ginny,' he advised. 'Frank will be fine. You know what he's like. Even if it does come to the worst Frank is brain not body. It's his mind that makes him what he is, not his legs. And it's not the main problem now. Let's cross that bridge when we come to it.' I was happy to comply.

Nelson had flown home to Monte Carlo but had arranged for Graziano and his car to be at our disposal for as long as we needed them. Since the car had a telephone we would be able to use it as a mobile office to both receive and make calls. That afternoon we used it to find another hotel, as the Mövenpick had no vacancies that night.

At four o'clock I was allowed in for a further precious ten minutes with Frank. His condition seemed about the same but he again asked about leaving. He seemed no happier with his treatment than I was. Again no medical staff spoke to me except to usher me in and out and there was no one in attendance at his bedside.

I was growing more and more agitated about our situation. Frank was isolated in a huge foreign hospital where the nursing bore no resemblance to what I pictured intensive care should be like. Although we all spoke French it wasn't the same as communicating in your native tongue. And no one seemed to feel the need to tell us what was happening. If the truth was that Frank was dying then we ought to be put in the picture. And if he wasn't, we should be told what they were going to do for him. Being kept in the dark like this was unacceptable. I had not even been able to get the wheels in motion to move him to England. I resolved to be a bit more assertive in my requests to see a doctor the next day.

We had booked into the Hotel Frantal and on my return from the hospital I found Susie and Hilary waiting for me in the lobby. Susie came towards me with her arms wide. I sensed that she was going to put her arms around me and commiserate and I froze, knowing I wouldn't be able to take it. I would just go to pieces. I shook my head at her.

'Don't say anything. Please don't say anything. Just don't give me any sympathy Susie.'

'All right,' she said. 'I understand.'

Peter went off to make a phone call and Hilary, Susie and I went through into the bar. Raucous music was blaring through

116

the speakers and we couldn't hear each other speak. My nerves, already frayed, suddenly snapped. Angrily I marched up to the bar and exploded, 'For Christ's sake turn that music down.' It was quite out of character for me. They must have thought, 'What a dreadful woman!'

I came back to the table and explained – though I suspect they already knew – that Frank was paralysed from the neck down. But still I refused to let Susie sympathize.

'I didn't want you to come here to say "Oh dear". I need you to boost me up and make me laugh.'

She nodded, 'Just tell me about it and I'll listen.'

So I did and for the first time I put my worst fears into words.

'He's dying I think Susie,' I said. 'But I have the feeling that if he dies it will be because he can't face living if he's paralysed. And if he lives it will be because he wants to live whether he's paralysed or not. I really believe that he will decide for himself which way it goes.'

I didn't want him to die but I didn't need to tell Susie that. She listened and understood. She let me talk about it when I wanted to and when I didn't she led me away onto different topics and we spoke about other things. It seems strange but in the end we laughed a lot that night. When Peter came back we went into the restaurant and all through the meal everyone joked and said things to cheer me up. They created a little bubble around me in which I felt safe. I *had* needed Susie to be there. I hadn't known how much. In a situation like that you want someone who will come up to your bedroom with you and listen. Someone who you've known for years and who you can cry in front of without any difficulty. For the last two days everyone around me had been a part of Frank's camp. Kind though they were, they were all still getting to know me. But Susie was in my camp.

She had come armed with Mogadon tablets and she gave me one to help me sleep that night. I was not used to taking pills but I didn't argue. 'I'm just going to give you one,' she said firmly. 'I'm going to ration them.'

I thought her remark was rather odd. Was she afraid I might try to kill myself? But I think Susie was just concerned that I wouldn't sleep at first and might take another one, and then, forgetfully, another, and compound the whole thing by ending up in the next bed to Frank. One tablet was sufficient. I fell deeply asleep that night in a Mogadon haze which proved very hard to surface from.

When I did regain consciousness it was to the sound of a phone ringing. Groggy and confused, it took me some time to realize that the kind lady speaking sympathetic words on the other end of the line was none other than Mrs Thatcher. She was brief but comforting. 'And how are you Virginia?' she asked. 'Are you being strong?' I felt bolstered by the knowledge that she could spare time from the business of government to be concerned about Frank's accident. Before she rang off she promised she would call again and would contact the British consul to see if they could do anything to help. I thanked her, wide awake now and hopeful again.

After breakfast the hotel receptionist passed over messages from other kind people who had rung to offer sympathy and encouragement. It heartened me to know that so many people cared about Frank. I thought briefly of phoning home but dismissed the idea. It was too difficult to contemplate yet. I had too many other things to deal with. I couldn't face hearing Claire say brightly, 'Hello Mummy' and having to switch into a bright pretence that all was well.

Peter returned with me to the hospital for my morning visit. There was no point in Susie coming, since Frank was still allowed no visitors but me. I was beginning by now to hate the Timone, I found it an alien and hostile environment. Everything seemed so disorganized. Even in the main reception area, there were always patients in varying states of undress shuffling around aimlessly, some of them pulling drips on stands after them. We took our place again in the dirty waiting room. There was no coffee shop and nobody offered you a cup of tea while you waited. As far as I could see there weren't even any loos. Visitors were definitely not encouraged.

In the waiting room everyone once again sat cocooned in their own unhappiness. We had been sitting there impatiently for an hour when Peter suddenly leaped up as though he'd been stung and stood in front of me. My face was nearly buried in his sweater. 'What are you doing?' I protested. Then I saw blood dripping onto the floor near one of the seats behind him. I stood up and peered round Peter. What was he trying to shield me from seeing? I sat down again quickly. Opposite us, as calmly as though he was peeling an orange, a man was cutting his wrists with a razor blade. There was some tut-tutting from his immediate neighbours but otherwise everyone continued to sit blankly as though nothing was happening.

It seemed an age before help arrived and the poor man was led out of the room protesting and moaning. My worse nightmares had rarely been as bad as the real life I was experiencing now. For the next twenty minutes we all sat silently contemplating the puddle of blood on the floor. Eventually a cleaner wearing bedroom slippers and with her hair tied up under a scarf came shuffling in. She had a mop and one of those buckets with a perforated section on one side. As she mopped the blood up and squelched the mop all the blood trickled through the holes into the bucket. I watched in horror. Nasty experiences like this were completely foreign to me. I was beginning to realize I had led a very sheltered existence.

At last the call came, 'Famille Williams'. Another nurse materialized and waited for me to get up and follow her. Again she said not a word. The French nurses seemed to have a completely different attitude to English nurses, perhaps it was the way they were trained. Maybe they were encouraged to stay remote from the patients and relatives to allow them to deal with death and distress better. Whatever the reason, in the whole time we were in France there wasn't one nurse who spoke to me comfortingly. Nor did I ever see a member of the nursing staff at the Timone show any other visitor the slightest sympathy or warmth.

I gowned up and went in to see Frank. His condition was alarming. His face was a horrible shade of dark grey and his breathing sounded desperate. When he saw me he tried to speak but his voice was now barely more than a croak. I had to struggle to make out what he was saying. 'I'm cold,' he gasped. 'It's freezing in here.'

I took his hand. It felt like the hand of a corpse.

He was whispering something else and I leaned over again.

'Get me out of this place.'

I looked around the ward. No nurse was visible. If Frank had suddenly stopped breathing no one would have seen him.

'Did anyone stay with you last night?' I asked.

'No . . . last night I wanted a nurse . . . to help me . . . there wasn't one . . . get me out Ginny,' Frank repeated. 'I'm cold . . . I can't breathe . . . do something.' There was panic in his voice now. Each short phrase was separated from the next by a rasping intake of breath.

I was galvanized into action. I was sure Frank was dying. Unless I did something to prevent it perhaps he would die today. I found myself thinking very clearly. I couldn't leave it to the medical staff any longer. To them, after all, he was just one more patient. But he was my one and only husband. I felt that staying at his bedside making pleasantries was wasting precious time. I whispered goodbye, kissed him and left. I had to find Peter and speak to him, then phone up Prof. and get things going. Frank didn't say, 'Stay with me.' I felt as if he too wanted me to go so I could fetch help.

Peter was still sitting in the waiting room. I marched up to him. 'We've got to do something. Frank can't breathe. He's freezing cold. If we don't interfere he's just not going to survive.' I wanted Peter to see him so he could form his own opinion, but the nurses wouldn't let him in. I demanded aggressively to see a doctor, and we were at last allowed in to see the resident anaesthetist for the Intensive Therapy Unit.

No one had yet explained anything about paralysis to me. Maybe I should have known that Frank's breathing difficulties were related to his broken neck but I didn't. I asked the doctor to explain why he seemed to have trouble getting enough air. His explanation staggered me.

'*Parce qu'il fume,*' he said with a shrug.

I was furious. If he didn't even know that Frank was a non-smoker how could he assess his breathing problems? Did he think Frank was just suffering from smoker's cough? I told him angrily that Frank had never smoked in his life. I assumed that he would react by jumping up and doing something. But not a bit of it, he merely leaned back in his chair and shrugged again.

Today I have more understanding of his attitude. It was probably the exception in that hospital to fight for someone who has broken his neck. If Frank had been the average Frenchman in the street in Marseille, he would have been allowed to die. I was to learn later that most people with Frank's degree of injury die within four days anyway. It is a question of just waiting it out. I don't think that the doctor could understand why, having been told what Frank's injuries were, we were all fighting so hard to try and keep him alive instead of allowing him to go peacefully.

'When can we take Frank back to England?' I demanded.

'Whenever you like,' he replied dismissively. 'It will be "heavy" for the hospital if Monsieur Williams dies here.' (Later I learned that the British consul in Marseille, prompted by Mrs Thatcher, had been in contact with the Timone which explained this last statement.)

But I could not believe I had heard correctly. 'Are you telling me you believe my husband is going to die?'

Again the shrug. '*Oui. Bien sûr.*' Of course.

There wasn't anything left to say. If he felt that way there was little point in hanging around.

Peter and I left the room. I asked Peter if he had the same understanding of the conversation as me. He did. It was obvious to us both now why Frank had no nurse. It wasn't considered worthwhile.

120

Out in the corridor I burst into tears, but it was only momentary. I felt outrage welling up. How dare the doctor talk like that. As though Frank's death were a foregone conclusion – not even worth a fight. We had to do something. I felt as though minutes counted now. There was no time to cry. Peter said he would call Prof. Watkins.

Graziano was waiting for us in our mobile office outside the hospital and we immediately put a call through to the London Hospital and pleaded with the Professor to intervene. I think he suspected we were over-reacting. However when he heard that Frank had no stand-by nurse and that I was only allowed two ten-minute visits a day, and was afraid Frank would die between one visit and the next, he decided to give us the benefit of the doubt. He arranged for Dr Paul Yates, an anaesthetist from the London Hospital, to fly down in Bernie Ecclestone's plane immediately and make a 'qualified' assessment of the situation. He could stay with Frank in lieu of a nurse until it was decided what to do.

I felt the weight on my shoulders lift a little with this assurance. It felt good to know that we were employing somebody to be with Frank through the night. The resident doctor wasn't exactly thrilled when we informed him that one of his peers was coming down to assess the situation. But as far as I was concerned that was just too bad.

On my afternoon visit Frank seemed no better than he had been in the morning. Speaking was still a tremendous effort, but he was plainly relieved to hear that an English doctor would be arriving in a couple of hours. He wanted desperately to go 'home'. I promised him it wouldn't be too long though he was so weak now that I couldn't imagine how it would be feasible to move him safely.

Banished once more from the ward, Peter and I found ourselves with a couple of hours to kill before Dr Yates was due to arrive. We decided to go shopping. Despite having spent a large part of the night of the accident considering what I would need to wear in France I had brought a ridiculous selection of clothes with me. I had forgotten to pack any knickers or socks, had brought only one pair of jeans, countless summer tee-shirts but no sweaters. It was completely unsuitable wear for cold March mornings in Marseille. Peter too was in need of a change of clothes. He still had on the blood-stained jeans he had been wearing when the accident happened. We had little option but to spend a couple of hours browsing around the shops. I was feeling disorientated and somehow guilty too. It seemed wrong to be even thinking of trivia like clothes. I said to Peter, 'We shouldn't be doing this.'

'What are you talking about? We have to carry on living,' he replied. I knew he was right. Gradually despite myself I relaxed as Peter tried on over-priced denims and I searched the boutiques for socks and sweaters.

Dr Paul Yates arrived at the hotel shortly after we returned with our shopping. His face was grave. He said he had already been to see Frank and was very concerned about him. 'Fluid is pooling in his lungs,' he said. 'It should be suctioned out frequently but as far as I can see no one is doing it on a regular basis. It's the reason Frank is having such difficulty breathing.'

He agreed that Frank would get better care in London, but dismissed my suggestion of an ambulance plane.

'It wouldn't be safe to even contemplate moving him until his condition has stabilized. It's out of the question.'

It seemed we were likely to be staying in Marseille for some time. Paul's immediate plans were to have some supper and then go back to the hospital to check Frank out. If necessary he would spend the night with him.

I felt quite relieved to have temporarily passed on the burden of responsibility. 'Let's have supper together,' Peter suggested.

'Why don't we meet up in twenty minutes? Afterwards Paul can go back to the hospital.' Slightly cheered I went up to my room to put on clean socks. I opened the bedroom door and stopped in my tracks. Frank's briefcase and spongebag were on the dressing table. For a moment my mind played tricks. Everything was all right after all. His briefcase was here. Any minute now he would walk out of the bathroom. I called out his name.

Then reason returned. I realized the briefcase must have been retrieved from the wrecked Sierra and brought to my room while I was out. I felt sick as the reality hit me once more. Frank wasn't in the bathroom – he was in hospital dying. I fought to stay in control of myself. He needed me. I mustn't break down.

Susie and Hilary joined us for supper and again we discussed our options. I pressed Paul to find a way to get Frank home if it was humanly possible but he was still adamant that it would not be safe.

'He'll have to show some improvement first. Then we can think about it,' he said firmly.

When we left the restaurant I went straight to bed and slept once more with the aid of one of Susie's magic pills. I was comforted by the knowledge that Paul was at Frank's bedside and would ensure his lungs were suctioned when necessary.

The telephone's ring woke me at six a.m. It was Peter, asking me to look for Frank's passport in his briefcase and then come down to the lobby to meet him. Still half-drugged I struggled out of bed and found the passport. I dressed quickly and took it down with me in the lift. As the doors opened into the lobby I was confronted not only by Peter but by Susie and Hilary as well.

'Oh my God,' I thought. 'Now what?'

Peter moved forward as I stepped out of the lift.

'Ginny, there's been a change of plan. We're going to fly Frank back this morning.'

Eight hours earlier I had been told it was 'out of the question'. Paul had said that flying would kill him. Now suddenly it was on. What was happening? I heard my voice starting to scream hysterically at Peter demanding an explanation. He tried valiantly to calm me down. 'Come on,' he said. 'Let's go through into the coffee shop.' People waiting to go in to breakfast were beginning to stare. I followed him to a table and sat down obediently. Susie held my hand while Peter explained that Paul had rung and said that Frank had not had a good night. Consequently he felt it would be a better idea to go now and take the chance.

'What's different. What's changed since last night?' I demanded.

'Nothing, Ginny,' Peter insisted. 'Stop worrying about it. There's just been a change of plan. Paul thinks it would be better this way.'

I was convinced that Peter was keeping something from me. Half-an-hour later Paul arrived back at the hotel to get washed and changed. He had foreseen my reaction to his decision.

'Look, don't get upset about it,' he said. 'I've changed my mind that's all. He's not going to survive in this hospital. We've got to get him back to London. I know it's hard, but try not to worry. There's a good chance that we can do it.'

One night in the intensive care unit at the Timone had convinced Paul that Frank had no chance at all if he remained there. While it would be a risk to fly him out it seemed to be his only hope. He tried to reassure me about the plane journey .

'I'm pretty confident Frank will cope with it. The plane is equipped to cover any emergency. There's a respirator on board if we need it.'

If he thought that news would bring me comfort he was wrong. To me the word respirator was terrifying. It suggested comas; human vegetables; life and death decisions about turning the machine off. I begged Paul not to use it. He attempted to calm my anxieties, 'Ginny, don't worry about the respirator. We'll only use it if we have to. It's nothing to be afraid of. It's not something Frank would be on forever. It would just buy him a bit of recovery time until he could do without it.' I felt he was humouring me. I wanted to say, 'I'm not five years old. I know what a respirator is for God's sake.'

Peter was brilliant. He had already been working hard on the phone that morning making arrangements to get the air ambulance Lear jet on its way from Geneva. Two nurses had been found to accompany Frank during the journey. Bernie Ecclestone's plane, carrying Peter, Susie, Hilary and me, was to follow the Lear jet back to England. I was not to be allowed to travel in the air ambulance in case Frank had to be given emergency treatment. Frank, who always complained when he had to wait at airports, would have liked the VIP arrangements. On learning of the journey the British embassy had arranged a police escort from Marseille to the airport where his flight was to receive special clearance. It had all been planned with military precision. Peter told me that Mrs Thatcher had telephoned again and had been informed of the travel plans.

Susie came back to my room to help me pack and for the first time since the accident I broke down completely. Up until now I had cried only briefly. I had always been able to make myself stop. To listen to the voice inside me saying 'Pull yourself together.' But now, terrified of what might happen, I lost control and just cried and cried. Shaking like a leaf and hardly knowing what I was doing, I threw things at random into my suitcase. Susie let me get it out of my system. Then, satisfied the storm was over she picked up Frank's briefcase and we all piled into Nelson's car and drove to the hospital. Time was pressing. I had to face another ordeal.

At the hospital I knocked on the door of the duty anaesthetist's room and went in. 'We have decided to fly Frank home to England this morning,' I told him nervously.

He looked at me with hostility. 'Do what you like. It's not my business,' he said. It was understandable. Hospitals do not appreciate having their authority undermined or their routines interfered with. I tried to ignore his words as I gowned up for the last time and went in to see Frank. Paul had not told him of the plans. I was to be the one to let him know that he was going home to England.

Frank's breathing seemed slightly improved after Paul's suctioning during the night. There was not as much panic about his efforts to get air, but he still gave me the impression of being very close to death. I told him what we were going to do and he listened intently. Then he said something in a low whisper. I had to ask him to repeat it.

'Where are my clothes? What have you got for me to wear?'

'Frank. You don't have to get dressed.' I exclaimed.

He let that sink in. Then he spoke again.

'Have you got your American Express card to pay the hotel and hospital bills?'

I couldn't believe him. Here he was, dying, and he was concerned about wearing his trousers and paying the bills!

The journey had been organized into a series of carefully ordered moves. Firstly, Paul had to get all the drips unhooked and replace the glass bottles with unbreakable plastic ones. The procedure would take some time. He suggested that I went down and waited in the car so that I would be ready to follow the ambulance as soon as Frank was loaded in.

I kissed Frank goodbye. 'I'll see you again at the airport,' I promised. An hour later I sat with the others in Nelson's car and watched as Frank was loaded into the ambulance. Carefully, Paul handed the drips and all their yards of plastic tubing in after him. His body had been wrapped in foil and layers of blanketing for insulation. With lights flashing and sirens wailing the escort took us straight through the centre of Marseille to the airport. When we arrived on the tarmac we found the little red Swiss ambulance Lear jet already sitting waiting for its cargo. Susie and I looked at each other and shuddered. Somehow ambulance planes look serious. People don't get moved around in air ambulances unless they are really ill.

Frank was taken out of the ambulance and his stretcher was rested on a trolley on the tarmac for a moment before being loaded on board. It was the first time Susie had seen Frank and I felt her go rigid with shock at his appearance. I ran up to him and gave him a kiss. In daylight he looked even worse than he had in the unit. I felt doubt rise up again. Could he really make it?

Getting Frank into the Lear jet did not look easy despite the specially adapted double entrance door. His stretcher, surrounded by all his drips was loaded feet first up the steep steps and then had to be manoeuvred through a tight turn to come to rest into the correct position for the journey. At last he was edged safely into place and the doors were shut. Almost immediately the plane taxied away to the start of the runway. We stood in a forlorn little group watching it as it took off and disappeared into the clouds. Slowly we walked back into the terminal building.

All of us travelling in Bernie's plane would have to go through normal customs procedures before being cleared for departure. This would result in us arriving half-an-hour after Frank's plane. Unknown to me this was all part of the master plan so that if Frank did not survive the flight I would not have to face seeing his body being unloaded onto the tarmac when I arrived in England. We discovered there had been an additional problem that morning; there was fog over the south of England. Weather reports were being monitored and at one point it seemed likely that we would have to divert from our planned destination of Biggin Hill but the gods decided to be kind to us. Had we set off an hour later we would have found all airports in the south of England closed.

We prepared to go through customs. It was time to say goodbye to Graziano, Nelson's chauffeur, who had always been in the right place at the appointed time and for whom nothing had been too much trouble. I don't believe he had been to bed for three nights. He had been ready at all times to drive or to assist us. How we would have managed without him and Nelson's car I don't know.

I had many unpleasant memories of Marseille but against that the concern so many people had shown for Frank, and the flowers and messages of sympathy that had been constantly arriving at the hotel had made a deep impression. We had been treated with extreme kindness while we were there by so many people who wanted to help, even in a small way. As we boarded the plane we found a picnic had been thoughtfully put on the plane for us by some kind person. Although no one had much appetite we picked at it and tried to keep our spirits up during our flight home.

But through all the chatter I was constantly aware of that little red jet just a couple of hundred miles ahead of us. I prayed we had taken the right decision.

CHAPTER 9

By the time we touched down at Biggin Hill Frank had already left, once again under police escort, bound for the London Hospital in the Whitechapel Road.

I said goodbye to Susie and Hilary, on whom I had leaned so hard for the past three days. (Hilary told me later that on returning home to Ascot Susie collapsed in tears for an hour having suppressed her own feelings up till then in order to support me.)

Peter accompanied me on the drive into London. We were both subdued and said little during the journey. I had no idea what the London Hospital looked like but while enduring the rigours of the Timone I had had plenty of time to speculate about it. I pictured a smart hospital with modern facilities and hotel-like decor. I imagined lots of simple comforts for relatives like lavatories and cups of tea. I had in my mind something along the lines of The Harley Street Clinic. I remarked to Peter that apart from the benefit to Frank it would be more pleasant for us to be in a good hospital. I had been shocked at the general dirtiness of the Timone, and the frequent sight of patients on trolleys left lying semi-conscious in passageways.

Peter, who was more worldly-wise than me, and had a greater knowledge of National Health hospitals said cautiously that he hoped I was not going to be disappointed. I soon discovered what he meant. Medically the London Hospital is a brilliant centre. The Intensive Therapy Unit has the highest staff-to-patient ratio in the country. But it is set in a poor and run-down area and all their medical miracles go

127

on in an antiquated Victorian building which must sometimes make the doctors there despair. Even walking in through the entrance I could see that a little bit more than a coat of paint would be required to restore The London to its former glory. A strange sickly smell permeated the building which I was to notice on every visit.

The porter informed us that Frank had arrived some time ago and had been taken up to the Intensive Therapy Unit on the fourth floor. He was still alive! My dismay at our surroundings vanished. To be critical of flaking plaster suddenly seemed pernickety. We got into an ancient creaky lift which in the brief time it took to reach the fourth floor I decided never to use again. It had to be safer to climb the stairs. The lift doors shuddered open and we announced our arrival at the doors of Frank's new home. I was not asked to gown up as thoroughly as in France, the nurse in charge merely handed me an apron – and she did it with a smile which restored my spirits. We were back in England.

Peter was not to be allowed in today. He sat on a chair in a long cold glass-walled corridor outside the Intensive Therapy Unit – or ITU as it was referred to by the staff. It was as well for my peace of mind that I had no idea then how many hours Peter and I were both to spend sitting shivering in that cold corridor over the next three months.

I followed the nurse into the ward. There were more patients here than in the intensive care ward in France but I saw Frank at once. He was installed in a bed in the right-hand corner, a nurse hovering in attendance. I felt absurdly pleased, remembering how nice it had been at boarding school when I got the corner bed.

Frank was awake, but tired. He could barely manage a smile as I kissed his cheek. His breathing sounded little different to before but at least there was someone else here now to listen to it and assess his condition. Frank's first duty nurse, a plump and cheerful young girl called Carole introduced herself to me.

'How are you? Would you like a cup of tea?'

I nodded gratefully. While I sat by Frank's bed sipping tea she explained how the ITU worked.

The ward was run on a conventional shift system. Each nurse worked for eight hours taking two breaks during that time when a back-up nurse would replace her at Frank's bedside. No nurse would leave Frank under any circumstances until relieved by another. In contrast to the short-staffed Timone unit the London ITU had over seventy nurses to take care of nine patients. For every two patients

128

there was one extra nurse to cover breaks and help in an emergency so, in effect, Frank would have one-and-a-half nurses continually watching over him every hour of the day and night. Supervising all the patients on the ward were two nursing sisters and a nursing officer. In addition there was always a resident anaesthetist on call who had sleeping accommodation on the ward.

I asked about all the machinery surrounding Frank and for the first time I learned the significance of some of the screens monitoring functions like heart and blood pressure, and of the six or seven tubes attached to his body feeding in saline solution and removing waste products. As Carol explained its functions some of my terror of the mysterious hi-tech equipment left me and I felt a surge of confidence brought about by his new surroundings.

By the time I had finished my tea Frank appeared to be asleep. Maybe he felt more confident too. I had not seen him sleep at all in the Timone. It had been arranged for me to meet Prof. Watkins that evening so after a few more minutes I left and retrieved Peter. Together we made our way through what seemed a hundred miles of dark passages to Prof.'s office. Prof. greeted us in friendly fashion. He seemed satisfied that the transfer had gone well. 'So far, so good,' he smiled. It had been a long day for all of us. No one felt like an extended formal interview and Prof. offered to take us for a drink and something to eat at the doctors' local pub in the Whitechapel Road – nicknamed with medical humour 'The Grave'.

During the hour or so we spent there, Peter took over the role of my nurse and tried to force-feed me some lasagne and a glass of wine. Prof. encouraged him, 'You need some food inside you Ginny. Build yourself up.' But it felt as though my throat was blocked. I was unable to eat more than a couple of mouthfuls.

At ten-thirty Peter left to go home, promising he would be back in the morning with a portable telephone which would save us having to shuttle to and fro to the public call box to make calls. The Williams organization had booked me into the Tower Hotel on Tower Bridge, but I had no intention of going back there yet. There were no visiting restrictions at the London Hospital and after being separated from Frank for three days I wanted to be with him as much as I could.

Hospitals take on a very different feeling at night. In the whole time that Frank was at the London Hospital I always felt threatened there after dark. During the day there was bustle; patients being transferred; cleaners at work; specialists, shadowed by students, wandering around visiting their patients. All these activities made me feel safer. But the stillness, the eeriness of the echoing corridors at night, made me shiver, even on that first evening. Someone had told me that the majority of people die in the early hours of the morning. I found it easy to believe.

It was just after eleven o'clock when I reached the ward. A new nurse called Mary was sitting on a chair by Frank's bedside. Her eyes never seemed to leave him except to glance occasionally at the monitor screens. If she required anything, even if it was positioned a yard away, she called her back-up nurse to take over the vigil. Frank was still asleep. I noticed again, as I had in France, that his chest was not moving. He seemed to be breathing with his abdomen. I asked Mary why. 'It's because of his paralysis,' she explained in a soft Irish accent. 'The pectoral muscles in his chest can't work any longer so the diaphragm has to come to the rescue. It's pushing his lungs up and down from underneath.' It was one of the human body's clever back-up systems. There were going to be many things to learn.

The lights in an ITU are only partially dimmed at night and casting my eye around Frank's 'dormitory' companions I realized that Frank was not the only desperately ill patient. It was my first close encounter with serious illness. My total experience of hospitals before this week had been visiting private nursing homes with bunches of flowers to see friends who had had babies or routine minor operations.

Tonight two patients in the ITU were recovering from heart by-pass surgery, nicknamed 'miracle' surgery because patients in critical condition prior to the operation can be sitting up and demanding a cup of tea the next morning. However the middle-aged lady in the next bed to Frank had not been so lucky. She lay semi-conscious, connected to even more tubes than him, her skin an unnatural translucent grey. Mary told me her three daughters were spending their fifth night in the hospital praying for her recovery.

Frank opened his eyes and whispered something. Again he was complaining of the cold although I found it unbearably hot in the ITU. His breathing was becoming more laboured. Mary watched his painful efforts to get air and decided to call the physiotherapy team who were also on twenty-four hour stand-by and arrived within minutes – two pretty girls in their early twenties.

I was partly prepared for what they did because I had seen the same treatment meted out to a poor girl in the next bed to Frank at Timone. The two physios set about vigorously clapping his chest, first on the left side and then the right. As they turned him I saw for the first time the wide scar stretching down his back from his hairline. I recoiled. I had thought the scar on the front of his neck bad enough. This was twice as long and twice as ugly. After several minutes of clapping, the physios put a suction tube down his throat to clear the mucus which their treatment had loosened. They gave him a brief respite to see if it had improved things but when his breathing did not change they rolled him onto his side once more and started clapping again. He was in agony. He looked towards me imploringly like a child, appealing to me to do something to end his suffering. Tears streamed down his face.

There was nothing I could do. I found myself crying in sympathy. Mary looked over and suggested gently that I should go to the relatives' room because it would be too upsetting for me to stay and it would restrict the physios in their treatment. I argued. I couldn't understand why they wouldn't leave him alone and let him sleep. The saying 'Sleep is the greatest healer' kept coming back to me. Naïvely I felt they were interfering with nature's own mending powers. I did not know that Frank was literally drowning in the secretions from his own lungs.

I walked up the glass passage-way, which was freezing now from the frosty air outside and went into the visitors' room. It was a far cry from the cosy Harley Street waiting room image I had painted in my mind; a spartan little room with a few chairs, and adjoining it a smaller room with a bath and a wash basin but no loo. It didn't matter. I had given up going to the lavatory by this stage. My body seemed to have shut down in sympathy with Frank's.

Sitting in the waiting room were the three teenage daughters of the heart by-pass lady. After five days they had made themselves quite at home there with sleeping bags, sandwiches and crisps, and a kettle. I felt I was intruding, and started to back out but they beckoned me to stay. 'No don't go,' one of them said. 'Do you want a cup of tea? Come and sit down. Is that your husband?' They were dreadfully upset about their mother but they wanted to know about Frank's accident and they took it upon themselves to look after me. Over the next week we spent long hours in that little room together drinking endless cups of tea while they consoled me and mothered me with East End kindliness. Not one of them can have been older than eighteen.

It was half-an-hour before Mary came to collect me. When I arrived back at Frank's bedside I almost wished she hadn't. He was shivering with cold, and crying and moaning with pain. I sat beside him not knowing what to do, powerless to help him. It was a terrible feeling.

Mary seemed to understand and came over and sat beside me and held my hand.

'The physios will be coming back every hour now to try and keep his chest clear,' she said gently. 'Try not to get too upset about it. It's all for his own good.'

I was horrified. How could he tolerate that treatment every hour?

When the team came back I was sent out again to sit with the girls in the waiting room. On my return Frank was once more in terrible distress. He stared into my eyes and begged me, 'Don't let them do it again. I can't stand it. Don't let them do it, Ginny please.' I was distraught. What was I supposed to do? My husband, whom I had always obeyed, was demanding one thing and the experts were insisting on another.

Anger welled up inside me against everybody who was subjecting him to this torture. I was still convinced that what he needed most was sleep. I hated those physios with a vehement loathing. The pretty little head physio with the sweet smile,whose duty that night was to try and keep Frank alive,became my mortal enemy. I had always thought of physiotherapists as people who soothed away aches and pains with gentle massage. I had no idea of the part they played in intensive therapy or of the fear and hate that they often inspire in their ITU patients.

The night dragged on. It was obvious even to my unqualified eyes that Frank's condition was deteriorating. After each session of chest clapping, nurses were forcing suction tubes down his throat and into his lungs to try and clear the accumulation of fluid. Despite this his breathing had now become barely discernible and his face had taken on a frightening, almost black tinge. For the first time I seriously doubted the wisdom of the decision to have him flown back.

Doctors, nurses, and physios worked on Frank constantly through the night. From time to time the anaesthetist placed an evil looking black face-piece over his nose and mouth and pumped the attached black bag up and down to force oxygen into his lungs. Mary told me they were fighting to keep him off the respirator. But the battle was being lost, halfway through the night the respirator was brought in and placed beside his bed in readiness. Seeing it filled me with terror. I knew that a patient on a respirator or life-support machine cannot speak or communicate. I was sure that was all that was keeping Frank going now. His lifeline was being able to talk to me, however weakly and infrequently. If they took that away he would have nothing left to live for. I begged them not to even consider using it but it stayed at his bedside threateningly. I developed a phobia of the apparatus. I couldn't bear even to look at it.

Mary handed over her shift at 6 a.m. At that time they noticed that Frank's urine bag which hung down beside the bed draining his bladder was empty. The nurses decided to press down hard on the bladder to force the contents out. As they did so I saw for the first time the long livid scar across his left hip. It was a relic of the operation to remove the bone which Prof. Vincintelli had inserted into his neck. One more grotesque souvenir of the moment of distraction which had left him upside down, paralysed in that field near Marseille.

The changeover procedure involved the duty nurse giving a full and detailed account of the patient and the care given during her shift. Half an hour was allowed for this so that the report could be as comprehensive as possible. I strained to hear what Mary was saying as she gave a résumé of Frank's injuries. Then quite clearly amongst all the discreet whispering I heard the word 'quadriplegic'.

I felt bile rising in my throat and looked around for somewhere to be sick. There was nowhere. I took deep breaths. It was the first time I had heard that word used in connection with Frank. It seemed suddenly to make his condition formal. Quadriplegic is a word like cancer or death that is harsh and uncompromising and allows no more pretence, no more believing that things will get better if you ignore them. Until that moment I think I had honestly believed that Frank's paralysis would cure itself once he got stronger. Other people might be paralysed for life, but not Frank. He had never been like other people. He had always scraped through. He would surprise everyone.

Now I glimpsed reality. I was aware enough to know that quadriplegia was permanent. Hoping that Frank would recover was as ridiculous as hoping that an amputee could grow a new limb.

I sat in shock in my chair in the corner and looked at Frank, the father of my three children, my best friend, the man who ran ninety miles a week, who never stayed still or in the same place for a minute. To think of him as a quadriplegic . . . Oh God help us, there has got to be a mistake. Frank's eyes were shut. I had no idea whether he was unconscious or merely asleep.

It was too much. I wanted to get out. To go to my hotel room. I felt an urgent need to escape, to go to the loo, have a bath and clean my teeth. I looked for my bag and realized I had left it in Prof.

Watkins' office on the other side of the hospital. In order to reach the administration wing it was necessary to take the lift down two floors, cross the building and take another lift up one floor. It was like trying to find your way through a rabbit warren. Everywhere was dark and still. I completely lost my bearings. Not a soul was about, and in growing panic I opened doors into strange quiet laboratories and empty offices. I started to cry from a mixture of fear and fatigue. I felt very alone.

At last I found Prof.'s office. I dried my eyes, picked up my bag and headed out of the building. As I left I said a prayer asking God to take care of Frank while I was gone. As an afterthought I asked him to find me a taxi too. He did. No wonder they say there are no atheists on the battlefield.

Peter had booked an adjoining room to mine for my brother Jamie feeling I shouldn't stay at the hotel on my own. Jamie had arrived early that evening. He woke up when he heard me coming in and came next door to see me. I collapsed against him, almost hysterical. The word quadriplegic kept repeating over and over in my head. 'Frank can't be quadriplegic Jamie,' I sobbed. 'It's not possible. It's just not possible.'

There was nothing Jamie could do for me except to run my bath and order me some toast. We sat on my bed and while he buttered my toast he told me soothingly that all was not lost.

'Frank still has his family Ginny.'

I was doubtful that it would be enough.

I hadn't eaten a proper meal for two days and my brother counted out the slices of toast and insisted that I had 'Just one more piece' rather as one speaks to one's children. I thought it was very funny and laughed. My mouth was unaccustomed to food and every bite made my mouth hurt, but obediently I did as he said. Once I was bathed and fed, I felt refreshed and wanted to return to Frank, but I submitted to Jamie's insistence that I snatch some sleep. He promised to wake me in two hours and drive me into the hospital if I did as I was told. I took another of Susie's Mogadons and curled up in a little ball to go to sleep. A desolate thought crept up on me. Whatever was it going to be like not to be able to sleep in the same bed as Frank? Never again to feel the comforting warmth of his body next to mine? I slept before an answer came.

Jamie took me back to the London Hospital soon after nine o'clock. There is always a lot of activity in hospital wards in the morning so I was not surprised at being asked by the sister on duty to wait outside the ITU.

Peter had already arrived and set up his new office with portable phone on the solitary chair in the glass passage. His role was to relay news of Frank back to Patrick at Didcot and also to field the constant enquiries from reporters. We had decided to stick to a strict 'no comment' for the time being. All we had told the Press so far was that Frank had been badly injured in a car crash. Patrick felt that it might be difficult to keep Williams running normally if the full truth leaked out. No one doubted that Frank would want it to be business as usual, so we faced no real dilemma in deciding to keep quiet about his paralysis. Not declaring it of course also helped me keep the vestiges of hope alive. But rumours had reached the papers and they were avid for more information. I was glad of Peter's presence to defend me from them and also to respond to the enquiries and kind messages of friends. I had no energy left over to deal with that.

I learned that Prof. Watkins was in the ITU examining Frank, which was the reason for the delay in letting me in. Some time later the doors opened and the Prof. accompanied by another senior doctor – whom I later learned was Brian Simpson, his deputy – and by three junior doctors came out. He stopped in front of me.

'Ginny, I've just been to see Frank. I've decided to call in a colleague to perform a tracheotomy.'

For a moment I was sure I was going to pass out, but Prof. Watkins continued to speak in a reassuring, matter of fact way.

'It will make life easier for Frank as well as for us. He's having so much trouble breathing and we can't clear his lungs any more just by suctioning through his throat. This way the suctioning will be more efficient and we will also be able to feed oxygen through the incision.'

I was allowed in to see Frank for a few minutes before the surgery was carried out. It was to be done without moving him to an operating theatre. They said the paralysis had now crept still further up from the point of lesion so there was no need for any anaesthetic.

The night had taken its toll. This morning, though awake, Frank seemed unaware of my presence. I held his hand. It felt alarmingly stiff. His knuckle joints seemed to have seized up and the whole hand was very flat. There was a crusty build up of dead skin at the ends of his fingers. Even his nails looked dull and lifeless.

The ENT specialist who was to perform the tracheotomy arrived. I left Frank's bedside and resumed my vigil in the glass passage. I expected the surgery to take at least half an hour so was surprised when five minutes later the sister came out.

'The operation has been carried out,' she said. 'The doctor would like to speak to you inside the unit.'

I followed her back inside where the specialist stood in the ante-room leading onto the ward. I was totally unprepared for what happened next. I was expecting gentle words of encouragement but instead he looked at me murderously and thundered, 'Just how much more effort do you want us to make to keep your husband alive?'

When people raise their voices at me I tend to get cross in return. 'I want EVERY effort made,' I shouted back at him. Infuriatingly I felt tears betraying me. I realized that this doctor felt Frank should be allowed to die and couldn't understand my stubbornness in wanting to fight for him. While I howled back at him, he shook his head and muttered grim predictions.

'Have you bothered to think about the sort of life you would be subjecting him to if he survives?' he demanded.

I was shocked at his words but also terribly angry. How dare anyone suggest that Frank's life was not worth living? Let him be the one to decide that, not some doctor. Frank's words when I first saw him after the accident came back to me. 'Now I shall have another forty years of a different kind of life.' Of course he wanted to live.

The sealed entrance unit where our 'interview' took place had soundproof glass doors. Peter seated on the other side saw me bursting into tears and being led away by the nursing officer into her office. He assumed that Frank had died and was extremely relieved a few minutes later when I came back out through the doors and told him the true situation. I fell on his shoulder, sobbing.

'Do you think we should let him die Peter?'

Peter was positive. 'No I don't Ginny. Frank would want to live. I'm sure of it.'

'But the doctors seem to think he'd be better off dead.'

Peter shook his head. 'We know him better than they do. There'll be a lot of adjustments to be made. You can't get away from that. But he has a lot to live for. He still has his children. He has the trees and the sunshine. Everybody loves him. He's very special. He's too determined himself to want us to give up so easily Ginny.' He smiled, 'Anyway, knowing Frank, he may surprise us all.'

It was what I needed to hear. I felt as though I had been pulled back from the brink of an abyss. But I was still very close to the edge. The situation was too appalling for me to contemplate in any depth. I thought back to some of the 'disasters' in our life before the accident. Even our worst problems and struggles now seemed trivial. I felt at a very low ebb. Both Frank and I had expected things to start miraculously improving once we left France, but by the hour the situation seemed to be worsening and there was nothing I could do. I dried my eyes, left Peter and took up my seat once more beside Frank.

I was beginning to have a better understanding of the role of the physiotherapists, and could recognize for myself when Frank needed to have his chest cleared. Despite my anger at the pain they inflicted, I had to admit there was a marked improvement in Frank's breathing when they had finished. It was an exhausting task for them. One stood either side of him while they took it in turns to clap his lungs and listen through a stethoscope to locate the pooling mucus. The tracheotomy opening was held open by a plastic vent stitched into his neck and it was plugged with a spigot which meant he could still talk. Although the wound looked unpleasant and bloody I realized that it had simplified the suctioning process. Now by removing the spigot they were able to pass a suction tube directly down the windpipe into his lungs and he didn't seem to notice them doing it. Before, passing it down his throat had caused him terrible distress.

The physios continued to work on him at regular intervals throughout the morning but I was no longer asked to leave. I still felt an instinctive dislike of them but I had come to terms with what they had to do. However distressing the treatment might be I did not want to leave Frank. I felt that I had to know everything that related to his condition.

Frank's bladder was continuing to cause problems and it was decided to catheterize him every four hours. Only a male nurse or an anaesthetist was allowed to pass a catheter into a male patient and since male nurses were in short supply the duty usually fell on the overworked doctors. I worried terribly about it and kept checking his abdomen when the four hours were up, becoming frantic to get the job done. His belly looked so distended I thought it could kill him. The possibility that other patients in the ITU might have more urgent needs for the doctors to attend to did not cross my mind.

Frank had started complaining of pain in his shoulders and by the evening it had become so bad that it was preventing him sleeping. I couldn't understand why they wouldn't give him painkillers, not comprehending that in his weakened condition they might prove fatal.

137

I was very impatient and showed little understanding towards the nurses but they were sympathetic. Probably they had seen protective wives like me before.

During the day Peter was allowed in to visit Frank for short intervals and while he talked to Frank I walked down to the visitors' room to stretch my legs and share a cup of tea with my teenage friends. Peter left late in the evening and suggested, prompted by the nursing sister, that I did not stay on the ward that night.

'You'll be better with a night's sleep Ginny,' he persuaded me, but I was deaf to his arguments. I wanted to stay.

The duty was taken over at ten p.m. not by Mary but by a new nurse called Sarah. I learned that the nurses are rotated around the patients in the ITUs so that they do not become too involved with any one patient. The job is stressful enough without that since one out of every three patients who come into intensive care dies. Sarah encouraged me to help Frank into a more comfortable position. We shifted his pillows and massaged his shoulders. It felt good to be able to do something useful and Frank appreciated it. The massage helped ease his discomfort a little.

He was still being physio-ed every hour but his terror of 'the team' had gone now. He appreciated that he felt better afterwards. After their midnight visit I could hear him praying in whispers before he fell asleep and I joined in his prayers. Unlike Frank I had no Catholic faith to call on but reciting the familiar words gave me comfort.

Still I could not bring myself to go. While he was sleeping Frank hallucinated several times, talking to himself in agitated whispers. Sarah and I strained to hear his revelations. We were amazed to hear Mrs Thatcher's name mentioned. He kept repeating that he'd let her down. One phrase recurred: 'Tell Mrs Thatcher I've left it under the hedge.' Could Frank have found time to be a secret agent in between Grand Prix meetings? We managed to laugh over his nightmares and Sarah told me of other unlikely confessions she had overheard in the unit.

She was planning to study obstetrics and with the long night stretching ahead of us I started telling her of my childbearing experiences. I felt quite a bond with her. She was sympathetic and fun and brought me unofficial cups of tea back after her breaks. Her friendliness was characteristic of most of the nurses on the unit.

By four-thirty in the morning Frank was sleeping comparatively peacefully. For the first time I started to feel tired and I agreed to go to the hotel for a couple of hours' rest.

This was only the second evening that I had made that journey out of the hospital after dark but already I hated it. Up the long cold passage, down four interminable flights of stairs, my footsteps echoing, trying to ignore the constant feeling that there was someone behind me.

On the ground floor a couple of tramps were huddled asleep in the corridor to escape the cold and I was happy to reach the porter's desk. Tonight I was unlucky, there were no taxis. I stood in the Whitechapel Road for a good half hour before giving up and heading back inside the hospital feeling that it would be very unsafe to start walking at that hour. I planned to return to the relatives' room and try to sleep in a chair, but the porter said he would phone for a minicab. Shortly afterwards a very rough looking driver in an ancient rusty Corsair turned up to collect me. I collapsed onto the heavily stained fake fur back seat and resigned myself to being murdered or at least raped. I was almost too tired to care. I was pleasantly surprised when the driver woke me to say we were at the door of the hotel. It was nearly five thirty a.m. I collected my room key and went up in the lift. Not surprisingly, no light showed under Jamie's door and I decided not to disturb him.

I had no energy to undress. I climbed wearily onto my bed and waited for sleep to carry me away.

CHAPTER 10

*F*rank's condition was now officially 'stable'. The nursing officer informed me of his new status when Jamie returned me to the hospital the next morning. A baby's respirator had been introduced into the tracheotomy to help his oxygen intake and his blood oxygen level was being tested every hour.

'The doctors have decided that Frank needs a blood transfusion,' the nursing officer told me. 'We are going to make a start on "topping up" his blood today.'

I couldn't understand the need for a transfusion. I thought they were only given to people who were haemorrhaging, or during operations. I was seriously worried about the risk of infection. The newspapers recently had been full of stories of people who had contracted Aids from blood transfusions.

'Can't you use my blood? I could donate some today,' I pleaded. I was sure family and friends would contribute as well, but it was not possible. The doctors wanted to start transfusing that morning and there was no time for the cross-matching and testing required. They tried to reassure me that all blood underwent rigorous testing but I wasn't convinced. I glowered at the bottles as they were set up behind Frank's bed, considering them to be yet another threat.

I was surprising even myself by my reactions to the hospital establishment. For most of my life I had been fairly respectful of authority and willing to do as I was told without too much argument. Now I was questioning nearly all the decisions that were being made.

I simply could not accept that what people were telling me was right just because they were in a position of power. I challenged constantly, demanding that everything be explained and justified. I sensed that some people were already becoming thoroughly tired of Frank's difficult wife but I could not back off. My protective instinct overcame my sense of propriety. If it was necessary to fight to get the best for my husband then that was what I was going to do, whatever people might think of me.

The physios continued to keep Frank's chest clear all through the day. They were having difficulty pinpointing the mucus pools and decided to call in an X-ray team to film his lungs. To take the X-rays they had to manoeuvre the plate underneath Frank's chest, shoulders and neck which he found excruciating. I found it hard to sit passively by and watch his suffering. When the film was developed the head physiotherapist in the hospital, a tall blonde lady called Karen took me over to see it on the illuminated screen and outlined the areas of pooling it revealed. I was grateful for her attempts to involve me. At least now I could appreciate the reasons for all the pummelling and slapping that followed.

For the last two days the nurses had been keeping a careful eye on Frank's heels where there were signs of pressure sores developing. By now they were seriously concerned about them and it was decided to bring in a special bed, known as an air loss bed, to help relieve the constant pressure. A pump caused air to circulate continually inside it preventing a build-up of pressure on any one part of the body. I did not appreciate the seriousness of pressure sores until the duty nurse showed me a group of pictures of neglected sores on paralysed people. The realization that here was something else that could end up killing Frank added to my worries and I promptly started a daily search for any red areas which might herald an imminent sore.

Pressure sores are caused by lying in the same position for too long. To prevent a recurrence Frank was now to be turned from one side to his back and then over to the other side as often as possible. It took four nurses and myself to move him; three of us on one side, one supporting his head and shoulders, and another to change or straighten the bedding under him. Pillows were positioned between his legs where they rested on each other, and more behind his back. Being moved was agony for him and caused a lot of pain in his neck. I didn't have enough confidence at this stage to take his head during the turning. It was crucial that the nurse holding his head kept in time with the other three. If she got it wrong Frank would groan in pain. Trying to get him comfortable was a long unhappy process. When the turning was completed I used hot flannels on his face and rubbed ice cubes on his lips, but he was still not allowed painkillers and my ministrations were no substitute. I continually questioned the staff about the lack of analgesics but was always told 'Not yet'.

Slowly the first week in the unit passed. Peter took dozens of phone calls from friends and relatives wanting to know if they could visit. Frank's father rang to ask if he could do anything and I spoke to him briefly. His mother was desperately upset and rang once or twice every day. For the time being Prof. Watkins had advised that Frank was not well enough to receive visitors but he did agree to make an exception in the case of Sebastian Coe. Frank was getting rather low mentally and we thought that a chat with Seb could cheer him up. It proved very worthwhile. Sebastian was cheerful and encouraging and joked with Frank that he might beat him yet. We all felt that it was important at this stage to keep Frank optimistic about his chances for recovery, whatever the hard facts indicated.

Every day Prof. Watkins paid Frank a visit and prodded his shoulder with a pin to ascertain at what level he started to feel any sensation. I watched intently, praying every time that Frank would suddenly swear at him as the pin went in. Unhappily, I had to admit that the level at which he felt the pin was getting higher.

After each session of physiotherapy Karen would try to find some sort of response in the muscles of his upper arm by lifting up the arm and manoeuvring it about to see if there was any reaction. She explained that if he could only recover some use in his biceps it would make a tremendous difference to his prospects. But stubbornly, day after day, his arm remained flat and lifeless.

I did see something encouraging. It seemed to me that now and again, especially when he was asleep, his toes moved. Excitedly I pointed it out to Karen but she shook her head.

'It's just a muscle spasm,' she said. 'He's not controlling it.'

I refused to believe her. To me it was cause for hope. And I was still clinging to hope against all the odds. If I started to come to terms with this horror I felt it would become a reality.

Frank's breathing seemed to have become considerably better with all the physiotherapy he was getting, which made it easier for him to talk. I told him of the enquiries and the well wishers and of all the flowers which had arrived and had been sent down to the children's ward since no flowers are allowed on the ITU. He seemed pleased and asked me to read him his cards. He had more awareness of what was going on now but was still far from alert and spent a lot of time sleeping.

Not once so far had Frank mentioned the accident or what had caused it. Nor since that first day I saw him had he mentioned the word 'paralysed'. I too avoided it. I felt he must bring the subject up when he was ready, not me. I was beginning to feel almost schizophrenic in my attitude to Frank's injuries. The rational voice within me said that paralysis was a probability and I had to face up to it, but my heart stubbornly rejected even the possibility of quadriplegia. And while he was continually facing life-threatening crises it was not too difficult to push it to the back of my mind.

I deliberately did not press any of the medical staff to tell me what Frank's future held. Talking to one of the nurses I had learned that there were two possible kinds of injury to the spinal cord. One was a partial severance, the other a complete severance. Frank's appeared to be complete but until the swelling from the injury settled down it would not be possible to be one hundred per cent certain. If it was only a partial severance he might well recover some movement below his neck. I clung to that hope. I told friends and relations that there was a definite possibility he might recover the use of his limbs. The more times I said it, the easier it was to believe it. For the most part his friends seemed happy to believe it too. Most people who knew Frank could not accept that such a fate as quadriplegia could befall him. It was unthinkable. I was told on several occasions that a personality as powerful as Frank was strong enough to overcome even a medical certainty.

I was uneasy about their assurances – sensing we could be trapped in a conspiracy of self-deception. I wanted to test the story on someone who was not involved, to get an unbiased reaction. In my taxi to the hotel one night I found myself telling the cabby that my husband had been in a bad car accident and was paralysed from the neck down. I don't know how I expected him to react. Perhaps by saying something bland and reassuring about disabled people he had met and how well they coped with life, or miracle recoveries he had heard of. But he responded quite differently. He peered curiously at my reflection in his driving mirror.

'You must be married to Frank Williams then. Oh dear! Oh dear!' He shook his head sympathetically.

I was astonished to be identified. Astonishment was rapidly replaced by terror. What if I woke up and found myself the subject of a story in *The Sun*? 'Williams wife in heartbreak taxi revelation.' I hardly waited for him to come to a halt in front of the Tower before I leaped out and dashed thankfully into the anonymity of the hotel. I had learned the need to be circumspect.

A pattern was emerging to my days and nights. I would leave for the hotel at around two a.m., and sleep for a few hours at the Tower, returning to the hospital by eight a.m. I sent Jamie home after three nights. There was little point in him being at the hotel when I only used it to sleep.

As soon as I arrived on the ward I would help the duty nurse give Frank a bed bath. In those early days the duty nurse and her back-up would carry out this routine together. I found it irritating to watch them. Instead of talking to Frank they would chat about various tit-bits of hospital gossip and their social lives. They behaved as if there was a body in the bed rather than a person. I felt it added to the indignity of his position and I took over the role of back-up nurse. I washed his face and shaved him, and because I cared, tried to make it a pleasant experience instead of a humiliating one. My help was not welcomed by all the nurses. One in particular seemed to resent me and one day she took me out of the room saying, 'I'd like to talk to *you*.'

When we were out of Frank's earshot she said aggressively, 'You must understand that nurses become very possessive of their patients and don't like other people interfering with their care.' Furiously, I retorted that she might like to consider that I felt quite possessive of my husband too! It was true. I was finding myself increasingly jealous of the attention the nurses were giving him. If there was anything I could do for him then I wanted to do it. If I didn't know how, I wanted to be taught, whether it was chest clapping, turning him, or positioning his pillows. I felt a strong primitive urge to mark my corner, to make it clear that Frank was my territory, not theirs. I was often a real thorn in the side of the duty nurses but with the odd exception they tolerated my activities with good humour.

On Wednesday 19 March, one week after we had left Marseille, Prof. Watkins took the decision to move Frank out of intensive care. It was the milestone I had been praying for. All my misgivings about the flight home vanished. We had done the right thing after all. In France they had predicted death and yet here he was in London a week later about to be moved onto a ward. Once again I pushed thoughts of paralysis away. I regarded Frank as being on the road to recovery. It is very hard in a hospital environment to have a full appreciation of what it means when your body isn't functioning. All the other patients there are lying in bed being ministered to as well.

144

Frank didn't look very different. For most of the time I just thought of him as being dreadfully sick.

Very slowly and carefully Frank was moved into a side room on the ground floor in the neuro ward. I was told I could bring in a stereo player and the charger for the portable phone. We put all his get well cards up on the walls. They hadn't been permitted in the ITU because of the dust they would collect. Many were from friends but there were also hundreds from ordinary motor racing fans; people who had never met Frank but had loyally followed the fortunes of Williams. There were letters too, offering prayers and words of encouragement. I was touched by the number of people who were thinking of us.

Sebastian continued to visit Frank regularly and in the middle of the get well cards he pinned up the number 359 that he had worn in the 1984 Olympic Games when he won the 1500 metre race.

Frank could only see clearly what was pinned directly above his head. He had some peripheral vision but seemed fairly oblivious to what was going on in the ward around him which was fortunate since there were some disturbing sights and sounds in the head injury ward. One poor man made a dreadful quacking noise all day long. Peter and I christened him 'the duck'. I found the noise very upsetting and worried that it would disturb Frank but he showed no sign of hearing it.

On the new ward there was no longer 'around the clock' nursing. I didn't share the doctors' confidence that Frank could survive without constant monitoring and for the first forty-eight hours he was there I felt unable to leave. It was obvious I could not keep up my vigil indefinitely so Peter and I decided to employ agency nurses so that Frank would not be left alone. There was nowhere for visitors to eat in the hospital and I was conscious that my jeans were becoming looser by the day. The visitors' lavatory seemed to be used by most of the bagmen of the Whitechapel Road which meant I had started to avoid even the cups of tea offered by the nurses in order not to have to use it.

I was aware of feeling light-headed. I guessed that I was using the back-up of adrenaline which seems to keep people operating in dire situations. Despite my virtually non-existent calorie intake I seemed to have bags of energy. It was almost as though I was on a high. From time to time Peter would frog-march me over the road to the 711 for a bun but all hunger had by now disappeared. It had become hard work even to swallow.

Frank, although on glucose and saline drips, had not received any food since the accident and was wasting in front of my eyes. I asked when they would start feeding him but no one felt able to predict that. His swallowing mechanism had gone, though this, they said, was almost certainly just temporary. Until it returned any food would have to be tube-fed directly into his stomach. But it would not be for a while yet as his body had not recovered enough to cope with the added challenge of digestion.

My time on the ward was now largely taken up with arranging and rearranging Frank's pillows a hundred times a day in order to try and take some of the pressure off his neck. This pressure was his main complaint. The hospital pillows were in limited supply and I decided to go up to Harrods on Friday morning to buy extra pillows and a stereo.

I had again exhausted my supply of clean socks so I went into the hosiery department first, picked up the first few pairs that came to hand, and went to the cashier to pay. An elegant lady in front of me was debating with the assistant the relative merits of two pairs of black silk tights – both very expensive, one with seams, the other with bows. She wanted the assistant's opinion on which would look better with which dress. I fidgeted impatiently, waiting for her to make up her mind. I thought of the contrasting worlds that I was flitting between. One where dedicated doctors and nurses on minimal salaries fought to keep people alive, and the other where ladies like this one could comfortably spend half an hour and £50 on a pair of tights. I wanted to hit her.

I continued my shopping feeling more and more off-balance. I felt detached from everything going on around me. I found the crowds thronging through the store very disconcerting. An hour later, laden with pillows and parcels I returned to the safety of the hospital. Safety! I realized I was becoming institutionalized.

I had bought a portable stereo cassette-player which was very well received. Frank was pleased to have some background music. I put on a Mozart tape which I had picked up in Harrods' music department and turned the volume up loud enough to drown out the noises from the brain-damaged patients in the head injury ward. I was finding it increasingly upsetting but coped with it by telling myself that they were not in as much distress as their relatives were. Some of them appeared not to have much awareness of anything and to be quite happy in their own strange worlds.

That weekend the first Grand Prix of the year was taking place in Brazil. It would be the first race Frank had not attended since that Argentinian Grand Prix when Walter Wolf had exiled him ten years

146

ago. He had been so looking forward to this season. It was bitterly cruel that he would have to miss it. Patrick had kept him informed with full details of the team's progress, not wishing to stress him with decision making but anxious to reassure him that things were under control.

Peter loyally decided to miss the race so that he could stay with us, and took telephone calls from Patrick and Sheridan in Rio who gave us information to pass on to Frank. On Sunday 23 March, the two Williams cars lined up second and third on the grid behind Ayrton Senna's Lotus on pole. Peter had been invited by the BBC to watch the race as it came through on their monitors that evening. The race started at 1700 hours British time which, because of programme schedules, meant it could not be broadcast live, but highlights would be shown the following day. I sat with Frank tensely waiting for Peter to phone through news of the race's progress.

Soon after seven o'clock a nurse popped her head round the door.

'Peter just phoned,' she whispered to me. 'There's a message. He says that one of your drivers has won the race.'

I glanced at Frank who appeared not to have heard.

'Which driver?' I asked.

She shrugged. 'I wouldn't know. I haven't a clue what he was talking about anyway. I think that's all he said.'

I couldn't trust such sketchy information. I didn't want to tell Frank and then find that the nurse had misheard. I left the ward and put a call through to Reuter World Press who confirmed that Nelson had won. Frank went very quiet when I told him. It was a bittersweet victory for him. He must have felt superfluous. It was a good ten minutes before he spoke and then he asked me drowsily, 'Ginny did you say we'd won?'

'Yes Frank. Nelson won.'

'I can't believe that,' he said and lapsed into silence again. I went out to the corridor, took the portable phone out of charge and brought it back into the ward. Then I put another call through to Reuters.

'This is Frank Williams wife,' I told the man on the sports desk. 'Would you mind telling me the result of the Grand Prix again? I'm going to hold the phone next to Frank so that he can hear the result for himself. He won't believe me.'

I put the receiver against Frank's ear and overheard a very emotional voice say, 'Mr Williams? Congratulations. You have won the Brazilian Grand Prix . . . and all the best.'

I burst into tears. Soon afterwards Peter returned with a bottle of champagne, a present from the BBC. We gathered up the toothmugs and Peter and I, together with Brian Simpson and a couple of nurses toasted Frank and the win.

Peter filled us in on the race details. He told us that five minutes before the start all the drivers and constructors had assembled in front of the grid holding a banner up to the TV cameras which read 'Don't worry, Frank. We're minding the shop.'

A few sips of champagne on an empty stomach went straight to my head. It was some time before the effects began to wear off and I became slowly aware that all was not well with Frank. He looked terrible; very grey and tired. For the first time since we had transferred to this ward I felt quite worried about his condition. I couldn't put my finger on it but I felt certain there had been a marked change for the worse.

We were employing an agency nurse again that night but I didn't feel happy about her competence and was uneasy about leaving him. Peter offered me a lift back to the hotel but I decided to stay. Since the ward was shortstaffed I suspected that Frank might be left alone during the tea breaks.

I sat on a chair very close to him and put my head on the bed, feeling close to exhaustion. I dozed, as close to sleep as it was possible to get in that position, surfacing now and then to hear Frank talking to me.

'God is punishing me Ginny,' he murmured. 'He's punishing me for having led such a selfish life.'

'No he isn't Frank,' I protested. 'No one is punishing you. It was just an accident.'

'If I get through this Ginny, I'm going to be a better husband and a better father.' He paused for air. His breathing sounded noisy again as it had done in his first days in the ITU. 'I'm going to take you back to Cumbria for a holiday. Would you like that?'

'I'd love it Frank,' I said, torn between laughing and crying.

Three months before the accident, after much cajoling I had persuaded Frank to take me to the Lake District for a weekend. It was the only time in fourteen years that we had ever been away together except to races. At the last minute he decided he could only spare one night, instead of the two we had planned, and we left five hours behind schedule, arriving too late for any dinner. The following day we left before lunch. And in our abbreviated 'weekend' he managed to fit in a sixteen mile run and make £150 worth of telephone calls!

148

On the way back he bought a postcard and sent it to Jaime with the message, 'Mummy and Daddy are having a lovely time!'

I had to drop him at Castle Donnington in the afternoon to meet up with Nigel Mansell. The pair of them flew off to Italy while I drove alone back down the M1 wondering why I had been so naïve as to expect it to be a romantic holiday.

Frank was obviously now feeling some remorse for his behaviour. As he fought for breath he promised that when we went back again it would be quite different. How could I tell him that I wanted it to be just the same? That I almost felt nervous of this new contrite man. Because the Frank that I loved was the old one. He was the man I had fallen in love with and married, and infuriating as he could be, I did not want him to be anything else.

As daylight broke at about six a.m. and the day staff returned I went back to the Tower hotel for a sandwich and a cup of tea. I sat at the dressing table, decided against the sandwich, but put four sugar lumps into my tea for energy. There was a box of flowers on my bed. It was becoming a regular occurrence. Kind friends often sent flowers to the hotel and Mobil sent a new arrangement every week. I really appreciated them. They seemed the only things of beauty in my life at the moment.

When I had finished drinking my tea I undid the white satin bow which was tied around the box and opened it. Inside were a dozen beautiful white lilies. I stared at them in horror. 'Funeral lilies' I thought. With a shudder, I opened my door and threw them out into the passage.

I sat down on the bed, shaking, and at that moment the telephone rang. It was Jane, the ward sister. Her voice was grave. 'Ginny, Frank isn't very good. I think you should get back here as quickly as you can.'

I was losing my sense of reality. Surely it was only in films that one was told that one's husband was dying and was asked to rush to his bedside? I didn't want to be in this film any more. I hadn't yet had time to undress. I ran panic-stricken down the stairs, feeling as though I was outside my body watching myself. I rushed through reception and found myself on the end of a queue of businessmen waiting for taxis. It was pouring with rain. A taxi drew up. I hesitated, then just pushed blindly past the queue and jumped in. I couldn't face explaining to them. 'Take me to the London Hospital,' I gasped to the cabbie. I hoped they would hear my destination and forgive me.

The ride seemed never-ending. I sat in the back of the taxi praying the taxi driver wouldn't question me. Praying that Frank would still be alive when I got there.

The driver dropped me on the far side of the Whitechapel Road and I had to weave my way across the rush hour traffic in teeming rain to the hospital steps. Thanking God that the neuro ward was on the ground floor I rushed through the ward doors and in through Frank's door, only to be pushed back out by Brian Simpson. But not before I had seen that Frank was surrounded by a team of unfamiliar people and had noticed a truly appalling smell in the room. I thought instantly that it must be the smell of death that I had heard people talk about.

Brian led me away and told me to sit down. I refused angrily.

'No I won't bloody sit down so that you can tell me Frank is dead,' I said. I remained defiantly standing while Brian told me that Frank was having severe breathing problems. The resuscitation team were with him and he was going back up to the Intensive Therapy Unit as soon as they were ready to move him.

'You must prepare yourself for him to be put on a respirator,' he warned. Dumbstruck I stared at him.

'Ginny, please sit down. You look as if you need to,' Brian said gently. I felt as if I needed to. I sank heavily onto a bench. Brian had to return to Frank but he called a nurse to stay with me.

I hugged myself on the hospital bench feeling a hundred years old. My mouth had dried up. My teeth ached. My body felt as though it was collapsing in on itself. We waited there silently. The nurse didn't speak to me. She looked upset herself. Somewhere in the background 'the duck' quacked on obliviously.

Moments later Frank's door opened and he was pushed out on a trolley surrounded by people. One of them was holding a manual respirator which someone else was pumping. Frank was wrapped in a silver thermal blanket. I stood up. Brian Simpson glanced over to me as they pushed him into the lift.

'Meet us up in the ITU,' he nodded. The lift doors closed behind him. I panted up the stairs to the fourth floor. The doors into the unit were always kept closed and you had to get permission to go in. I rang the bell and after a couple of minutes the nursing officer came out. 'It's better if you don't come in just yet,' she advised. 'Let us try to stabilize him first.' She disappeared back into the unit and closed the door behind her leaving me on the chair in the glass passage.

Peter arrived looking white and shaken. He had appeared at the neuro unit at his usual time and had walked into Frank's room to find himself looking at an empty bed. He was terribly shocked. It was obvious to both of us that this was a very major step backwards. After some time Brian Simpson came out to talk to us.

'I'm afraid he has developed pneumonia,' he said. 'Frankly Ginny it's touch and go. We have to face the fact that we may be going to lose him.'

'Is he on a life-support machine?' I asked in terror.

He shook his head. 'For the time being we're not going to put him on a respirator. I want to avoid it if we can.'

'I don't want you to use it,' I pleaded. Every instinct told me that a respirator would kill Frank, not keep him alive. I wanted Frank to have to stay alive by himself. That was all I still had faith in. Frank's own will to live. Only that could pull him through now. I was sure of it. Peter disagreed with me. He thought that the respirator would give Frank's body recovery time but I was immovable.

It was hours before I was allowed in. He was in a little side room and his bed was still surrounded by people. I kept out of the way of their work as much as possible. The nurses and physios were using the power suction to clear the mucus from his lungs; pushing sterile tubes through the tracheotomy opening. As soon as one was withdrawn he was given a few breaths of oxygen and then the tube was replaced by another.

Frank was barely with us. The nurses told me his veins were breaking down which meant the drips were kicking out and had to be repositioned. I watched helplessly, still not knowing what half the drips contained or how vital they were. No sooner had a new needle been inserted than it kicked out again. They were running out of sites to insert them.

There was no sheet covering him and even his stomach looked alarmingly black. Every now and then someone injected something into his abdomen. I was told they were anticoagulant injections to stop blood clots from forming.

I stayed sitting quietly in the background for hour after hour, no longer conscious of time passing. My friend Sarah, the maternity nurse, was on duty and at some time long after midnight she turned to me.

'He's all right,' she said. 'We're looking after him. He's stabilizing. But who is looking after you?'

I started to cry. Quietly she led me out of Frank's room. 'Keep crying,' she said. 'It will do you good.'

She put her arms around me while I sobbed.

'Listen,' she said after a while. 'I think you should go away now and rest. You have to look after yourself as well as Frank. You have to learn to pace yourself or you'll be no good to him when he starts to get better will you?'

I left almost with relief at being ordered to do so. To my surprise Peter was slumped half-asleep on his chair in the passage. He drove me back to The Tower. I had no desire to go to bed so we went into the coffee shop, their only customers at that early hour of the morning. I can't imagine how dreadful I must have looked under the appalling glare of the neon strip lighting. I hadn't slept or cleaned my teeth or changed my clothes in thirty-six hours. My eyes were red-rimmed from exhaustion and crying. Peter did not look much better.

He ordered tea and a club sandwich and we sat in silence for ten minutes. Then our eyes met and he gave me a little wan smile, 'It can't get much worse Ginny.'

I was so pleased to see him smile. Unexpectedly I found myself laughing. 'You had bloody well better be right,' I said.

CHAPTER 11

At eight o'clock the following morning I crept apprehensively into Frank's new room in the ITU. I was greeted by the sight of a hundred helium filled metallic balloons clinging to the ceiling. Five of the balloons carried a coloured message, visible only to someone lying flat on his back, 'HANG ON IN THERE FRANK.' Mobil could not have timed their gesture better.

It was very comforting to know that people were still thinking of us. The unit with its strict 'no flowers' rule always looked spartan and the red, white and blue Mobil colours cheered up the whole room. The nurses had thought twice about allowing them in but decided they might give Frank some of the fight he needed and had helped arrange them. They looked quite incongruous floating above the hospital machinery.

It seemed to me that Frank's breathing had slightly improved since the previous night. Although the respirator was still parked outside the door it had at least been moved away from the emergency position next to his bed. Over the next few days it was to shift like a yo-yo between the two positions as Frank's condition fluctuated. The nurses' preoccupation during the whole of this time was the battle to stop his lungs filling with fluid. It was a week before the pneumonia was finally overcome and everyone once more began to think in terms of his long-term recovery.

Peter started to bring in The *Daily Telegraph* and *Autosport* magazine to read to him. Frank's attention span was limited but as the pneumonia retreated he was becoming more interested in events in the world outside. I had tried reading to him myself but found I was too tired to concentrate. It was good to have a break from my vigil and I would walk down to the relatives' room to stretch my legs while Peter relayed the world and motor-racing news. Every day he also passed on the latest telephone messages from Patrick. I was pleased Patrick was keeping the information flowing. He was obviously managing superbly in Frank's absence, but he realized that keeping him up to date on the team's activities would motivate his recovery as nothing else could. He also visited the unit several times, becoming, like Peter and Sebastian, an honorary 'next of kin' for the occasion.

The time had arrived for me to attempt some of the nursing tasks involved in caring for a paralysed patient. Karen decided to teach me first how to use the suction machine. I was apprehensive since I am naturally squeamish but I was determined to do my best. The suction tubing was connected to a glass bottle on the wall. A catheter had to be attached to the other end of this tubing, introduced through the tracheotomy opening, and manipulated down into the lung. The suction was then switched on and the contents of Frank's lungs would pass up the catheter tubing. As it drained into the bottle on the wall the nurses would carefully scrutinize the mucus for any sign of blood.

I was terrified of getting it wrong. The sterile procedure alone was extremely complicated. Karen watched me like a hawk to make sure I had first put on gloves, then had opened the catheter packaging in the correct way. Next I had to remove the spigot from the wound and insert the catheter without letting it touch the outside of the tracheotomy incision. If it did I would have to start all over again. I was desperate not to hurt him and took ages pushing the catheter gently into his lungs. Although I did not enjoy it I gradually gained confidence and soon Frank preferred me to do it as he found it less painful than with some of the nurses. I did take extra special care. If it hurt him it also hurt me.

My mother was relaying news from home and reassured me that everything was going smoothly. Susie had arranged for Pauline, a capable girl who had often helped me out during school holidays, to move in and run Boxford House for as long as I had to be away. Sarah was there too, looking after Claire and Jaime.

Over three weeks had passed since the accident and at last the doctors decided to introduce a nasal gastric drip in order to get some calories into Frank. I was vastly relieved. Now that the swelling had subsided he looked as though he was made of skin and bone. I estimated that he weighed about eight stone compared with his pre-accident weight of eleven and a half stone.

All Frank's pain was located above his shoulders. Perhaps when there is no sensation anywhere else in the body the intensity of the pain you can feel is increased. The process of inserting the nasal gastric tube up the nostril and down his throat was agony for him. A container of milky protein substance was added to the bank of bottles already hanging above his head. To start with, only a couple of hundred calories was allowed into his stomach daily as his tolerance for food was built up.

Frank was starting to communicate more with the people around him. In the early days he had been so weak that the conversations had been mainly one-way. Now he would ask for suction when he realized his lungs were filling up and respond more frequently to questions. He was no longer in such continual discomfort and only suffered extreme pain during the hourly turning which was complicated by the numerous drips. But even that process we were getting down to a fine art. As his days developed a routine I allowed myself to feel a little more secure.

Then one afternoon I was talking to Frank and realized he hadn't answered my last question. I moved closer to him. His face seemed to have darkened in colour.

'Are you all right?' I asked, concerned.

He didn't answer. Instead he stared at me as if trying to communicate. Terror struck the pit of my stomach.

'Are you breathing?' I demanded.

He gazed back speechlessly and I screamed in horror. 'You're not breathing are you?'

Simultaneously his nurse realized what was happening and pressed the red emergency button on the wall. Within seconds the crash team arrived and set to work frantically with a portable respirator. By now Frank's face was quite literally black. I cowered in the corner, very deeply shocked. One minute we had been talking quietly and the next he had stopped breathing. The barrier between life and death suddenly seemed terribly frail.

Someone quickly pushed the suction catheter down into his lungs – no time for gentle persuasion now – and a strange milky white liquid started to trickle into the glass jar on the wall. Normally the lung fluid was either clear or yellowish depending on the level of infection present. The quantity of this fluid provided the answer. It was nasal gastric feed.

The crash team discovered that Frank's nasal gastric tube had slowly moved up out of his stomach and become lodged at the entry into his windpipe. The milky calorie-filled drink had been dripping steadily into his lungs. His secretion bottle filled up with a quarter pint of liquid. It had nearly drowned him. For the time being there was to be no more tube-feeding.

Nothing had passed Frank's lips for nearly a month and he was beginning to feel a strong thirst. The paralysis remained high and he could still not swallow. I did not know how to explain to him that no one could estimate when he would be allowed to have a drink. The best we could do for now to alleviate the thirst was to rub an ice cube over his lips knowing that if a small drop did pass down into his lungs it could be cleared out by suction.

One day I had a bright idea. I wondered if he could suck on a boiled sweet. That way he would get the flavour but not have to swallow much more than his normal saliva. I suggested it to the duty anaesthetist who had been up all night with a critically ill patient in the next room.

'I don't see why not,' he said distractedly. I rushed down into the Whitechapel Road and came back with a quarter pound of Frank's new treats. I put one into his mouth and one into mine. His face was a picture of contentment. At last his mouth was being lubricated and he was enjoying his sense of taste for the first time in four weeks. I congratulated myself on my brilliant idea and sat happily next to him companionably sucking on my own sweet.

Then disaster struck. Five minutes after I popped the sweet into Frank's mouth his face blackened and again the nurse had to push the red button to summon the resuscitation squad. This time no progress could be made with the suction equipment. His lungs simply would not clear. There was an obstruction. Fortunately the anaesthetist put two and two together and realized that the partially sucked sweet must have dropped down into a lung. The suction catheters are extremely fine and could not move something as solid as this. I extracted the sweet from my own mouth to give them an idea of the size of the object they were dealing with. It looked enormous. Larger catheters were imported from elsewhere in the hospital. They proved very difficult and painful to pass down the airway but eventually they did their job and the sticky residue was retrieved. After oxygen resuscitation Frank was once more able to breathe unassisted.

I was stunned by the enormity of what had happened. I had done everything in my power to keep Frank alive for the past month, and now, by my own hand, I had nearly killed him. I couldn't look at him. The guilt was too much to bear. I stood miserably staring out of the window with tears streaming down my face. His nurse told me it wasn't my fault but I knew it was. The duty anaesthetists work terribly long hours and the poor guy I'd asked had barely listened to my question. I hadn't thought it out. I had just acted on impulse and my impulse had nearly caused Frank's death. To make matters worse Prof. Watkins was called in. He marched into the room, and looked accusingly at the nurse and me.

'I will personally castrate the person who is responsible for giving Frank the boiled sweet,' he announced. By the time he had completed his examination of Frank, both the nurse and I were in tears. Frank was asleep.

At night it was always a toss-up whether I waited for a black cab or called for one of the dreaded mini-cabs. That night I waited in the freezing cold out in the Whitechapel Road. At first I had felt wary of the drunks outside the hospital but they were largely unfortunates with no aggression in them. They would often say, 'Hello Luv' now. I was becoming as familiar a sight to them as they were to me in those early hours outside the hospital.

I was feeling low after our near catastrophe. I crawled thankfully into a cab after a half hour wait and wearily told the cabbie to take me to the Tower Hotel. I could see him assessing me in his mirror. 'Now what would a nice young lady like you be doing going there at this time of night?' he asked knowingly. He had mistaken me for a hooker. I was too tired to protest. Let him think what he liked. God knows who he thought would have wanted me in my state!

I opened my bedroom door and took a step backwards. Another hundred helium balloons bobbed about on the ceiling. This time the message was for me. It read 'KEEP YOUR CHIN UP'. Mobil had saved the day.

Peter told me later that Dan Nelson, the marketing director of Mobil, had been conscientiously keeping abreast of developments at the hospital. He had regularly rung from New York to check on Frank's condition and when things were bad was the person responsible for coming up with these gems that kept us going. I sat on my bed, ate my regulation sandwich and worked hard on applying the balloons' advice.

I was starting to feel physically quite unwell, probably because I was eating so little. I was getting only a couple of hours' sleep each night, since invariably, on my return to the hotel in the early hours of the morning, I would find I was so worried or so revved up that immediate sleep was almost impossible. The best I could do was to rest on the bed. During those sleepless small hours I tried to avoid thinking about the future. The one thing I was sure of was that I desperately wanted Frank to live. I considered with contempt any suggestion by anyone, however well-meaning, that he might be better off dead. Only a few people said it outright. But others suggested it by their looks or manner. I was beginning to sense that among both friends and medical staff there was a distinct lobby of opinion that felt it might be a blessing if he went.

I was slipping back into a dream world where the only reality was my reality. Although with every day that passed it was becoming more and more certain that the severence of Frank's cord was complete rather than partial I refused to believe that there was no hope. No one had actually sat down and said to us yet, 'This is permanent'. I knew it could be permanent for other people, but Frank would be different. He would pull through. He was so strong, so tough. He just needed a bit more time.

I was in almost total ignorance of what spinal injury meant. I wasn't anxious to learn more. Deliberately, my questions to the doctors allowed room for oblique answers. I clung gratefully to their platitudes of – 'It's still too soon to be certain', 'No one can be sure'. I avoided asking Prof. Watkins questions because he was too straightforward. I sensed he wouldn't play the game and might tell me something I wasn't ready to hear.

Sometimes just before I fell asleep the words 'paralysed' and 'quadriplegic' cast shadows across my mind but I pushed them resolutely away. I could not imagine that I could ever come to terms with such a disaster. I had always had a terror of wheelchairs. I would cross the road to avoid a confrontation with one and I found it very difficult to have eye to eye contact with a person sitting in a wheelchair. There was a mental block there. I didn't want to know. I told myself that Frank would run out of that hospital. I kept repeating it.

My abandoned responsibilities were beginning to prey on my mind. I worried about the running of the house. Although Patrick was doing a wonderful job running Williams I managed to worry about that too. But most of all I worried about the children. The school holidays were looming up. I had spoken to them all several times on the telephone but I hadn't seen Jaime, Claire and Jonathan for a month.

I arranged for the children to come up to visit us at the weekend after their schools broke up. They would stay overnight with me at

158

the hotel and we would try to turn it into a treat. Detailed plans were laid. Pauline would drive them up to the hotel where Peter would meet them. He would give them hamburgers in the hotel restaurant before driving them over to the hospital. There I would talk to them first before taking them in to see Frank.

I was nervous of their reactions. They were only young. I was sure they would think we had let them down badly. Mummy and Daddy should be around for the Easter holidays no matter what. Who would hide the Easter eggs in the garden?

Frank's awareness of events occurring around him was still very limited. When he wasn't being treated he spent the majority of the time asleep. Thanks to the artificial lighting there is little difference between night and day in the unit and so little sense of time passing. I had told him the children were coming and he seemed pleased at the news, but I was not sure he would remember.

Special dispensation had to be given for the children to visit the unit since they are not usually allowed in. But Frank had been in there so long they made an exception. A week is the average stay in the ITU, by then most people have either died or recovered enough to be moved to a normal ward.

The nurses and I decided to do all we could to improve Frank's appearance so that the children would not be too frightened. Even after a month he had some nasty cuts about his face. He also had some minor but messy scalp wounds and the hair around these had not been touched. I had become used to them but I saw them now through a child's eyes and cut some of the bloody hair away. He still had a drip of blood or saline feeding into each foot and another attached to each arm so we shrouded them in white sheets. It occurred to me that he now appeared to have a ghost at each corner of his bed but it was the best we could do. We put a light cover over the tracheotomy opening and I tucked his drainage bags under the sheets. Not bad. I hoped optimistically that to them it would just look as though Daddy was in bed resting.

The nursing officer told me that they had arrived. I put on a bright smile and went out to meet them in the glass passage. I was confronted by three little terrified people. They looked strange and unfamiliar. Behind them Pauline, Sarah and Peter hovered tactfully at the other end of the passage.

I knelt down and held out my arms and gave each of the children a cuddle. I was making a big effort to be very cheerful and give the impression that there was nothing too much the matter. They were quiet and shy. Like strangers. Jaime held himself stiffly, trying hard to be grown up. Claire in contrast seemed close to tears, while Jonathan just looked bewildered. 'Oh God Frank, what have you done?' I thought.

I stood up, smiled, I hoped convincingly, and gave them my rehearsed speech. 'Daddy's in bed and he's still quite sick, but he's getting better. Are you going to come with me to see him?' They nodded solemnly and followed me into the ITU.

I prayed that there would be no emergency intake to the unit. The nurses had agreed that in order to protect the children from any disturbing sights they should pay their visit at a time when there wasn't expected to be any toing and froing. I led the way down the corridor followed by this little band of self-contained children, who seemed in four weeks to have grown disconcertingly together and away from me.

I held out my hand to Jaime and he dropped his grown up act and clutched it tightly. Jonathan, taking his seniority seriously, entered the room first followed by Claire, looking pale. Had she always looked like that? I felt a lump in my throat. Please Frank, try hard, I thought. Try to speak to them and reassure them. I can only say so much. The rest is up to you.

They stood beside the bed like rigid little sentries staring at him. I can only imagine how frightening he must have looked to them. I had become accustomed to it all but viewing the scene as it must appear to them I suddenly saw a very grim picture. He looked deathly pale and had lost so much weight since the last time they had seen him. It made him look old and gaunt. He had fallen asleep in the few brief minutes I had been away and I had to wake him. He smiled at the news that the children were there but he was unable to move his head and could not see them.

'Can you lift them up?' he asked me.

I lifted them in turn. Frank seemed lost for words. 'Hello' he said quietly as each little face appeared above him. Shyly they said 'Hello' back.

I tried to jolly things along.

'Have you seen that Daddy's got a special bed so he's floating on air? That's the whirring noise you can hear all the time.'

They examined it gravely.

I looked at Jaime. 'Daddy's a bit thin isn't he? He's nearly as thin as you were Jaime when you were born before you were ready.' Silently, Jaime stared back at me.

In the early Seventies I start to attend races with Frank (*Giancarlo Falletti*)

The Laundry House, rented from the Colman Estate in Hampshire in 1974, where we lived without carpets for a year!

Jonathan Piers Williams aged nineteen months with his proud father
(*Giancarlo Falletti*)

Silverstone 1979. Clay Regazzoni in the first Grand Prix win for Williams (*LAT*)

Battle House: bought in 1980, our first perk of success

Running became the second love in Frank's life after cars! (*Mike Nicholson*)

Frank and Sebastian Coe discover mutual interests (*John Dunbar*)

Patrick Head, Frank's partner and Williams' Chief Engineer (*LAT*)

Alan Jones, our first World Champion driver, with Beverley and Christian

Jaime allowed out of the Special Care Baby Unit in time for Christmas 1982

My favourite photograph. A rare moment, Frank relaxing with all his children

Boxford House, my dream home, seen through the trees from my daffodil bank

Pauline took this picture for Frank and sent it to the London Hospital to pin on the wall in the ITU

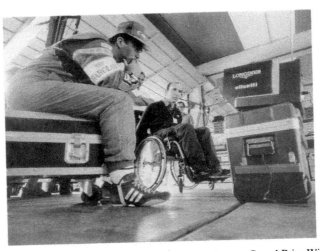

In 1987 Frank fulfilled his ambition to attend every Grand Prix. With Nigel Mansell, he watches the opposition practice on the TV monitors in the pit garage (*LAT*)

Silverstone 1987. Pauline, Frank pushed by Ian Cunningham, Jaime and myself (*LAT*)

Robin Kinnill, Frank's first full-time nurse, still with him after four years

Back home, Jaime easily adapts to his father in a wheelchair

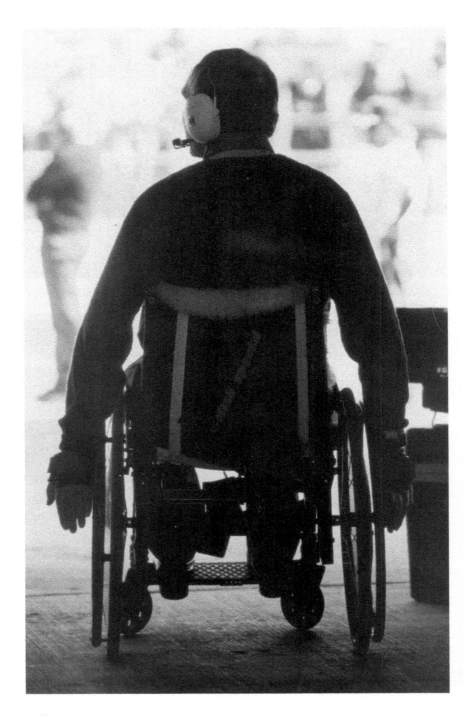

A different kind of life ... (*Nigel Snowdon*)

'That's why Mummy has to stay here and look after him,' I continued. 'It's the same as when they looked after you when you were in hospital. It's really fun being a nurse.' I could tell that Claire was sceptical but I struggled on.

'Daddy and I are both very proud of you all for being so grown-up and helping to look after yourselves.'

Frank did his best to support my attempt at reassurance. He told them how nice the nurses were and asked them how school was going but he was exhausted. After ten minutes he could offer no more.

I led the children back into the glass passage in silence. As soon as we got through the doors Claire burst into tears. Jaime looked confused and frightened. 'I want to go home,' he wailed. Jonathan stood quietly meditating.

I asked Peter to stay with Frank and took the children back to the hotel. I wanted to spend some time with them and gauge how deep the impact had been. We sat in the coffee shop for an hour. Up until now they had been kept in the dark about the nature of Frank's injuries. Maybe it was time to be honest with them. Perhaps it was time to be honest with myself as well.

'Daddy didn't look very well today did he?' I asked. 'He has been very ill indeed but now the doctors and nurses all think he's getting a lot better. They're very pleased with him.'

'When will he be coming home?' Claire wanted to know.

'Not yet. It's going to take a very long time because he was so ill to start with. And there is a chance that even when he is better, he won't be able to walk.'

I had said it.

I had been prepared for tears but the news didn't seem to disturb them as much as I expected. Perhaps Pauline or Sarah had dropped hints to prepare them for it. Something however was obviously worrying Claire. Eventually she came out with it.

'Mummy, what does "unknown male" mean?'

While she was waiting for me to appear in the hospital she had been reading the notice board which hung on the wall inside the unit and listed the patients, and details concerning their care. Next to Frank's details was some information about an 'unknown male'. It had obviously made a deep impression on her. She wanted to know why no one knew him and what had happened to him. The man had been brought off the street after a fight and was to die later that day, still unidentified despite every effort. Like Frank, he was in his forties but unlike Frank he had nobody who either knew or cared what had happened to him. 'At least Daddy will never be as unlucky as that,' I comforted Claire.

But something else was bothering her. Frank had been described correctly on the list as forty-one years old, but she was very concerned that his forty-second birthday was coming up in a couple of weeks. 'Will you make sure they change his age on the notice board Mummy?' she pleaded. For some reason it seemed of vital importance to her. I promised I would.

I went back to our rooms with the children and helped them have their baths. We talked about school as they got ready for bed. Afterwards I left them watching television with Pauline while I returned to the hospital. It was time to relieve Peter and assist with getting Frank into position for a few hours' sleep. He had nicknamed me his 'chief comfort officer'. I alone now had the knack of positioning his neck to his satisfaction. It could take a couple of hours. 'Are the children all right?' he asked. I assured him that they were. He looked as if their visit had taken a great deal out of him. I explained that I would arrive a bit late in the morning as I wanted to have breakfast with them. Perhaps, I suggested, it would be better if the nurses gave him his bed-bath before I arrived. But Frank was getting used to my attentions and wanted to wait for me.

I returned to the hotel and cuddled up with Jaime. He had sneaked out of the little bed specially installed for him in my room and had crawled into my bed without Pauline noticing. It was lovely to have him there. I needed him.

In the morning, after breakfast, I waved goodbye to them feeling painfully torn between my responsibilities as a mother and as a wife.

'When will you be coming home Mummy?' Jonathan asked.

'I can't tell you yet Jonathan,' I said. They looked at me reproachfully. I did my best to explain.

'Listen. I have looked after you all your lives until now haven't I?' They nodded.

'Well, now it's Daddy's turn. You will just have to try and be patient while I look after him and try to make him better. But I will come to Boxford soon I promise.'

I meant it. I wanted to see my home again. I wanted to see what the garden looked like in spring. I wanted more than anything to escape from this nightmare I was in. But at the same time I didn't want to go. It was as though there were invisible cords binding me to Frank's bedside. Since the accident I had not left him for more than a few hours at any one stretch. Stupidly, perhaps because of what had happened in France, I didn't trust anyone with his care except myself. Peter who had shared my vigil and had been quietly observing me ever since the accident was probably more aware than I was of the toll the strain was taking on me. He wanted me to take a break. Possibly the doctors had a word with him. Brian Simpson had often shown concern for me.

'You must learn to pace yourself better,' he would scold. Peter came up with the suggestion that I should go away for twenty-four hours. It was arranged with Susie that she should come up and take me overnight to a hotel near Bath where I could eat and sleep and talk to her for a day. They all felt it would be better than going to Boxford where the children would mean I would simply be exchanging old responsibilities for new ones.

I couldn't make up my mind if it was the right thing to do. I broached the subject to Frank.

'I don't want to go,' I said, 'but they think I ought. They want me to get a good night's sleep.'

Frank thought about it. 'I don't want you to go either, but I think they're right. It'll probably do you good.'

Finally I agreed that *if* Frank was in a stable condition and *if* Peter would stay with him for the full twenty-four hours and *if* he would promise to contact me if there was any emergency, then I would go. My batteries were running very low and needed recharging if I was to stay the course. The end was very far from being in sight.

At the appointed hour Susie came to collect me and I said goodbye to Frank.

'Enjoy yourself,' he said. I felt I was deserting him. He needed me and I was going away. I suddenly felt it had all been engineered against my wishes. I might be tired but Frank was paralysed – maybe dying. Why had I allowed myself to be manipulated?

Peter came in and sat down in my place beside the bed. The nurses gathered round and ushered me out. 'Get some rest and enjoy yourself,' said Carole firmly. 'Have a nice time. Forget about it.' I walked miserably away and the door of Frank's room closed behind me.

Susie and I set off along the Chelsea Embankment towards the M4. The deed was done. We had gone past the point of no return. As I accepted that fact I started to relax. The river looked more beautiful to me that morning, after my month of imprisonment, than it had ever looked before. I drank in the scene: the sunshine glinting off the water and the fresh green spring leaves on the trees.

We reached Bath in time for lunch, and spent the afternoon looking around the shops. Again I felt disorientated. It was like being in a world where I didn't belong but Susie shepherded me gently around and I allowed her to dictate what we did next. We were to spend the night at Ston Easton, a gracious hotel set in superb grounds in the midst of traditional English countryside. We arrived late in the afternoon. I had been booked into a bedroom overlooking the gardens. It was wonderfully cosy with a log fire and a four poster bed covered in the same pretty chintz I had used in our bedroom at home.

We ordered tea in my room and I unburdened myself to Susie. I told her of every fear, every worry. I hadn't left Frank behind at all. I carried him with me in my mind every minute of the day. I hadn't been aware till now how much I needed someone who would listen, rather than just offer words of consolation or advice. I told her of my fears that he might not get better. And I talked about how we could live if he did and was paralysed.

We discussed the word quadriplegia and the difference between that and paraplegia. It seemed to me like the difference between night and day. I had seen Clay Regazzoni since he had lost the use of his legs in an accident. I told Susie I could imagine Frank coming to terms with that. Wheels can substitute for legs. Frank could continue competing in marathons in a wheelchair if it was just his legs that were paralysed. I had seen people doing it. He would be able to drive a car too. With modern gadgets there seemed few limits to what the paraplegic could do. But losing the use of your arms – that was another matter. There lay the difference between independence and total dependence. I wasn't sure either of us could cope with it.

It was the first time I had faced up honestly to the possibility of total paralysis. It was a relief to get it out in the open. When at last, exhausted, I ran out of words, Susie put me to bed and I slept for an hour before she woke me up to get dressed for dinner. Pauline had brought some of my clothes up to London when she came with the children. I shed my well-worn jeans and gym shoes and climbed into a dress. It hung off my shoulders and my collar bones and shoulder blades protruded. I realized with a shock that Frank was not the only one to have lost weight.

My stomach had got used to being empty and I had no appetite for dinner but I appreciated the pretty dining room and drank a glass of wine. It revived my conversation and Susie and I chatted until eleven when she reminded me that part of the object of this exercise was for me to have my first good night's sleep in a month. She gave me a Mogadon and I snuggled down in my four poster. I pictured Frank in his air-bed in the unit a hundred miles away. Then the picture faded and I passed out for ten hours.

I was woken by a maid bringing me breakfast in bed. She pulled back the curtains so that I could look out at the wonderful view over the Mendip Hills. I ate my breakfast and luxuriated. Overnight the magnet pulling me back to the London hospital had lost its power. It would be so nice to stay here for ever, cossetted and spoiled, pretending I hadn't a care in the world. I got up and had a leisurely bath. It seemed a hundred years since I had enjoyed such a luxury. Quick showers had been all I'd had time for since the accident. Then, dressed once more in jeans and gym shoes I got into Susie's car. She drove me to Bath station where I was to catch a train back to London. This morning I found little to say. I did not want to go back, I felt quite sick.

Susie left me at the station entrance, kissing me goodbye and promising to come up to London and visit me soon at the hospital. Tense and unhappy, I sat on a bench on the platform. I felt terrified of leaving the comforting nest which had surrounded me for the last twenty-four hours. The thought of the hospital made my stomach turn over. I couldn't face it; the clinging smell of the unit, the sickness, the deaths, the revolting lavatories, the ghastly dark stairwell at night, the endless wait for a taxi at two a.m. in the Whitechapel Road. I missed Susie. How dare she leave me? I felt hideously sorry for myself.

The train arrived and reluctantly I climbed on board and just over an hour later found myself in Paddington. I was working on auto-pilot. I heard myself saying 'The London Hospital' to a cabby, just as I had on countless previous occasions. Today the journey along the Embankment did not fill me with joy. The river looked threatening, not beautiful. I was returning to the set of the horror movie. I paid the cabbie and went into a chemist on the pretence of needing toothpaste; anything to stall my return for a few more moments. But there was no escape. I found myself once more walking down the glass passage. Reluctantly I pressed the bell and sat down on 'Peter's' chair waiting to be let in.

It was a couple of minutes before the door opened and the nursing officer beckoned to me.

'Have you had a good rest?' she asked with a smile.

I nodded, 'Lovely, thank you. How's Frank?'

She gave a slight grimace. 'He's had a couple of serious breathing problems during the night. I'm afraid he missed you. He'll be better now you're back.'

Guilt at my shirked responsibilities and grudging return flooded over me. I rushed into Frank's room, his face lit up weakly as I leaned over him.

'I'm pleased you're back,' he said.

I kissed him and only then noticed a very ragged Peter sitting quietly in the corner. I realized he had never before seen Frank experience a breathing crisis. He appeared severely shocked and looked as though he could do with a little oxygen himself.

His nurse came to us and said that it was time for Frank to have his bowels evacuated and would we like to go out for a while. Since the accident Frank's bowels had completely given up functioning and once every four or five days what was graphically termed a manual evacuation had to be carried out. I took the opportunity to drag Peter down to the 711 for a cup of tea and a bun. He had supported me over the past weeks, always strong, always there. Now it was my turn to act as his support.

Over his tea Peter told me that he had nearly phoned me at the hotel. He had felt sure Frank wasn't going to make it through the night. He had been in great distress, great pain, and wanted to know where I was – he seemed to have forgotten my plans for a day away with Susie. Only the nurse's insistence that I must have my rest and should not be told had kept Peter away from the phone.

The breathing problems had become almost routine to me. In contrast, Peter, seeing one of Frank's crises for the first time had felt it was touch and go. I had been lulled into a false sense of security by having been witness to so many of these recoveries from the jaws of death. It seemed to me a foregone conclusion that he would continue to fight his way out of them. Now I wondered if Peter's assessment of the situation was closer to reality than mine.

One major breakthrough did emerge as a result of his deputizing for me the night before. He had managed to persuade the nurses to let us use the staff lavatory. I had never dared ask and when necessary had trailed up the passage to the filthy public loo. This new concession meant I could now allow myself to drink as many cups of tea as I wanted during the day and night. My delight at the new privilege must have seemed out of all proportion to Peter.

166

I settled quickly back into the hospital routine. Pat McCann, the chief nursing officer called, me into her office and told me that they had decided to recommence the nasal gastric feeding.

'I know you want to be involved in his nursing,' she said. 'I think you are ready now to learn how to pass a catheter through the urinary tract to empty Frank's bladder.'

I don't know what you look like when you blanch but I felt myself do it. She smiled. 'Don't worry about it. You manage the lung suction very well. I've every confidence you'll be able to learn. I wouldn't suggest it if I didn't think it was a useful step. The doctors think so too.'

Faced with such faith in me I could do nothing but agree, but secretly I hoped they might forget all about it.

First though there was the matter of the nasal gastric feed. Poor Frank suffered another painful tube up his nose. They had decided to add food colouring to the protein fluid this time so that any misrouting to his lungs would immediately show up in the suction bottle. Red was discounted because it could be confused with blood. Similarly green could resemble an infection in the mucus. In the end it was decided to use blue, and a ghastly looking bottle of blue milk was added to the set-up around his bed.

They did not forget my promised instruction course. Mark Harvey, an anaesthetist with a passionate interest in motor racing, was given the dubious distinction of teaching me to catheterize. It was not easy. Several attempts had to be aborted on the first try and the catheters thrown away because I had bungled the complicated sterile procedure. I found it very hard to master despite Pat's confidence in me. My hands were shaking so much I could at first not get the catheters out of their sterile packets without contaminating them. Frank lay there with his eyes firmly shut, not able to bear watching my fumbling attempts. He never had suffered fools gladly and may not have been too impressed at having this part of his anatomy in unsafe hands.

We tried it six or seven times. Eventually that first morning I had to give up altogether but Mark assured me that the next attempt shouldn't present me with the same difficulties. It was just a matter of practice.

I was dubious but he proved to be right. The next day we attempted it again, and the next, and by the fourth day I was less nervous and passed the exam, not with flying colours, but with a good average. From then on I was able to carry out the four-hourly catheterization for Frank myself, firstly under the scrutiny and supervision of a doctor and then, when they had sufficient confidence in me, on my own. It was a time-consuming business which occupied quite a big part of a busy doctor's schedule. Since the female nurses are not allowed to carry out this procedure on a male patient it was a help to them to be able to delegate this job to me. Pat was well pleased with me and I was quite pleased with myself. Even Frank declared himself impressed.

Since his first visit, Sebastian Coe had returned regularly to see Frank. A few days later he was waiting outside the unit with Brodie who was not allowed in yet but who paid frequent visits to the hospital. While they were chatting out in the corridor Frank had a major breathing crisis and once more needed the hand-held respirator. Brian Simpson was called in and asked the nurses to bring the life-support machine into the room. I kept out of the way in the corner of his room, apprehensive that even at this late stage they might still put him on the respirator. I did not feel the panic I once had at these emergencies but I did feel disheartened. I wondered how much longer this pattern of a few clear days followed by another drama was going to continue. He had been in intensive care for six weeks now. It was like a game of snakes and ladders. Surely it had to come to an end soon?

The immediate crisis appeared to be over. Frank was breathing on his own again. I left the room to tell Sebastian that he wouldn't after all be able to visit today. We were standing in the glass passage talking when Brian Simpson came through. Without warning he stopped in front of me and said wearily, 'Ginny, I'm terribly sorry. I just do not think he is going to make it. You are prepared for that aren't you?'

I was completely unprepared for it. I almost fell onto the chair as my legs gave way. I couldn't speak.

'Are you all right?' Sebastian's voice was concerned.

I nodded. All at once I felt dreadfully tired. 'It just seems to be going on and on,' I said.

I walked slowly back into the unit to sit by my dying husband's bedside.

That night we said our prayers together as we had when he first arrived on this ward from Marseille. I put on a tape of the Moody Blues and sat close to his bed listening to the same songs we had listened to all those years ago before we were married.

> 'Watching and waiting
> for a friend to play with.
> Why have I been alone so long?'

The words broke my heart. I felt a lump growing huge in my throat. I wanted my friend back. Tears streamed down my face. Frank was lying on his side watching me.

'Do you think I'm going to die?' he whispered.

It was too much. All my carefully nurtured self-control abandoned me. I sobbed uncontrollably, gulping and choking as I looked at him. I was incapable of answering.

Unable to put his arm around me, unable even to hold my hand, he looked steadily back at me. Tears ran down his cheeks too as he said quietly, 'I'm very sorry Ginny.'

CHAPTER 12

*F*rank defied death. Ever since the accident I had been sure that, however grim his future might look, Frank wanted to live. Now he proved it. He would not give up. He fought so hard and for so long over the next few days that sometimes I was afraid he might die from sheer exhaustion rather than from his injuries themselves.

It was a long anxious week before the monitors began to show steady signs of improvement. I dared not ask Brian Simpson each day whether he thought there was a better chance. Instead I watched the doctors' faces. Towards the end of the week I detected a slightly more relaxed atmosphere around the bed, the odd joke was being cracked, they seemed to be assisting him to breathe less frequently than before. The anaesthetist who was taking blood samples to check the gases' content returned to the room with better readings and the amount of oxygen being fed into his lungs was gradually reduced. Everyone seemed amazed at Frank's resilience. One of the doctors told me that only a man as fit as Frank had been before the accident could have pulled through. All that running had increased his lung capacity and strengthened his heart.

After seven days Brian Simpson told me with a smile, 'We seem to be making good progress now.' It looked, after all, as though Frank was going to make it. It was the end of April.

I felt as though I had been holding my breath for an eternity and with relief I started to let it out. Seven weeks of our lives had passed, time suspended, night merging into day, every minute spent with the constant background fear that Frank might die. During those weeks I had sometimes tried to imagine my life without him. I had even tried to picture his funeral. Myself, the children, standing at his graveside. Wondering if I could handle it.

I had never felt tired or hungry after the first few days. Any semblance of being well-groomed had disappeared, other things were more important. There had been little time for such vanities as washing my hair. Each night I had parked the same pair of jeans at the end of my bed and after two or three hours' sleep pulled them back on again, put on my gym shoes and returned to Frank's bedside. Always there had been the same apprehension when I arrived at the hospital – the terror that perhaps today I would walk in and find his bed empty. Apart from that one venture out with Susie the outside world had ceased to exist for me. The focus of my existence, the purpose of my life, had been to help Frank to live.

Now, with the latest battle won I started to dare to believe that he was not going to die. Like the nurses I sensed that Frank had turned a corner. And, believing that, I felt that I could leave his side without worry. The night away with Susie had done me good but its benefits had been undone when I returned. I needed another break. I wanted some more fresh air in my lungs. More than anything I wanted to go home and sleep in my own bed.

My car was delivered to the hospital. I planned to drive down to Boxford after settling Frank for the night and return at lunch time the following day. What had been unthinkable a week before now seemed perfectly feasible. It was as though I too had turned a corner.

There was no traffic on the M4 in the early hours. It was strange to be driving again. Strange to be away from my insular world at the hospital. Those last long miles through the country lanes to Boxford seemed never-ending. Then at last there it was. The familiar turn up the drive. I drove past the daffodils, still in bloom after the late spring, and stopped the car. The house, unchanged, was bathed in moonlight. In some ways it felt as though I had been away a hundred years and yet in others it was as if I had never left.

I had not wanted the children to know I was coming in case I had to change the plans at the last minute, so no one was waiting up for me. I put the key in the front door lock, turned it and stepped inside. Fred, the labrador, looked at me accusingly for a moment. I had been away too long. Then he relented and greeted me with familiar kisses. I knelt and hugged him. The house was so quiet. I went into each room somehow expecting it to have changed as we had done. It hadn't. It was the same. It was home.

I was starting to feel unreal again, in a dream. Perhaps I was going to wake up and find Frank was here and the nightmare was behind me. I climbed the stairs up to our bedroom. A book lay on the table beside the bed; *The Pacific War* by John Costello, its corner still turned down where Frank had finished reading it nearly two months ago. Piled up on the chest of drawers were his newly-ironed shirts. In the bathroom his toothbrush and shaving things waited for him. I opened his cupboard and buried my face in his jackets, my heart breaking, knowing now that I would not wake up. It was no dream.

I looked at our empty bed. Almost certainly Frank would never spend another night in that bed with me. My throat was burning. Shivering, I undressed and climbed in between the cold sheets and my feet touched something warm – a hot water bottle. Pauline must have known how cold I would feel. On the bedside table I saw that she had left a flask of tea and a plate of my favourite avocado sandwiches. I didn't sleep but lay in bed nibbling the sandwiches and watched the morning arriving. The sun at least still came up in the east – Carlos used to say that, I remembered.

At seven o'clock Jaime and Claire arrived on my bed, excited and demanding to know why I had come home and how was Daddy? I tried to tell them the truth as I knew it. That Daddy was getting better but it was looking more and more as though he might not walk again. I laughed with them and teased them, determined that I was not going to impose my anguish on them. After breakfast I took both of them to school. I stayed in the car as I let them out and drove straight off down the school drive again, anxious to avoid the curious stares or questioning of other mothers. Or worse – far worse – their sympathy.

Back home I spent the morning checking everything out, organizing the payment of bills and various household jobs with Pauline. I left at lunchtime but found it hard to head back up to London. There was a conflict just like the last time. Part of me wanted to be with Frank, but I felt a strong pull also to stay at home. For the moment however there was no question of it. Firmly I pointed the car out of the drive and put my foot down. I had no idea when I might see Boxford next.

I returned to find that Frank's care had entered a new phase. It seemed generally to be accepted now among the medical staff that at some time during the last week the tide had turned. The nursing emphasis had shifted subtly from survival to recovery. One by one

172

his drips were being removed. We were entering a new phase, and we developed a new routine to suit it.

In the mornings we would give Frank a bed-bath, a shave and sometimes a hair wash using an odd-shaped bucket which was attached to the end of the bed and slipped under the top of his head. By noon he was ready to see the physiotherapists who now spent less time clearing Frank's lungs and more on working towards raising him into a sitting position, supported by the adjustable bed. After two months lying horizontally Frank's blood was pooling. His blood pressure had lowered dramatically and he passed out if he was raised too high from the pillows. Progress therefore had to be slow. Each afternoon he was taken up a further inch, with his blood pressure being constantly monitored and a pair of anti-embolism stockings guarding against clotting in his legs. It took four of us to put these stockings on – the team around him was as large as ever.

Once he was tolerating a close-to-sitting position the next move was to strap him onto a tilting table and slowly change the angle until his whole body was nearly vertical. Only when he could tolerate this would he be ready for the next step, a wheelchair.

Frank could sense when he was approaching a faint but he was so determined to reach new heights each day that he doggedly refused to give the physiotherapists the correct feedback.

'Are you still okay?' they'd ask.

He'd nod his head confidently and then proceed to pass out cold!

For the first time he was allowed to have visitors other than Peter, Seb, Patrick and me. The only exceptions made so far had been when the children visited him. Now at teatime every day fresh faces appeared: Charlie, Brode, even Alan Jones who was back in England for a year. Each visitor was restricted to just a few minutes as Frank rapidly became tired. I had worried how people might react when they saw him. Frank had enough problems without having to deal with visitors who recoiled at his appearance. But we were lucky. There were no flinchers. Some of them almost went too far the other way.

'Right you stupid bugger – when are you running again?' was Alan's typical greeting. Most of the motor racing fraternity had visited intensive therapy units all too often and had developed a fairly black humour about it all. It did help lighten the atmosphere and encouraged Frank to see things in a different perspective. Me too. If it was permissible to joke about it then maybe it wasn't the end of the world.

After visiting time Frank would sleep for a couple of hours. Peter hired a television and video for the room. Since Frank couldn't see it properly from his horizontal position it made the incentive to sit up all the greater.

The nasal gastric feeding was still causing regular problems with misrouting. Five times in the two weeks after my Boxford visit the tube had to be quickly pulled out through his nose as blue fluid appeared dramatically in the lung suction bottle. Twenty-four hours later the tube would be replaced, each time causing Frank fresh agony. He was beginning to crave a drink, or anything by mouth. He was also beginning to get much more assertive – more like the old Frank. 'Come on Prof. When are you f—ing going to let me have a cup of tea?' he demanded one day. Prof. Watkins laughed, considered the matter, and decided to risk letting him attempt a few sips. But the paralysis was still too high. His swallowing mechanism refused to function and the tea passed straight down into his lungs. Once more he had to be rescued from drowning by the suction tube, and the cup of tea ended up in the glass bottle on the wall.

The doctors reassured me, they said it was not unusual in cases like Frank's for the swallowing reflex to disappear immediately after the trauma but to reappear later.

I believed them, because I wanted to, but it was hard to comprehend. I couldn't understand how they could talk about the paralysis being permanent and then say in the next breath that a paralysed throat might recover. I couldn't understand if paralysis was permanent why they kept sticking pins into him in the hope that he might feel them. There seemed so much paradox in what I had been told. I wanted more information. I felt now I was ready for it. I wanted for the first time to understand exactly what it was that had happened to Frank and what we could realistically hope for in the way of recovery.

My quest was answered unexpectedly one day when the door to Frank's room opened and James Palmer, brother of the Formula One driver Jonathan, and one of Prof. Watkins assistants, looked in.

'I've brought a visitor to see you,' he told us. Like a conjuror pulling a rabbit out of a hat he pulled a full size skeleton on a stand around the door. Frank grinned and I laughed. 'I want you to have an understanding of what the spinal column is all about,'

James explained. 'Then you can see just what it is Frank has done to himself.'

James told us that what had happened as a result of the accident was a complete severance of the spinal cord between the cervical vertebrae known as C6 and C7. The doctors no longer considered there was any possibility of it being just a partial break. The degree to which a person is paralysed is dependent on the exact vertebra at which the cord is severed. The nerves which control the different bodily functions leave the cord at different levels, so the higher the break the more functions are lost. The highest survivable break was between C4 and C5. If the break had happened at that level Frank would have been on a respirator for the rest of his life as the ability to breathe is lost. We had to be grateful for small mercies. Frank's break was two levels lower than this.

A severed cord cannot repair itself. Ever. So for Frank the functions that had been controlled by the nerves leaving the cord below C6 had been permanently lost. These included the use of his legs, his lower arms, and all of the voluntary movements of his body below the level of his upper chest. He would never be able to breathe again by expanding his ribs. And for the rest of his life he would be unable to cough, to sneeze, or to laugh.

The last loss, that of laughter, hit me harder than the others. It had been such an important part of Frank's personality. Laughter used to punctuate his conversation all the time. I had noticed that he had not laughed since the accident, but it had never occurred to me that it was because he couldn't. I thought it was simply that he had not had much to laugh about in the past eight weeks.

Frank was anxious to hear more, so James continued. There were some areas of uncertainty he told us. Functions which were controlled by nerves that were close to the break but above it, did sometimes disappear due to the trauma of the accident; however, provided the nerves were intact, they could return later. Swallowing was one of these functions. So was the contraction of the bicep muscle in the upper arm. There was every chance that Frank would get control of these activities back. We must just be patient. Suddenly I remembered the first time I had seen Frank at the Timone. I had been sure he had moved his upper arm towards me. He had been sure of it too. Perhaps I hadn't been imagining it after all and there was some small cause for optimism. But for the time being Frank would have to continue with the nasal gastric feed and close his eyes during the food advertisements on the television.

His condition had officially passed once more through 'critical' and enquirers were now being told that he was 'stable'. He had been so close to death that I saw the slight improvement through rose coloured glasses. I kept telling people gaily, 'Oh Frank's fine.' Peter and the doctors had to keep reminding me that he was still a great deal sicker than most people ever are in their lifetimes.

One day, Karen, who had been testing it every day, found a flicker of reaction in his bicep. There was massive celebration. She and all the other physios appeared so thrilled that had James Palmer not educated us, I would have assumed the word quadriplegic could be deleted from my vocabulary. I was uncertain exactly how much use one muscle in his arm was going to be. After all, his hands and lower arms couldn't work. Karen explained that the bicep muscles could be trained to take over many functions. If he was prepared to work hard to retrain and strengthen the biceps he might eventually, with the aid of special splints, be able to feed himself, and perhaps even more importantly, push himself about in a wheelchair. Life began to look marginally brighter.

The influx of visitors he was now allowed seemed to stimulate Frank. He talked more, although it was still only a couple of sentences at a time. He was much more aware of what was going on – and the news coming in was exciting. The season was going well. Nigel had only just missed winning the Spanish Grand Prix by a fraction of a second – in as near as you can come to a photo finish in a car race. Frank started talking about racing again. He started talking about the factory. He started talking about going home

No one except me took him seriously at first. We were told firmly that the second step in the treatment of a spinal injury patient, once the initial recovery period was over, was rehabilitation. This meant transferral to a specialist spinal unit like Stoke Mandeville where Frank would be taught to come to terms with his disability and through intensive physiotherapy to develop the maximum potential of those muscles which did still work. As far as the medical staff was concerned it was unthinkable for someone with Frank's degree of injury to even think of going home until at least twelve months after the accident – if then. The majority of quadriplegics they said were accommodated in long-term hospitals where it was possible to supply a degree of care impossible in a private home.

Frank was just not interested. When Prof. Watkins came in one day and said, 'I think the time is coming when we ought to think about transferring you to a spinal hospital' his reaction was immediate.

176

'Not for me thanks Prof. I would rather go home.'

As usual I backed him up. The thought of spending another nine months of our lives in an institution held little appeal for me either. And the name Stoke Mandeville struck terror in my heart. In my mind to send Frank there would be to categorize him first and foremost as a disabled person. Both of us wanted to approach his problem in a different way. We felt that he was Frank Williams first and disabled second. It was perhaps rather an idealistic and blinkered view but we would not be swayed. Prof. Watkins felt our attitude reflected only a lack of understanding of our problems. He said that we had, after all, been sheltered from the unpleasant facts of paralysis while the struggle for Frank's life was going on. We really had very little appreciation of the predicament Frank was now in and he felt sure we would change our minds when we had thought it out.

But we did not change our minds. We discussed it at length in the evenings and always reached the same conclusion. We both wanted to go home. Frank's whole world was motor racing and he needed to get back closer to that world. It was all he had ever lived for and he couldn't change now. No matter what the difficulties, they could surely be overcome. What could be done at hospital we would do at Boxford. We would employ nurses and physiotherapists. We could make Boxford just like a private hospital.

Our reasoning was in black and white. If Frank was permanently paralysed no amount of time in hospital was going to make him unparalysed. We might as well try and adapt as best we could, as early as we could. Whatever the limits to his recovery we both felt he would recover faster at home in familiar surroundings, picking up the threads of his life again instead of in some unfamiliar institution surrounded by other disabled people with whom he had nothing in common, and far away from his beloved cars. I knew that Stoke Mandeville did a wonderful job but just because it was right for some people didn't make it necessarily right for Frank.

I do not think at this time there was a doctor, anaesthetist, physiotherapist or nurse in the unit who considered it to be a good or even a feasible idea for Frank to go home. But though the medical profession was against us, most of our friends were on our side and with their encouragement I started to make plans.

The owner of our rival team McLaren, Ron Dennis, who was a good friend of long standing, offered to try to help us find the medical equipment and special bed we would need. Bernie Ecclestone promised to convince Prof. Watkins. It seemed unlikely that we would be able to leave in the immediate future but since we would have a lot of preparations to complete we might as well start them straight away.

Ron Dennis came into the unit to discuss with Pat McCann what needed to be done. She agreed to work privately for us for a short time and help organize the set-up at home. I believe Ron put her temporarily on McLaren's payroll. The first move was to go down to Boxford to decide which room would be the most suitable for converting to a hospital-like specification. We chose the dining room, since an upstairs room seemed impracticable. Together Pat and I listed the alterations that would be needed. The dining furniture was to be sent into storage and the carpets taken up and replaced with vinyl floor coverings. We needed banks of power points to accommodate suction apparatus and the air loss bed. In case of power failure we needed a back-up generator. In the corner we would have to instal a wash basin. On the windows the taffeta curtains would have to be replaced with blinds which would trap less dust and could provide instant privacy.

Frank was going to need at least two permanent nurses and it would be easier if they were resident. There was a two-bedroomed flat on the top floor currently occupied by Sarah. We could let the nurses use that and move Sarah down a floor. By the end of our first visit Pat McCann was quite satisfied that within Boxford House it would be possible to make a working unit.

I put the wheels in motion that day. On my return to the London Hospital I was able to tell Frank that the 'escape plan' was in operation. The only contribution required of him was that he keep improving. We estimated that the conversion work would take a month. By the time it was completed I hoped Frank's condition would allow us to make some predictions about when he could leave.

Convincing the doctors that our plan to go home was medically safe was proving very difficult. Their arguments in favour of Stoke Mandeville were so strong that occasionally I felt myself wavering. I discussed the options at every opportunity, weighing up the advantages against the disadvantages and asking other people's opinions. Most of the people who really knew Frank thought that for him the psychological benefits of being at home would outweigh anything else. Like me they were concerned that another nine months in hospital might drain the spirit out of him.

Patrick Head came in to talk to Prof. and they sat down together and made a pros and cons list. Patrick thought it showed decisively that Boxford was the answer. Faced with this wealth of feeling Prof. capitulated but he suggested that we keep the option of Stoke open in case we had too many difficulties. It seemed a sensible compromise.

The physiotherapists who had worked so hard to keep Frank alive put up the strongest opposition to our decision to go home. They had a good case but I didn't want to listen to any more objections. I wanted no more negative input from anybody. There were times when I left the room rather than face another confrontation. The atmosphere became strained but I resolutely believed that we had the right to make our own choice, even if other people believed it to be the wrong one. I felt it was unfair that I should be the one in the firing line since Frank was even more vehemently opposed to going to Stoke Mandeville than I was.

Frank was still suffering continual pain in his shoulders and neck. It was worst late at night and he struggled hard not to give in to self-pity. At long last they had judged him strong enough to be given drugs and he was dosed with temazepam at night to help him sleep. It had to be administered through the nasal gastric tube. There was a junction in the tube close to his nose which had to be opened and the drug was forced into the tube through a syringe. It was a very thick liquid which took some time to be forced up through his nose and he could feel its passage in the tube as it reached first his throat and then his stomach. He hated it more than he hated the urinary catheterization. Pat McCann reassured him by saying that neither procedure was likely to be permanent.

The nurses and I were trying to 'teach' his bladder to release its contents on demand. If we were successful it would greatly simplify one aspect of his care, but the reason was not solely convenience. To introduce a catheter into the bladder every four hours, however carefully one carries out the procedure, is to risk introducing infection into the body. We had to try and make the bladder work. Brian Simpson taught me a method of tapping with the edge of the hand just above the pubic bone. If you did this in a rhythmic consistent way it was supposed eventually to make the bladder release its contents naturally. Between each catheterization the nurses and I took turns to work on Frank's bladder at every opportunity. It was very tiring on the hand to continue for more than ten or fifteen minutes at a time and we had very little success. We had been told that it could take months before we saw any results but it was important not to get disheartened. It was a learning process for the bladder and these were its lessons – just as necessary in their way as piano practice for a reluctant child. During these sessions Frank would close his eyes and dream of faraway places. Fortunately he had never been modest and toughened quickly to the indignities that were now a necessary part of his life.

There was some cause for optimism. Frank was beginning to recognize when his bladder was full. When he said he needed a catheter, he was usually right. At this stage he seemed to be getting quite a lot of sensations from below the level of the injury. As well as the messages from the bladder he felt a lot of pain in his hands and legs even though he could not feel a pin pricked into them. Karen told us the discomfort was caused by nerve sensations, which still existed in a haphazard way, rather like an amputee's 'ghost pains'. But that they were there at all kept alive in both of us a flicker of hope that more sensations might return.

Dr Palmer's lecture was fading from my mind. All my life I had believed that God never sent you anything that you couldn't cope with. Since I doubted gravely my ability to live with quadriplegia I felt it was unlikely I would have to. Now, when I think of that time, I wonder if God was protecting us by sending Frank those sensations and giving us straws to cling to. We needed to be kept from reality for a little while longer. We needed time to accept. To lose all hope overnight was too hard. Instead over the next few months I feel He allowed our hopes to disappear gradually in a gentler way that we could deal with.

Frank maintained his stable condition but still slept a great deal. I made plans. The worst threat was over and I spent time walking in the Whitechapel Road with Peter. Friends appeared and took me for lunch. The sun shone. One night each week I went back to Boxford and spent time with the children and kept up with the alterations on the house. I had time to wash my hair, get some new clothes from home and most importantly of all, to smile. I had cried for weeks. It was enough.

One evening Peter took me down to Parsons Restaurant on the Fulham Road and we ordered quantities of food. The dreadful sick feeling which had hovered in my stomach for weeks had gone and I was starving. I ordered far more than I could eat. Jacket potatoes and sour cream, avocado dip with taco chips. Afterwards we hired videos to take back to Frank, carefully avoiding any plots which revolved around either food or sex. Although the topic of sex or its absence had yet to be broached I felt it was another appetite it would be tactful not to remind him of at present.

180

I felt as though we had made it through a minefield. And in some ways we had. I never allowed myself to contemplate the long-term future. Getting home was the limit of my vision.

Pat McCann set up an appointment for me to meet an occupational therapist to discuss possible mechanical aids we would require at home. I had never liked the idea of a wheelchair and I found myself averting my eyes from the aesthetically unpleasing equipment for the disabled. It provoked a strong negative reaction in me. Unlike the medical staff I did not consider Frank 'a disabled person' and I did not see that these badly designed ugly aids for the handicapped could ever merge happily into the Colefax and Fowler, nineteenth century antique world we had so carefully created at home. I visualized Frank being cosseted in linen sheets and lifted into the brass tapped Czech and Speake bath, not surrounded by chrome and black vinyl. It would have seemed rude to tell her that so I tried to appear to be listening intently. We made a pilgrimage down to the second floor of the hospital to the geriatric ward. It was a tactical error on the part of the occupational therapist. I watched aghast as an elderly man was prepared for his bath. He was suspended naked in a netting sack above the bath on a huge hoist, soaped and flannelled in that position, lowered into the water for rinsing, raised again to be dried and then finally the hoist was moved away from the bath and positioned so as to lower him into a wheelchair. It served its practical purpose admirably but with no consideration whatsoever for the dignity of the user. I was appalled. Unaware of my reaction the occupational therapist enthused on informing me how the hoist could also be positioned over a lavatory for manual bowel evacuation and a host of other purposes around the house. I tried to imagine Frank being swung around the house in a net and failed.

It got worse. She meant to be helpful, but I was left shocked that anyone could consider my husband to be a candidate for such grotesque equipment. I was determined it was not going to be like that. I returned to Pat McCann for tea and sympathy.

When you have a baby you are bombarded with literature and free samples. A similar thing happens, it seems, when your spouse becomes disabled. In recent weeks I had started receiving letters from 'doctors', mainly from the States, offering magic cures for paralysis. Spinal injury organizations too were sending me their literature. Often I found the text of their booklets very upsetting. One likened spinal injury to being 'like living with terminal cancer for many years'. Others demanded money to help fund research involving the transplanting of rats' spinal cords into human patients.

Pat would try to sniff them out before I had access to them but occasionally one slipped through her safety net. One, advertising an American nursing back-up organisation informed me that my future was that of 'a widow without the freedom' with, in addition, 'a massive workload for the rest of your days'. It was sometimes hard to keep smiling. Pat was not the only one sifting through the mail. Peter would usually try to check the get well cards before I saw them. But one or two found their way past his censorship system as well. One read, 'When I asked you to spend the night in London, I didn't mean in hospital!!!! Lots and lots of Love Maureen XXXXXX.' Had we not made such an effort to keep him alive I would have killed him!

Peter, sensibly, told me not to make an issue out of it. We had enough to worry about without trivial things like that. But I have to own up to a brief feeling of satisfaction that at least those particular naughty ways of his were probably at an end.

We were attempting to introduce a drink by mouth every third day now, always without success. I would spoon tiny spoonfuls of sweet tea into his mouth while a physiotherapist stood by, ready to suction his lungs to ascertain whether or not the liquid was getting into his stomach. It was not. Again and again we attempted it, setting Frank at varying angles on the bed to see if that would help, all without success. We felt that the nasal gastric tube might be preventing him swallowing and one day we removed it but it made no difference. I felt very despondent.

I stayed very late that night. He was suffering severe pain again and I didn't want to go back for a few hours' sleep until I was sure his sleeping drug had taken effect. Early in the morning I finally left him with his overnight nurse. On my way out the anaesthetist beckoned me into his room and asked if I wanted to share a pot of tea with him and Alison, the duty nursing officer. They had a rare quiet night on the unit and must have thought that I looked in need of a sympathetic ear.

We talked about going home and to my surprise they praised what we were doing. It seemed as though a policy decision had been taken that we should be encouraged now and not harassed, which was a considerable relief.

I brought up the subject of swallowing. 'When do you think we can expect a breakthrough?' I asked hopefully.

They looked at one another.

'I'm afraid you must consider the possibility that Frank may never feed by mouth again,' the anaesthetist said quietly.

It was perhaps my worst moment. Up until now I had always been careful to avoid asking questions which might have unwanted answers, but tonight I had been caught off my guard. Since James Palmer's demonstration with the skeleton I had always been confident that the swallowing would return one day. As he had said, it was just a matter of time. I was unprepared for this new prognosis. What would Frank's future be like if he couldn't swallow? What was there left? What was the quality of your life if you couldn't eat or drink? Couldn't even enjoy the most basic of comforts, a cup of tea? It wasn't possible. To think of Frank spending the rest of his life having fluid poured down a tube in his nose was too horrible for words. I was sure I was going to be sick.

They realized at once that they had delivered me a severe body blow and tried to comfort me but I would have none of it. I blamed it on them. They were my enemies. I had to get out of that room, back into the relative safety of the dark glass passage. In tears I fled down the staircase and into the night air of Whitechapel Road. I sat down on the entrance steps, not caring who saw me. My face was wet from crying. I needed help. But the only person I wanted to comfort me was lying, unable to move, in a hospital bed.

The porter knew me well now and coming out to look around, he saw me, and came to the rescue. He helped me up from the steps and led me into his little office. There he sat me down. 'Now love, what's the matter?' he asked kindly.

'They said that Frank might never swallow again,' I sobbed. 'He'll have to be fed by a tube for the rest of his life.'

He thought about it, then shook his head, 'I don't believe that, and you shouldn't either. He'll learn to swallow, you mark my words.' I smiled at him gratefully. It was what I wanted to hear. I desperately needed to believe him.

CHAPTER 13

My worries about Frank's swallowing were temporarily diverted the following morning when I opened the doors into the glass passage and saw an oversized clumsy wheelchair parked outside the doors of the unit. I eyed it suspiciously, hoping fervently that it had nothing to do with us. My wheelchair phobia had grown stronger over the last couple of weeks. The prospect of Frank becoming mobile failed to excite me. Although he looked seriously ill in his hospital bed, he did at least look reassuringly like the other patients on the unit. In a wheelchair he would look indisputably crippled.

The arrival of the physiotherapists confirmed my fears. The dreaded object was brought into the room. Frank had been making such progress on the tilt table – he could now spend several minutes at a close to vertical position – that they felt he was ready for the next step. The wheelchair was a specially adapted one they had sent down from the occupational therapy unit which offered more support than conventional ones.

Carefully, the same team of five which manoeuvred him each day onto the tilt table now lifted him into the chair. The back was angled since he was not yet ready to tolerate his upper body being vertical and the foot rests were brought up so that his legs could be horizontal. We supported his head with pillows, fastened a chest and waist security harness around him and Karen gently pushed him towards the window which overlooked the hospital car park. It was his first glimpse of the outside world in over two months.

184

Frank put up with the manhandling with an air of resigned tolerance. Movement still made him feel faint and ill and he was less excited at the prospect of a change of scenery than were his carers. All the physios seemed exhilarated by the fact that at last Frank was able to view something other than the ceiling in the unit. Despite my initial reservations I found I was infected by their attitude. There was a boy scout enthusiasm about the team which was catching. It did feel like a breakthrough.

'What do you think?' asked Karen. 'Shall we try for the corridor?'

Frank was noncommittal but I nodded. Having got this far I suddenly wanted to stretch his horizon beyond his four walls.

We asked the advice of the duty anaesthetist who said we could go, provided we carried portable oxygen and a suction unit with us. Surrounded by his faithful gaggle of attendants he left the security of the unit. We pushed him excitedly up the glass passage, his one remaining drip following him on a stand, while a bemused Frank experienced all the sights and sounds of the hospital. Twice around the lift shaft we circled. Then a peep into the relatives' room. All the places he had heard of from me but never seen.

I noticed that as we passed, people in the corridor were averting their eyes. I was conscious again how I had become used to Frank's appearance. To them he looked a desperately sick man; but they hadn't seen him a few weeks before. My spirits refused to be lowered. We were on our way. It marked a beginning. In the space of a few minutes the wheelchair had ceased to be a threat to me. Now it represented freedom.

We returned to the unit and to Frank's prison walls. He was both mentally and physically exhausted. He had not said much during his trip but must, like us, have felt it was a breakthrough. Now he slept away the rest of the afternoon, recovering from the unaccustomed stimulation. Meanwhile the physiotherapists and I congratulated each other on the achievement. Later in the week we planned a trip into the hospital garden and the sunshine.

My fears about Frank's swallowing did not go away. Prof. Watkins was still checking daily to determine the paralysis level. Since the accident it had crept slowly above the level of the bone injury and was now hovering around the level of his lower jaw. How much higher could it go?

Then one day during our daily attempts to get Frank to drink, a few sips of tea, as if by magic or divine intervention, by-passed the passage into his lungs and entered his stomach. I held my breath. No choking. No turning blue. There was no immediate way of telling whether it was good luck or whether the paralysis level had lowered one level and returned him the use of his throat muscles. We had to cross our fingers and wait patiently for the next attempt the following day.

It was not luck. The next day he took more by mouth and we knew with glorious certainty that he could swallow again. I had never told Frank of my traumatic conversation with Sister Alison and the anaesthetist. No doctor had warned him that he might never recover the ability to take food and drink by mouth, so our celebrations of his reprieve were one-sided. He remained quite unaware of how close he had been to losing that most basic of functions.

My hopes were revived. I told myself optimistically that only God knew how much further the paralysis would retreat.

I had started to notice that Frank never looked at any part of himself now. Instead he looked to the side or to the ceiling. There were times when I too found it difficult and distressing. I was unfamiliar with this paralysed body. It seemed at times to bear no resemblance whatsoever to my husband's body, the one I had known as well as my own for all these years. He looked horribly emaciated. All the lean hard muscle built up by years of running had gone. When he lay on the bed his body appeared oddly flattened. Gravity was pulling down on his internal organs but his abdominal muscles were unable to counteract its influence as they do in a normal person. For the same reason when he sat in his wheelchair he appeared to have a most uncharacteristic low paunch. Despite his loss of weight, his thin limbs when we moved him were extremely heavy; mere blocks of unconscious flesh ignoring all messages sent from the brain.

Dead skin cells had built up on his extremities. Normally the everyday movements of the body would slough then off but with Frank they had to be daily removed from his fingers and toes, taking great care not to break the skin. His healing powers were seriously weakened and any cut would take months to heal and could allow infections to invade.

The reasons for his constant complaints of the cold in Marseille had become clear. Frank's body thermostat had been destroyed and was giving him random messages of extreme cold or heat irrespective of the true room temperature – which was always a steady 70. To compensate for his body's misguided reactions he was forever being either wrapped in space blankets or stripped naked and cooled with damp towels.

186

His unfeeling body had developed a safety mechanism. Any bodily malfunction below the level of the injury manifested itself in a headache. At the onset of one of these headaches his body had to be carefully checked. Usually it was a routine problem– the wrong position of a limb, a full bladder or bowel, the beginning of pressure build-up that might lead to sores. But the possibility was always there that it might be due to something more sinister. It was odd to think that Frank's body could be suffering from gall, kidney or bladder stones and the only pain felt would be a headache. And if he needed an operation there would be no need for an anaesthetic – the cut of the knife too would register only as a dull pain in his head.

The risk of an infection was even more of a worry since it could be entirely without physical symptoms in the early stages. Consequently Frank's blood and urine were regularly checked for signs of bacterial invaders. One day one of his cultures showed the dreaded multi-resistant Staphylococcus, a hospital 'bug' named after its resistance to all known drugs. A large sign appeared on Frank's door 'BARRIER NURSING' and we all, including visitors had to clothe ourselves in plastic gloves and aprons. Every one of Frank's body fluids proved on testing to contain the germ. At this stage it was causing no serious problem but if his condition weakened it might take too strong a hold and kill him. He was put onto heavy doses of intravenous antibiotics in an attempt to keep the infection under control.

Soon the doctors were confident enough of his swallowing mechanism to remove the nasal-gastric feed tube. It looked as if it had been on the sea bed for a hundred years as it withdrew from his stomach and emerged through his nose. Normally in Intensive Therapy Units there are no hospital meals as most patients are too sick to eat. But Frank was to be an exception. Pat offered me the job of buying and preparing food and I was also to be allowed to use the nurses' kitchen. I was excited at the novelty of the prospect. The last meal I had cooked for Frank had been tagliatelle. This time the menu was less adventurous – tomato soup. Apart from being easy to digest it could be quickly detected in the lung fluid should it misroute. Thankfully the tomato soup presented no problems and found its way, a small spoonful at a time, straight into his stomach. He enjoyed that first sensation of taste, it was as if he was discovering a new sense and he was eager to experiment with as many foods as possible. Being able to swallow made a big difference to his routine and reduced the boredom considerably. He was able to drink tea or soup at any time of day, hot chocolate at night, and before long I bought a blender and started to liquidize cooked vegetables with chicken or fruit. It was like preparing baby food again. I was not given strict orders as to what to feed him – just told to stick at first to light and easy foods. He was quite hungry when meal times came but a small amount satisfied him. I was told that because so few muscles are working the energy requirement of a quadriplegic is only about 700 calories a day. Although he would need to eat more than this to replace his lost weight it would be best if he did not overdo it or he might overshoot his target weight and have to diet – not easy when your calorie requirement is so small.

Day by day as the food went in Frank was getting visibly stronger. He was awake for longer and did not tire so easily. I felt sure that the time was approaching when we could think seriously about leaving. Pat McCann had a small office in the unit and over the weeks had been building up a supply of begged and borrowed equipment that we would need at home. There was barely room for her to sit amongst the oxygen cylinders, incontinence sheets, suction units and blood pressure reading apparatus. She had a long list of our requirements and nearly everything on it was ticked off. The conversion work had been completed at Boxford House. Both Frank and I were eager to go.

On Monday 19 May the medical staff met to discuss our case and Prof. Watkins told me cautiously that provided Frank continued to improve he could leave in ten days' time. First however he wanted us to meet a Mr Gardner, a top spinal injury specialist from Stoke Mandeville who would spell out in block capitals the problems we faced with home nursing. It was a last ditch attempt to get us to change our minds and use the Stoke Mandeville facility. I was now mentally totally committed to going home and was frightened that Frank would change his mind. Ultimately though, the choice between home or Stoke had to be Frank's decision, not mine. Mr Gardner duly arrived and spent several hours painting a very gloomy picture, warning of the dangers of infection and the difficulties of nursing in a home environment.

If only he had been more positive and suggested that the benefits of going to Stoke outweighed the disadvantages of another few months in hospital he might have won the day. Frank and I were both ignorant of the meaning of rehabilitation. To us the word meant painting pictures with a brush gripped in your teeth. Had Mr Gardner spent his time educating us I think in retrospect that Frank might have been persuaded. We did not realize the full range of facilities on

188

offer at Stoke or have the slightest grasp of the concept of mental rehabilitation which they also offer. I think we both just felt a blind confidence that once we got home, we wouldn't need any help to adjust. Boxford would do it for us. Looking back I find it sad that no one found a way of getting through to us how unprepared we were for what was to come.

After an hour's lecture from Mr Gardner on bowel management I felt so close to screaming that I had to leave the room for the safety of Pat's office. I was fed up of hearing the negative medical side. What about our LIFE? I wanted to start living it again. However I couldn't put pressure on Frank. The responsibility was too great. Mr Gardner left at last and I returned to the room apprehensively to discover Frank's views unchanged. No amount of professional persuasion was going to alter his viewpoint. Home was in his sights. We were both stubbornly convinced we were right.

Shortly afterwards our local GP, Dr Britz came up to the hospital. He was obviously in some trepidation. I sympathized. He had been informed we were returning to his patch and he, too, would be faced with a big responsibility. He voiced his concerns but we were getting practised at dealing with them now. When he realized we were set on this course he said, 'Well if you're really sure, I'll be behind you to the best of my ability.' With a busy Newbury practice that meant a considerable commitment and we were grateful for his pledge.

Dr Britz had already made contact with a physiotherapist called Penny Lilly who lived near Newbury and had provisionally agreed to take us on to her list. She had experience of spinally injured patients who were living at home and was treating Dick Hern, the racehorse trainer who had not long before been partially paralysed in a hunting accident. On the Saturday before we were due to leave, Penny came up to the hospital to meet us. She was a blonde, bright, capable lady in her early thirties. Just the sort of confidence-inspiring figure I needed. One of my major terrors about going home was what we would do if Frank ran into serious breathing problems that were too much for the nurses or myself to cope with. Penny instantly laid that fear to rest.

'Don't worry. I can be on call twenty-four hours a day,' she said. 'If you do have a bad crisis you can just ring me and I'll be there.' Another medic was on our side. My confidence strengthened.

The most persuasive argument that had so far been presented in favour of a Stoke Mandeville rehabilitation period was their well-tried programme of intensive physiotherapy to strengthen and retrain the remaining working muscles. It had to be done within the first year if maximum benefit were to be obtained. If it was left any later Frank's full potential would not be realized. I determined that with Penny's help we would put our own physiotherapy programme into action which would rival anything Stoke could offer. I asked the physios how many hours a day would be spent on physiotherapy at Stoke. They said two. I instantly resolved that we would do four. And we would start it immediately we got home. Nearly three months had already passed since the accident and his medical problems had meant that virtually nothing had been done in the way of working on these muscles. I felt that the vital first year was already slipping away from us. From now on working with the physiotherapist would become our first priority.

As departure time approached I started to be niggled by last minute doubts. I'm sure Frank was too. He was heavily dependant on the hospital and unavoidably he had become institutionalized. He had a lot of time during that last week to reflect on the attractions of being cared for by doctors, nurses, and anaesthetists in the twenty-four hour safety of a hospital environment.

In contrast, I didn't have time to dwell on it. I was too busy rushing about buying dozens of towels and sheets. I was well aware of the quantity of washing which left Frank's room each day. It had not occurred to me until now how I was going to cope with all this laundry. My own domestic automatic washer was certainly not up to the job. I hastily phoned the buyers at the Williams factory and asked them to make arrangements for industrial washing machines and clothes driers to be installed at Boxford House immediately.

Next I journeyed up to John Bell and Croydon, the surgical chemist in Wigmore Street who furnish most of Harley Street with surgical supplies. I was dazed by the array of disabled paraphernalia laid out on display. It was a new and most unwelcome world. Everything was ugly and utilitarian. I could feel the assistant's eyes on me wondering what I wanted. I wondered myself. In confusion I muttered, 'Um, my husband is paralysed from the neck down. I'm going to need quite a few things.' Goodness knows what they thought!

I had no shopping list and I purchased everything I could lay my hands on. I was buying security. I planned to be prepared for every unforeseen situation. No disaster would floor me. If a nurse said, 'I need this' I wanted to be able to say, 'Oh I've got that!' Half an hour later I struggled into the taxi weighed down with every brand of incontinence pad ever produced, catheters by the ten-pack, special drinking vessels, toothbrushes, different shaped bowls and containers,

190

and dressings of every size and description. It was, by and large, a waste of money. Most of it turned out to be unsuitable when we got home and we ended up giving it away to the local hospital. I was a complete novice, but it was not entirely my fault. No one had offered me advice on what or what not to buy. Maybe because this was such an unprecedented event, no one knew any better than me, or perhaps no one felt it was their responsibility to tell me.

I did my shopping in the mornings that week, excusing myself from the morning routine of bed-bathing and shaving. Frank submitted to the nurses doing it, understanding that I was busy. In the afternoons we pushed him in the wheelchair to the lift, down to the ground floor and into the central garden of the hospital. There with his attendant team of me, two nurses, the oxygen and portable suction machine, and the ever-present drip, Frank would spend an hour or so in the sun. Around us, other patients, some still lying in their beds, were also pushed out to enjoy the early summer.

In the evenings now I started to sort out and pack things for Peter to take away. It was like preparing to move house. Somehow we had been allowed to ignore all the normal strict sterile precautions in the ITU. There were letters, cassettes, magazines, all the accumulation of nearly three months of life in hospital.

One day around that time, we quietly celebrated the removal of Frank's last drip. It seemed a minor landmark. One less symbol of dependancy.

Pat McCann had drawn up a nursing rota. Mike and Carole, two of the nurses from the ITU, were to come home with us and stay for the first week. They would work out the day shifts between them while I would look after Frank at night. After a week they were to be replaced by another pair of nurses from the ITU, and for the third week two more volunteers would substitute. After that we were on our own. By then we planned to have arranged our own long-term private nursing care.

A private ambulance was booked and on Monday 26 May I returned to Boxford one last time without Frank, to take delivery of all the equipment and to check that the beds organized by Ron Dennis had been delivered and were operational. Ron had ordered them from America. Frank's bed was virtually identical to the air-loss bed he had been using at the hospital – a huge piece of equipment costing £11,000. We had discussed my own sleeping arrangements. I wanted to sleep in the same room as Frank. A bed had been made for me which fitted up beside Frank's bed at the same height.

On Tuesday we spent a last quiet evening together in his room. People called in to say their goodbyes – nurses, doctors, even the cleaning ladies. The door kept opening and another head would peep round and smile, 'Bye, all the best, good luck.' I felt suddenly very alone. Both of us I think were frightened and unsure. We looked at each other silently, aware that this was our final chance to call it off.

Frank was given his sleeping drug – by mouth now – and twenty minutes later he was asleep. I waited a while longer to make sure, before making my way back to the hotel. The hospital corridors were familiar to me now. I walked past the darkened doors leading into the other wards, pausing to look into the little untidy relatives' room, which was unoccupied tonight. My friends, the daughters of the heart by-pass lady had long since gone home with their mother. Down the stairs and past Prof. Watkins' neuro ward on the ground floor, where Frank had nearly died. I felt a pit growing in my stomach. In those first weeks the hospital had threatened me. Now it seemed like an old friend. I had expected to be filled with elation as our departure approached. Instead, as I stood in the dark of the Whitechapel Road and waited for a taxi for the last time, I felt sad and frightened.

I arrived back early the next morning but before I could enter Frank's room I was intercepted by Pat McCann.

'Frank's had a bad night,' she said. 'He's had breathing problems. I think it's because he's worried about leaving, but I'm not going to call it off. I think if we delay it for two weeks it will only happen again the next time he's due to leave.'

I understood better than she knew. It was proving difficult for me to leave the womb. How much more terrifying must it be for Frank?

We said goodbye to a lot of people who had become very important to us over the last weeks. Every one of them in their own way responsible for saving Frank's life. Then, perhaps hardest of all, I had to say goodbye to Peter. I felt he had saved *my* life. Without him I wouldn't have made it. He had carried me on his back. He had always been there when I needed him, yet sensed when I needed to be left alone. He knew when to speak and when not to speak. Best of all he had made sure that I still laughed.

We took Frank on a stretcher down to the waiting ambulance at the main entrance. The hall porter winked at me and gave me a thumbs up sign. Mike, Carole and I were to travel in the ambulance with Pat McCann and an anaesthetist following behind by car. Slowly, our speed never rising above twenty-five miles an hour, we drew away from the hospital, leaving the East End of London behind. Past the Tower Hotel, my home for so long. Past the Embankment. And then, in bright May sunshine we made our way steadily down the M4 to Boxford.

Two hours later we were there. Across the drive a banner, suspended from the trees by the children with help from the adults proclaimed 'Welcome Home Daddy'. On Wednesday 28 May, twelve weeks after that terrible day in the South of France, we carried Frank's stretcher through the front door. In the hall were two enormous displays of white roses. In front of the flowers Pauline stood smiling. She produced some champagne and glasses and followed us as we carried Frank into his new downstairs bedroom.

Carefully Frank was transferred into the air-loss bed and we stood around him in a semi-circle to toast his return in champagne. He was tired but he had made it. Our eyes met and he smiled at me. We had dreamed of home for weeks and finally we were here. The sun streamed in through the dining room windows. Fred the dog popped his head around the door to see what was going on. Soon afterwards Claire and Jaime came home from school and came in to see their Daddy, wreathed in smiles. Jaime, overcome with joy at Frank's return, jumped onto his bed. Frank looked at me over Jaime's head.

'It's fantastic to be back,' he said.

In all his forty-two years Frank had never before needed his home. I had sometimes felt he regarded it as a passing place, something little more than a hotel room. But now he did need it, and it was waiting for him.

BOOK
3

CHAPTER 14

I was surprised at how quickly I adapted to being back at home. As the first day drew to a close, the hospital already seemed far away, pushed to a remote corner of my mind. I sat beside Frank in his new room as dusk fell and looked out of the window at the garden and the surrounding countryside with fresh, more appreciative eyes. I loved Boxford House that day. With its solid stone walls embracing my family once more I felt safe.

Both children were now asleep, their daily routine unaffected by the hustle and bustle around Frank. I felt confident that we would slide back easily into being a family again. Frank seemed tired but content. I took a deep breath and let it out slowly. It was a big jump from the ITU to home. It was down to us now. No resident doctors, anaesthetists, sisters and physiotherapists to come to our assistance at a moment's notice. But there was no concern on Frank's face and at that moment I felt none either. It was what he had wanted. I felt ready for whatever I had to cope with.

There was still a strict nursing routine to be adhered to. Urinary catheters had to be passed every four hours. Frank was to be turned as often as possible and he had to have chest physiotherapy and passive joint physiotherapy. All this was in addition to feeding him and making sure that he was taking in sufficient liquids throughout the day to guard against kidney or bladder infections.

With so much to do it was very late before Mike and Carole retired to bed that first night leaving me alone with Frank. I changed into a t-shirt, climbed into my bed and lay down beside him. Physical closeness was impossible. It had taken us so long and needed so many fine adjustments to get him comfortable for the night that I dared not even lean over to give him a goodnight kiss. It felt strange not to be able to touch him but it didn't matter. We were together again.

He fell asleep quickly on his customary dose of temazepam whilst I lay next to him, my brain on overtime, planning our new domestic life. It felt as though I had only just dozed off when I heard Frank's voice call softly, 'Ginny? Are you awake?' It was time for his chest physiotherapy and turning. Clapping his chest was routine now and took about fifteen minutes. In the hospital we had always followed it with suction to clear the loosened secretions, and we had acquired a portable suction machine, expecting to have to continue the procedure at home. But within hours of exchanging the London atmosphere for Boxford's country air, Frank's chest had miraculously cleared. Although I still had to do the clapping, he had been able to bring up the reduced amount of lung secretions himself. He could not cough them up as an able-bodied person would but he could achieve what was known as an 'assisted cough', a sort of repetitive clearing of the throat. Amazingly, the suction apparatus was never to be needed again.

Chest clapping required no great physical effort. Turning him proved less easy. At the hospital in the last few days two of us had been able to alter his position with ease. But now, trying it for the first time on my own, my ingenuity was tested. I was taken aback by the strength it required and struggled without success to pull him over towards me in the conventional way. In the end I clambered onto his bed and bending double, stood over him, one foot on each side of his body, while I put both my hands under his back and used all my strength to shift him on to his side. It was not too good for my own back but it worked.

Nearly an hour had passed by the time I got Frank comfortable again and I was wide awake and desperate for a cup of tea. But I dared not leave him alone in the room. It was the first lesson learned. The next day I resolved to bring a kettle and tea-bags in for my night shift. I couldn't get back to sleep, but I didn't mind. I lay quietly on the bed, luxuriating in our unaccustomed privacy and peace.

I had left the blinds up and as the dawn light crept into the room I glanced over at Frank and saw his eyes flicker open. Saw him staring out of the window at the views across the Berkshire fields. For one brief instant I expected him to jump out of bed. We were home now, all had to be well. But he remained where he was. Wordlessly contemplating the world outside. What could he have been thinking? I dare not ask him. I felt too guilty to move. It seemed too cruel for me to get out of my bed while he lay there helpless.

For me, probably for both of us, the word paralysis took on a more realistic face that morning. My bubble of blind optimism burst. Frank wasn't going out for a run. He wasn't going to drive his car to work. He wasn't going to bound in later on full of news of some deal or victory and give me a big hug in the kitchen. He wasn't even going to get out of bed.

It was a moment of truth. While it was still sinking in, Mike and Carole came into the room, each with a bright, 'Good morning'. I slipped out of bed and left Frank in their hands to dash up the staircase to the safety of my bedroom. Locking my bathroom door I sat on the edge of the bath and wept as I thought of everything we would miss – everything that might have been. I sobbed uncontrollably for five minutes until a glance at my ravaged face in the bathroom mirror made me pull myself together.

There was a great deal to be done. We were a large household now and I was at the head of it. There were children to be organized, shopping to feed our increased number, visits from the doctor and the physiotherapist to be scheduled. Crying was a waste of precious time. I wiped my eyes with a cold wet flannel and went back downstairs.

With no smooth routine established it took us nearly four hours that first morning to prepare Frank for the day. It was a long haul, attending to bladder, bowel, bed-bath, shaving and finally our first attempt at getting him dressed. We had chosen a soft loose navy tracksuit that would not constrict him. It was far from smart but it was one more step towards normality. In hospital he had never worn more than a sheet over him. Dr Britz arrived and I led him into the bedroom where the nurses were attending to his patient. He smiled at Frank.

'So! How does it feel to be home?'

'Great!' Frank gave a broad grin. 'But it'll feel better still to be back at the factory.'

I saw the doctor furrow his brow.

'Yes. Well, perhaps one step at a time. Don't you think?'

'Not for me Doctor Britz. I'm going to work this afternoon.'

Horrified glances ricocheted around the room.

I knew Frank was keen to get to Didcot but had assumed there was no likelihood of it happening for at least several weeks.

'Frank? Don't you think you should let things settle down first. Get used to things here?' I suggested hesitantly.

Frank gave me a withering look. 'No. I want to go and I'm going. I've been off work long enough.'

Dr Britz seemed dismayed. I could read his thoughts. What had he let himself in for? He had assumed at least that Frank was sane. Realizing that Frank was not going to be dissuaded he made a defeated gesture.

'Just understand that I want nothing to do with this,' he said. I think it's utterly foolhardy, and I won't be held in any way responsible if you insist on going. It is absolutely against my advice. I can't say that strongly enough.'

Frank gazed at him blankly, completely unmoved.

But his plans were to be unexpectedly foiled. At noon Penny Lilly arrived to give Frank his first full home session of physiotherapy. As she started to prepare him she discovered that the nurses and I had lined his tracksuit trousers with incontinence pads to collect any urine which might leak between catheterizations. She was horrified.

'He'll get terribly sore if you start using these things,' she exclaimed. 'Hasn't anyone told you how to collect urine?'

No one had told us. In hospital it was not a problem that had arisen, since Frank had not been dressed and the sheets were changed so frequently. When I had seen these pads in John Bell and Croydon they had seemed the obvious answer. I had thought we were doing well and felt rather put out at being criticized.

Penny explained that for male paralysed patients there was a much easier solution: special condoms which drained into plastic bags attached inside the trouser legs. Simple, discreet, and less likely to cause problems than pads. She dispatched me off to Newbury Hospital to get supplies.

'And hurry up about it,' chivied Frank. 'I want to get to work this afternoon.' I drove off on my mission. It was dawning on me that we were very ill-prepared for life outside hospital.

At Newbury an occupational therapist produced condoms in a range of sizes from one to ten and lined them up for me so I could select the size that looked appropriate. (Embarrassing business this quadriplegia I thought.) A nurse showed me how to attach the leg bags, and with sufficient supplies for a month I drove back to Boxford to practise. The afternoon had passed and to my relief the trip to Didcot was postponed. But only until the following day. There was no question of Frank being talked out of his plan.

That evening Mike and I sat in the kitchen and discussed how we would get Frank into the car. It took three of us to get him into his wheelchair and fitting him into a front passenger seat through a cramped car door was not going to be easy.

'Where there's a will there's a way,' I told Mike. The will was all Frank's. But it was up to us to find the way.

I looked forward to being alone again with Frank that night. I had remembered to put tea-making equipment in our room and after Mike and Carole went I made us a cup each. I lay on my bed spooning his tea into his mouth and listened as Frank talked about his plans to get back into harness. I didn't mind not sleeping. The nights were quiet. The children didn't need me. I wasn't hurried. Giving him his tea was rather like feeding a baby in the middle of the night. I had always loved doing that when the children were tiny – waking up and feeding them by the fire, looking out of the window in our own private little world where no one else was awake.

I had decided that before the nurses came on duty in the morning I would try to make a start on bowel evacuation. I had been taught how to do it in the hospital and it had been assumed by the nurses and by me that I would share this routine with them. But it was not a success. I was Frank's wife, not his nurse, and I found the process too distressing and embarrassing to cope with. I alternated between fits of giggles and tears. We mutually agreed to leave the process to Mike and Carole in future. I would use the time to have a bath and perhaps an hour in bed to make up for the lack of sleep.

The morning passed in a bustle of activity. The children came in to see Frank before going to school, and he told them he was going back to work. Any hopes that he might have forgotten his idea were dashed. It was early afternoon before he was ready, dressed once more in his tracksuit. Gently we lifted him into his wheelchair and pushed it outside and up to the passenger door of his car. Then, Carole, Mike and I, with perspiration dripping off our faces, lifted and tugged and pushed, until somehow he was precariously balanced on the car's front seat. How we managed it I don't know. He sat there with a triumphant smile on his face while Mike scrambled into the back seat supporting him as best he could from behind. Frank's head wobbled all over the place. He looked like a new-born baby in the body of a man.

Dr Britz had warned us that Frank might black out in the car. He wasn't used to sitting for any length of time, and the manoeuvring to get him in might have affected him. 'Whatever you do, don't exceed thirty miles an hour,' he had cautioned.

Nervously, I drove down the drive and very slowly around the first corner out onto the road. We were still within a mile of home when Frank's voice sounded crossly in my ear.

'For Christ's sake Ginny, can't you drive any faster than this?' He swore at me all the way up the A34 until by the time we approached Didcot we were cruising at ninety miles an hour. I laughed hollowly to myself as I remembered a friend's naïve suggestion that the accident might have left Frank with a fear of car travel!

Frank had insisted that I was not to tell anyone at the factory of his visit. He wanted to spring a surprise. We drove in through the factory gates and parked around the side of the building in order to remain unnoticed. Mike, Carole and I lifted Frank out of the car and into his borrowed National Health wheelchair. It weighed a ton and had a very high back to support quadriplegic patients and a safety harness to prevent him falling out. It made him look very disabled – more disabled than I considered him to be. I thought pessimistically that the workforce's reaction was more likely to be horror than surprise.

The Honda engine workshop was situated on the side of the building where we had parked and as we man-handled Frank into the chair I glimpsed out of the corner of my eye one of the Japanese mechanics walking out into the car park. He stopped in his tracks when he saw Frank and turned and ran like a scared rabbit back into the safety of the factory. He must have told his colleagues that he thought 'the boss' had arrived and, seconds later, two more Japanese mechanics came out to check the unlikely story. Within a couple of minutes a score of Williams and Honda employees had poured out through the door and gathered around Frank's wheelchair smiling an uneasy welcome. No one seemed to know the appropriate thing to say.

It was understandable. It must have been very hard for them to see Frank. I had watched him pass through all the changes day by day, but they had last seen him looking fit, well and fifty pounds heavier three months previously. Our refusal to publicize the true nature of his injuries meant they cannot have been prepared for what they saw. Frank looked desperately sick. Mike had to stand behind him and support his head to stop it lolling sideways while Carole hovered nearby carrying portable oxygen. He looked about 120 years old.

We wheeled him through the side entrance door and into the race-shop bay area where the cars are stripped down between each

202

Grand Prix. Word had spread, and more of his workforce came smiling to greet him. Peter Windsor appeared, his expression switching from shock to pleasure. Frank's skinny face broke out in the familiar grin, he was happier to be back at the factory than he had been to get home. He was in his element, back where he belonged.

The 1986 season was showing a lot of promise. Nigel had won the last race in Belgium and was third in the Drivers Championship. Only three points behind him was Nelson in fourth place. More importantly to Frank we were hanging onto McLaren, tailing them by just one point in the Constructors Cup. There was every reason for him to be eager to return.

Slowly Peter wheeled him once around the race shop so he could get re-acquainted with what was going on. Patrick appeared and chatted for a while. Then, our mission completed, we took Frank back to the car. Already he was tired and made no protest. He had achieved his goal. Over the next week we repeated the trip each day. He wanted the workforce to know he was there. Back in charge, taking an interest and participating in decisions. Each day the process of getting Frank prepared for his day ran a little more smoothly. By the end of the week it was still taking most of the morning but we were developing a routine, which I found easier to live with than the near-chaos of the first couple of days.

The nursing shift changed and we said goodbye to Carole and Mike and welcomed Anna and Kathy. No male nurse I realized. It was too late to do anything about it so I had to be constantly on hand to help them with lifting. That meant there were no snatched daytime naps as there had been during the first week. Now it was a twenty-four hour day every day. Before the second week was out I had decided that looking after a quadriplegic was *not* quite as nice as feeding a baby in the night. One of the pleasures in those days had been crawling back and snuggling up to Frank's warm body afterwards for another four hours' sleep. This time I had no such consolation.

By the end of that week I was beginning to wake up to quadriplegia and to realize its implications for me as well as for Frank. He depended totally on other people to support his life now and that meant that we had waved goodbye forever to our privacy and freedom. Both so precious to us. Both until now almost taken for granted. A petulant little voice inside me wanted them back. Demanded them back. I wanted a dramatic improvement. I made jokes.

'Okay Frank. The game's up. Would you please get off your bum?'

'Yes. Fine. Just give me a few more minutes,' Frank would say. But underneath, for both of us it was no joke.

I was finding the loss of privacy hard to bear. I was used to privacy in my own home. I had accepted the lack of it in hospital but somehow the invasion of Boxford House by this army of carers was more intrusive. Frank and I had always been rather solitary, enjoying our quiet times together. We had few friends outside motor racing and though we entertained people to dinner we rarely had anyone to stay. I was not used to having people popping up in every corner of the house as they were doing now, treating my home as their own. It was not their fault. We needed them. But would it always take this many people to cater for Frank's needs?

I continued to assume the role of his night-nurse. I would get ready for bed upstairs while Anna and Kathy prepared Frank but I found it embarrassing to get into bed in my t-shirt in front of them. Frank might be a patient but I wasn't. Sometimes I had to lie in bed for an hour or more while one of them physioed him. It began to play on my nerves. I resented their intrusion into our bedroom, I couldn't relax. After spending the previous twelve hours in the nurses' company I had nothing left to say to them. But if I didn't keep up a flow of bright conversation I felt they might sense my irritation. There was no solution. Frank needed full-time nursing. I would just have to get used to it.

One night very late I attempted to pass a urinary catheter and got into difficulties, unable to get the tube past the prostate gland. Doctor Britz came out at one a.m. and took over. It was two a.m. before we had the problem under control and I decided it was too close to morning for me to bother getting undressed. After that I stayed dressed most nights, partly because I was too exhausted to climb out of my jeans and partly because, since there was no question of a few hours' sleep, it seemed pointless. In between turning Frank or giving him drinks I had the opportunity only to catnap.

Penny, seeing how ragged I was getting, suggested we employ a night nurse but I obstinately refused to consider it. It would mean one more stranger in the house and yet another mouth to feed, and more importantly, if someone else was in the room at night it would remove the last little bit of intimacy Frank and I could enjoy. I knew I would not be able to sleep with him while a nurse hovered nearby. I would have to move out of his bedroom and back upstairs and I did not want to do that. What we needed more urgently than a night nurse was a full-time private day nurse. The arrangements for the third pair of nurses from the London Hospital had fallen through and when Anna and Kathy left there was no provision for them to be replaced. Pat McCann had been looking on our behalf for a suitable candidate and telephoned me one day to say that a young man called Robin Kinnill was interested in the job. He had experience of similar nursing and sounded suitable. Pat had arranged for him to come down to Boxford for an interview on Saturday afternoon. I was very relieved. The girls and I had been really struggling this week. Frank only weighed eight stones now but moving his unco-operative body was like trying to manipulate an eight stone block of concrete. We needed male nurses, the stronger the better. I looked forward to Saturday and what I hoped would be the answer to a lot of our difficulties.

The weather was glorious that week and we started to cook a main meal in the middle of the day and wheel Frank outside into the garden to eat it. I felt he needed some sunshine as well as feeding up. But another of my good ideas went awry. One day was particularly hot. After a couple of hours we took Frank back inside and put him to bed and I noticed that he was very red. I was puzzled. He had never been liable to get sunburnt.

Penny arrived for his physiotherapy session and was shocked and cross to see how burnt he was. 'Frank's skin can't defend itself against sunlight now,' she explained. 'Someone should have told you.'

He suffered from a quite badly burned face for the next few days. His hands too were red and angry but of course he could not feel them. The burns exaggerated the itching that he felt continually on his nose and scalp and the all-consuming desire to scratch nearly drove him mad. We had to locate the itches for him and massage them gently to avoid breaking the skin. All sorts of trivial actions that one normally does automatically, without a second thought – brushing away a fly, wiping one's mouth after a meal, blowing one's nose – were now impossible for him, and we, his helpers, had to take them over.

On Saturday, Frank stayed in bed until after midday – he still spent the larger portion of his day there. The candidate for the nursing job was due to arrive at lunchtime and I waited anxiously, praying for a knight in shining armour. At twelve-thirty a powerful Yamaha motorcycle roared up the drive and screamed to a skidding halt, dispersing the carefully manicured gravel in all directions. I watched from the kitchen window as the rider parked his machine and strode purposefully to the front door. He was dressed in black leathers from head to foot. I assumed he must be delivering documents. As I opened the front door he pulled off his helmet to reveal a punk hair cut and a cheerful unintimidated smile.

'Mrs Williams?' he held out his hand. 'I'm Robin Kinnill. I've come for an interview about the nurse's job.'

I invited him in, unable to think quickly enough of an excuse not to. He informed me that he had ridden down from London, but as far as I was concerned it was a wasted journey. He seemed quite unsuitable. I could not envisage this biker fitting into our quiet rural community. And I certainly couldn't imagine him living in my house!

Out of politeness I felt I had to talk to him and offer him a cup of tea. But it was my firm intention to pay his expenses and return him whence he came. To pass the time I made a pretence of telling him about Frank and the requirements of the job. To my surprise his qualifications were excellent. He had worked for several years in Intensive Care. But the discovery did not sway me. He was not for us. I was used to clean-cut male nurses in white coats. Robin Kinnill did not fit the image. I said I would introduce him to Frank before he went and we would be in touch with his agency. The classic 'Don't call us' line.

He followed me into the dining room. Frank, lying on the bed opened one eye, took in Robin's appearance, and asked, 'Can you handle bladder and bowels?'

Robin nodded. 'Yes, no problem.'

'Okay. How about starting on Monday?'

I was very nearly speechless.

In a last-ditch attempt to baulk his employment I decided to show Robin the chintzed-up guest bedroom and bathroom where he would be expected to live, condemned to look out on peaceful pastoral views. He belonged in the Kings Road. I felt sure our environment would be quite foreign and unappealing to him and would make him think twice. But not a bit of it. He put his helmet back on, said 'See you Monday then,' and jumped back on his bike to disappear down the drive in another flurry of gravel.

Despite the air of farce about the interview, I really was quite worried. In two days' time we would turn Frank's care over from nurses who had looked after him throughout his stay in London to one unknown man. I knew that without a team of helpers we could not possibly have brought Frank home. But I hated bearing the responsibility of choosing the right staff. If I made a bad choice Frank would be the one to suffer. He was at the mercy of whoever looked after him. The thought made me nervous.

It was essential that we find a back-up nurse for Robin Kinnill. I had not yet worried too much about this, assuming that the nursing relief agencies could supply them to order. Once again I was wrong.

I spent most of the weekend when I wasn't with Frank sitting at the kitchen table telephoning around the Reading and Oxford nursing agencies. I spoke to endless very well-meaning female nurses who had no experience of spinal injury and were not trained in the necessary procedures. I had not realised suitably experienced nurses would be in such short supply. I was very discouraged. I knew that the doctors in London and Stoke Mandeville were watching us closely. They were expecting us to find the problems insurmountable and to come screaming to Stoke with our tails between our legs. I was determined that I would not give them that satisfaction. I would just have to attach a large L plate to my back and set about learning as quickly as I could. Neither of us had received any education whatever on living with quadriplegia. We had left the London Hospital totally unprepared and wildly optimistic. But it had been our decision not to go for rehabilitation. We were going to have to learn the hard way instead, by trial and error.

Robin arrived to take up his employment early on Monday morning carrying all his worldly possessions in a black leather holdall strapped to the back of his bike. Within minutes he had rolled up his sleeves and set to work. I watched rather disapprovingly. He was still wearing his black leather trousers and obviously had no intention of putting on a starched white coat. I sneaked back to the kitchen and settled once more on the telephone to bully the agencies into finding me someone more suitable.

But by the end of the day my panic had diminished. All had gone well, Robin's manner belied his appearance. He was surprisingly caring towards Frank, and was gentler in his handling of him than some of the women who had looked after him. He was very thorough in his nursing techniques too. He knew what he was doing. And most importantly, Frank obviously recognized that and was able to relax.

Robin made a great impact on Pauline and Sarah who sat giggling in the kitchen over this strange good-looking alien imported into their midst. That evening when he went off duty he visited The Bell, the village pub, where he caused quite a stir. Colour in the village at last! Word spread and before long the entire teenage female population turned out to check the new arrival. Tall, dark and handsome, he broke hearts on day one. Over the next few weeks as I saw Frank's confidence in his new nurse grow and as I recognized his competence myself, my initial prejudices were overcome. Nearly four years later, as I write these words, I have to admit I was wrong about Robin. He, and his motorbikes, are still with us!

CHAPTER 15

*A*stiff upper lip had always been Frank's forte and to a certain extent mine too. Determined to stay on top of the situation, I was trying hard to present a controlled front not only to Frank and the staff, but especially to the children. We had decided before Frank left hospital that they must be affected as little as possible. I felt that they would not suffer unless they saw that Mummy or Daddy appeared to be suffering, and we both did our best to maintain a cheerful acceptance in front of them.

Frank's days were spent similarly to before, except that now it was Robin rather than me who got him up and ready in the mornings. After the night shift I was just too tired and there was too much else to do. There had been no outside pressures on me in hospital. Now, as well as night nursing, every day I was faced with organizing lunch and dinner for seven or eight people, spending time talking with the children when they came home from school, responding to the piles of mail, and making and taking phone calls. All small things in themselves but they added up. After a month at home, despite all our helpers, I was starting to wilt from lack of sleep. Pauline, who had originally come on a temporary basis, agreed to stay on as our housekeeper and her presence relieved some of the pressure.

Every day Penny continued Frank's physiotherapy, though to my untrained eyes it seemed to be showing little benefit. She would start with passive exercising of his limbs. This was to stop the paralysed muscles atrophying and the joints from stiffening and becoming inflexible. In turn, she worked on his legs and feet, arms and hands. I questioned the value of the work one day and she told me to look twice the next time I saw someone in a wheelchair whose hands were flat or whose feet seemed to have dropped downwards until they were in line with the leg. That, she warned, was what happened when physiotherapy was neglected. She felt it was very important for Frank's own self-respect that he should work to keep his body *looking* as normal as possible even if it was not functioning properly.

After the passive exercise Penny would start more active physiotherapy, in which Frank was expected to participate. He struggled to lift his head and hold it up for a second or two in order to strengthen his neck muscles. Aware that the 'floppiness' of his head was one of the most disabling aspects of his appearance Frank worked quite hard at that exercise but he grumbled incessantly about some of the others. In particular, he did not share Penny's enthusiasm for getting his biceps to work. 'I want you to feed yourself by Christmas,' she told him firmly. Frank would grunt rudely and do his best to ignore her. He did not like strong-willed women and neither did he like other people to set his targets for him. But she persevered. She made him try to swing his arms from his shoulders as they hung down limply by his side. The specialist wheelchairs were very light and a development of that movement would eventually be enough to propel his own chair. Next she would hold his arm out sideways while he tried to use the slight spasm he could produce in the biceps to jerk the arm upwards. It was still only lifting an inch or two and even if she got it to move further I failed to see how he could ever get enough control over its direction to connect with his mouth.

It was important that we developed a safe routine for moving Frank from one sitting position to another. Penny taught Robin and me to use the technique known as the 'one man standing transfer'. Robin mastered the skill almost straight away but it was several days before I got the hang of it. I had to stand facing Frank, grip his knees tightly between my own and link my hands behind him in the small of his back. I then used a rocking motion to swing both of us into a standing position and with his knees still locked between my own, I could shuffle his feet and mine around and sit him down in the new situation, whether wheelchair, or car seat, or bed. Strength helps make it easier but the prime requirement is good balance. Most of my first attempts to get him into the wheelchair ended up with Frank and me landing back in a heap on the bed. But

Penny cajoled and encouraged me that I would get there in the end and I did.

Soon, on most afternoons I was putting Frank in the car by myself and driving him up to the factory. There I would push him around the workshop so he could keep himself up to date with what was happening. I think Sheridan and Patrick found his presence very difficult during those early months. He was still extremely weak and was unable to do much at all except to exert his authority – the 'I'm the boss' syndrome. His office was on the first floor, which presented a problem. It was decided to install a lift, but in the meantime four strong mechanics were recruited each day to carry him precariously up the stairs.

We had many visitors at home and I welcomed them gladly. They helped Frank to pass the long monotonous hours of his day. However they added to the already heavy burden of the housekeeping at Boxford. Despite Pauline's capable help I was overstretched. I knew it was too much for me but I was quite unable to resist the urge to be superwoman. I wanted to be seen to be doing a brilliant job, it was part of my nature. But I was starting to pay the price for it. In those first few weeks at home, exhausted, confused and realizing with mounting terror that this was for *life*, I would frequently lock myself in the bathroom and cry miserably. I wanted my husband back. This way of life was just unacceptable and my mind continually rebelled at the horror of it.

I was alarmed by my own tearfulness. Normally I never cried. I had always been one of life's optimists. What was happening to me? And if I thought I had problems then how much worse must Frank's be? I couldn't burden him with what I was feeling. My duty was to cushion him from the harsh reality. I felt that he should only see me smiling and joking. I would leave the bathroom having rubbed yet another cold flannel over my face and recommence trying to be the best wife of a quadriplegic in the world.

I needed to talk to someone. I wanted to unburden my anxieties to a sympathetic ear instead of bottling it all up inside me. But there was no one I felt I could discuss it with. Because I was housebound, I was becoming isolated from my friends now, and I could not bring myself to confide in any of our helpers. During my childhood there had always been a quite marked division between our family and the staff whom my parents employed. We were never allowed to cross over the boundary lines between employer and employee. There were no intimacies, no friendships, between us. 'Not in front of the servants' was the rule. Those days were gone now but it had left me with a legacy I could not escape. To maintain my authority in our household I felt I had to remain in complete control of myself. At no time could I allow a nurse, nanny or housekeeper to be party to any distress I might feel.

So I disguised my real feelings, making less of our problems than I really felt. Perhaps I was trying to deceive myself too – forcing myself to believe that we were ably coping with this situation when the reality was very different.

My head ached continually. I took painkillers, and when they didn't work, more painkillers. Without realizing it I was becoming dependent on them. Soon I was taking twenty tablets a day of a strong non-prescription analgesic. The whites of my eyes began to turn yellow. I was in very bad shape. I longed for an unbroken night's sleep. Just one, that's all. Please Frank. Don't wake me up tonight.

Robin would give Frank some sleeping medicine before leaving us together for the night. Having taken it, Frank would sleep well for perhaps three hours and then wake up, rigidly uncomfortable, and needing to be turned, to have his arms stretched and to clear his chest. From that point on he found it very difficult to settle back to sleep. He didn't want to keep waking me but had no option. Dimly in my drugged semi-slumber I would hear, 'Sorry Ginny' and know that it was time to reposition him.

We really needed a night nurse. I knew it. But I still fought against it. We had managed to get a succession of day relief nurses so Robin could take time off but obstinately I considered that employing a night nurse would mean admitting that Frank needed twenty-four hour nursing. I refused to admit that he was that disabled – that we were both so totally dependent. Not when we had fought our way back so far towards a normal kind of life. I was wrong. He did need it, and his needs should have been my priority. One night, I was so tired after the first three-hour turning procedure that I picked up Frank's bottle of sleeping medicine and downed three enormous swigs. On top of my nightly fix of codeine and paracetamol it put me out into a semi-coma. In the morning Robin breezed in to find Frank in desperate straits having been calling upon me for hours to help him. I was virtually unwakable and when I did groggily surface had to crawl upstairs to sleep it off for a couple more hours.

I was finding it hard to cope with the attitudes of some of our friends. I recognized my own former attitudes in the majority of them – like them in the past I would prefer to have avoided a difficult confrontation. I had turned my head away from disablement. A year or so earlier I had found myself sitting in a coffee shop in Knightsbridge when a black nurse had pushed a blonde woman in a wheelchair to my table. I had recoiled, bolted my food and disappeared as quickly as I could. Much later I discovered with shame that the object of my horror was the cellist Jacqueline du Pré.

Now the boot was on the other foot. On more than one occasion I saw people actually cross the street to avoid speaking to me. I had always thought people who said that had happened to them must be paranoid but now I saw 'friends' do it. Visitors to the house showed signs which varied from discomfort to pure terror at the prospect of seeing Frank for the first time. Their concerns to me seemed largely trivial. Should they try and shake Frank's hand? (No) Should they mention the accident? (Yes, why not?) Rather than visitors trying to console me it was often falling to me to put them at their ease. I sometimes sensed their relief at having 'got it over with' as they left for the safety of their cars and that other world away from disablement and its uncomfortable reminders of human frailty. I wished I could leave it behind me as easily as they did. I had to work hard not to feel bitter, it was not our friends' fault that they could enjoy a normal life and we could not.

One of the most surprising reactions to Frank's disablement came from Fred the Labrador. Before his accident, Frank was the one who fed him and took him for a run, and when he returned from work Frank would always get a huge welcome from the dog. But from the first day we came back from the hospital, Fred had completely ignored his master. When Frank came in from the office now he didn't even bother to get up.

'Do you know, I don't think Fred knows who you are,' I said to Frank one day. Frank was philosophic about it. 'As far as Fred is concerned I'm as good as useless now,' he replied.

But I think it was more than that. Frank smelled different now. His voice sounded different. He behaved differently. Fred simply did not recognize him.

Frank was far braver than I was throughout this time. He seemed to be developing a barrier between himself and his paralysis. He preferred to think of it as a minor irritation which had to be borne but would not be allowed to interfere with Frank Williams and his racing. It was the best way he could cope with it – perhaps the only way.

'If I let myself think about it, if I start feeling sorry for myself, or think about the next thirty years, it would be the start of the slippery slope,' he said to me one day. Frank refused to pass the brink of that slope, but there were times when I felt I had already toppled halfway down it and was struggling to claw my way back up.

On many occasions when I got enmeshed in some real or imagined difficulty Frank would say, 'Ginny, for God's sake. If I haven't got a problem, I can't think why you should have.'

His words pulled me up short. The cross I had to bear was as nothing compared with Frank's. I must stop feeling sorry for myself. I decided to try and adopt his policy and not spend too much time examining the inside of my head. We had to live each day as it came. Some days would be hard work, and some would be sad, but every now and then if we were lucky a good day would come along to lighten the gloom a little.

One lovely summer afternoon Nigel Mansell came to visit. The children waited eagerly to hear the first distant sounds of his helicopter approaching Boxford. There was a large flat grass lawn to the north west of the house which made a perfect helipark but Nigel's pilot decided to be different and make his descent towards the front of the house so the welcoming party had to make a quick dash round to greet him there. The house was bordered by a wide terrace along which stood six enormous antique stone urns. The previous autumn, Tony, our gardener and I had spent a week filling them with hundreds of black tulip bulbs underplanted with pink forget-me-nots, a scheme I had copied from Sissinghurst. They had just bloomed and looked truly wonderful that day. I hoped that Nigel would be suitably impressed.

To my horror, as the helicopter descended, the petals began to fly, caught in the slipstream from the rotor blades. Not a flower remained intact. The urns were full of hundreds of green stalks and the lawn was awash with a sea of black tulip petals. For a few seconds I had to fight to keep my welcoming smile in place but then I saw the humour of the situation. I don't think Nigel quite grasped the gravity of the disaster – I tend to take flowers rather more seriously than most people. In the end we had a good laugh about it over a cup of tea and it was a happy afternoon.

Since Frank's return home, the boys had been having a charmed season on the circuits. In Canada, Nigel had won, with Nelson in third position. In Detroit they were less lucky. Nelson crashed out after a difficult pit stop and Nigel could manage only fifth place. But in France two weeks later they were back in form with another first and third. Williams now had the lead in the Constructors Championship and Nigel and Nelson were running second and fourth respectively in the Drivers Championship.

Frank was determined to get back to the racetrack before the end of the season. The British Grand Prix at Brands Hatch was on 13 July and we had set our sights on it. It was too soon really, but if we waited for a later race it would mean a trip abroad and Frank was certainly not ready for that yet. Getting to Brands Hatch would be important psychologically; a milestone attained. It was what the previous four months had all been directed towards; the return to racing – that all-consuming love that even a broken neck could not take away. Everyone joined in to help make it possible. On the Friday before the race, the first qualifying day, Bernie Ecclestone sent his helicopter to pick Frank up. The children rushed excitedly around the lawn waving white sheets to indicate to the pilot where he should land.

Brian Simpson, who called to see us at home quite often, advised us to take oxygen on the flight in case Frank had any breathing problems due to altitude, but in the event we did not need it. The skies were clear and blue all the way from Boxford to Brands Hatch. We knew we were getting close when we started to see other helicopters through the windows. They swarmed around the circuit like gnats, circling the track, the pits and the paddocks as they awaited their landing slots in the helipark.

We landed gently and Robin and I transferred Frank to a waiting car and headed towards the pits. It was a slow journey. A large happy crowd was already wending its way towards the track. Only participants' cars were allowed inside the perimeter fencing and people were looking curiously through the car window hoping to spot a driver. Several people recognized Frank. He was greeted with continuous calls of 'All the best Frank', 'Terrific Frank' and he smiled back at the wellwishers. We made our way steadily through the tunnel under the track and into the pit area and now there were familiar figures, mechanics, other constructors, drivers, gathering around, all greeting him, giving him thumbs-up signs. We were surrounded by smiling faces. Then perhaps best of all on an enormous advertising hoarding opposite the pits, we saw the words 'Welcome Back Frank' in letters three feet high. Tears prickled my eyes and I saw Frank swallow hard.

At the end of 1986, *Autocourse*, the annual journal of motor-racing contained a description of Frank's arrival. 'For once practice was not about the man on the pole,' it said. 'The high point was seeing the owner of his team, Frank Williams make a welcome and at times emotional return to the Grand Prix paddock when he came to Brands Hatch to see his cars in action. More than that he faced the Press, and the standing ovation gave an indication of the appreciation of this brave act and the esteem which the Formula One world held for the Team boss as he continued to make a long and slow recovery from his road accident.'

It seemed as though it was destined to be Frank Williams weekend at Brands Hatch. God smiled on us. Nigel and Nelson went out in their Williams-Hondas on Friday and qualified them in first and second positions on the grid. Frank flew in again on the Saturday. He spent both days in the pits garages with the cars, the drivers, and the mechanics, just soaking the atmosphere in. I tried to imagine how he must feel. But no one could really put themselves in Frank's shoes that weekend. He had lived through a unique experience and what he was feeling now was a completely personal and private sense of elation. By Saturday evening he was very tired. The circuit was warm and crowded and overwhelming. It was a long way from the protection and seclusion he had experienced at the London Hospital and latterly at Boxford House. He recognized his own exhaustion and, deferring to medical advice, agreed to stay at home on the Sunday and watch the race on television. I was as relieved as Brian Simpson. A third day may well have put him at risk. Most people with high level spinal injury are in hospital for over a year and Frank had driven himself to be 'back at work' in a third of that time.

Jonathan was home from boarding school and was thrilled at the prospect of coming to the race with me. The helicopter picked us up on race morning. We wished Frank luck before we left for the circuit. It must have been very hard for him to see us go.

120,000 motor racing fans had arrived at Brands Hatch that hot July Sunday hoping to see a British driver, Nigel Mansell, repeat Jim Clark's achievement at the same track twenty-two years earlier when he won the British Grand Prix for his nation. To the British crowd this was the Grand Prix that counted – the big one.

It is an unwritten rule that people not directly involved with the preparation of the cars make themselves scarce during the morning of a race. Jonathan and I crossed the track through the underground tunnel from the pits into the grandstand area on the pit straight. We spent an hour or so browsing anonymously among the stands which sold all the race paraphernalia, umbrellas, stickers, model cars. Jonathan picked up Williams badges and stickers for his school friends before we returned to establish a good position to watch the race. Jonathan had gone to his first Grand Prix at the age of four and, by now, he could have gone on *Mastermind* on the subject of motor racing – he could probably tell you who finished twelfth in every Formula One race in the past ten years. Today he was desperately trying to contain his excitement. Under no circumstances are children allowed in the pits during a race and we searched for an alternative position. A steward allowed us up onto a flat roof area halfway up the stairs to the winner's rostrum, where we had a marvellous view of the start, the pit straight, the run into Paddock Bend, and then up the hill into Druids. We found ourselves standing next to Barry Sheene, another thrill for Jonathan.

The green light flashed on and we watched as Nelson and Nigel powered past us in the lead. Seconds later it was obvious that the start had gone wrong. On the second half of the grid, just to our left, car after car was piling up on the track. Pile-ups are not an uncommon sight during the first lap of a race and are the reason most drivers' wives don't watch it. More often than not everyone is able to get out of their cars and transfer to a spare car in order to restart. This was not the case on this occasion. One car had hit the guard rail heavily in front of us and the driver seemed to be trapped. I did not recognize it, but before long to my horror, news reached us that it was Jacques Laffite. His Ligier was surrounded by support vehicles, medical crews and marshals so we could see little, but it looked bad.

I felt quite sick. I had been speaking to Bernadette only an hour earlier. 'Anything, but not Jacques too,' I prayed under my breath. The thought that he might be paralysed haunted me. Six months previously I would have prayed for his life. Now I found myself praying for him not to suffer the same fate as Frank. Not Jacques and Bernadette please God. No one should have to suffer that. It took thirty-five minutes to free Jacques from the wreckage and get him into the helicopter standing by to airlift him to hospital. Bernadette went with him. It was another hour before the word filtered back that his injuries were badly fractured legs. I was weak with relief. It was bad enough (in fact it was to cause Jacques to retire from motor racing) but at least he had escaped my worst nightmare.

I did not find out until later that a strange quirk of fate meant that Nigel profited from Jacques' misfortune. His drive-shaft had broken at the precise moment the accident happened. Had it not been for the restart his race would have been over on the first lap. Now, with Nigel in the spare car, the Williams team set off again. By the third lap they had re-established themselves in the first and second positions. On lap twenty-three Nigel overtook Nelson and raced for home. He was never in any danger of being caught. I doubt whether Brands Hatch has ever heard such cheering from any crowd as it did when Nigel took the chequered flag that day.

Jonathan and I returned to the pits and I pushed him in front of me to the area in front of the winner's rostrum so that he could see the presentation and the champagne spraying. I was intercepted by Patrick Head.

'Ginny. Would you join the drivers up on the rostrum? I'd like you to accept the Constructors Cup on Frank's behalf.'

216

'Oh no. I couldn't,' I said shaking my head appalled. The thought of being the focus of all that attention terrified me. Even when he was well I had never wanted to share Frank's limelight. I certainly didn't want to replace him in it now. But Patrick was insistent.

'Everyone wants you to do it. It would be the right thing to do. Honestly.'

He promised to stay with me to provide moral support. Much against my wishes I found myself being escorted onto the rostrum to stand in front of Nigel, Nelson and Alain Prost who had finished third. Nigel had driven his heart out and was in a state of total exhaustion and had to be supported on either side by the other two drivers while the national anthem was played.

When the anthem came to an end a sudden hush seemed to descend on the crowd. My legs felt gelatinous. I dared not look towards the drivers. Somehow I kept myself under control as Peter Cooper, the secretary of the RAC, gave a short speech and presented me with the cup. I held it aloft for a brief moment. I was told afterwards that we all received a standing ovation from the grandstands but I was only aware of a stifling tightness in my chest and a feeling that my heart was about to break. I battled to control the tears welling up behind my eyes.

Nothing more was expected of me. I handed the trophy to Patrick and left the rostrum as quickly as I could to rejoin Jonathan, who had positioned himself in direct firing line of the spraying champagne and was waiting for me soaked through and wearing a broad grin. With relief I became once more a part of the faceless crowd. I was glad, after all, that I had done it. Afterwards I had only one regret. I wished I had had the courage to look across to Nigel and to Nelson and to say, 'Thank you.' I had wanted to but I knew that if I had I would have broken down completely. I'm sure they knew what was in my heart.

It had been a day filled with emotion. Even in the midst of triumph I grieved that things could not have been different. I knew that I would never again be able to watch Frank's familiar figure sitting on the pit wall, listening intently to his headset, his face set in its customary impassive expression. Never again see him stand up with a huge happy grin as the chequered flag dropped. Never again see him striding about minutes later formulating a strategy for winning the next race. From now on he would have to watch all his races from the sidelines, or worse, like today, on television.

So many adjustments to make. So many losses.

CHAPTER 16

*P*enny Lilly continued to work very hard at Frank's physiotherapy. She was tough with him, tolerating neither excuses nor procrastination and, because of this, their relationship sometimes became strained. He didn't enjoy his exercise sessions at all. Penny was very opposed to doing too much passive exercise, whereas I think Frank would have preferred it to be all passive, and Penny expected him to do things for himself. She also expected him to be ready for her when she appeared for their morning appointments. She had a lot of expectations of him. In contrast to me and most other people, she made very few concessions to his disability. He was rather peeved by this, although it was probably the best thing possible for him. Penny was very used to seeing disability. She met it every day, and was in no way intimidated by it. She treated disabled people according to the same rules that she applied to the able-bodied. There was no indulgence. Her manner was cheerful, no-nonsense and optimistic. There were times when Frank really didn't like her at all.

She had declared her goals for him in the first week he was home. Christmas day was our first target. By then she wanted him to be able to feed himself and be starting to wheel his own wheelchair. Building up Frank's biceps so that they could perform jobs normally achieved by a complete set of arm muscles was hard work and there was no short cut. The biceps is the muscle that runs down the front of the arm from the shoulder to the elbow, normally it works in conjunction with the triceps muscle which runs parallel with it but behind the arm. The biceps is not designed to work alone but it can be taught to do tricks, jerkily lifting the arm up towards the mouth. Penny daily bullied and cajoled Frank into exercising himself further towards a degree of independence. It was going to take months but I could see she was making progress. Little by little he was inching closer towards her goal. Once the height was established she would work on getting him to hold the arm in that position rather than letting it crash heavily down as it did at present. She promised him that once he could manage that, she would get him some hand-splints and he could start to feed himself. Using these splints it was possible by next year that he might even be able to sign cheques again. It was a shrewd suggestion. The thought of signing cheques probably gave Frank much more motivation than being able to feed himself.

I was disappointed by Frank's lack of interest in physiotherapy. I had assumed that he might use these exercises and targets as a substitute for his running. It would require similar dedication, but he showed no enthusiasm at all. He belittled the whole idea of feeding himself, it was so much effort for so little reward. And what the hell, there would always be someone around to feed him.

Doggedly Penny persevered. Despite their intermittent clashes she seemed to be the only person now who could discuss with Frank how he felt about his injury. She would chat away as they worked together and force him to confront his reactions. I would sometimes come into the room and find them in deep conversation about various aspects of paralysis, usually when he saw me he would clam up. I tried several times to get him to talk about what was happening–about the problems we were both facing–but it was like meeting a stone wall. He absolutely refused to discuss it with me. Our lines of communication, which had grown stronger than they had ever been before while he was in hospital, seemed to be breaking down. It frightened me that we didn't seem able to discuss anything except on a very superficial level.

I was sure that one of the reasons for this situation was the new control I had over Frank's life. He had always been the dominant one in our partnership. What he said went. Now, overnight he found that Ginny had the last say on everything. He felt totally at my mercy and he hated it. He said once to a visitor, 'If Ginny pushed me into the middle of the garden and left me on the lawn, I would simply have to sit there until I died.'

I understood his feelings. But I felt it was unfair. I had not chosen my new power. Nor did I enjoy it. It had been his hand that had forced me to be in charge.

Penny began to act as a go-between for Frank and me, transmitting worries that we couldn't talk of directly to each other. I found myself confiding in her. For the first time I let down my 'front' as I recognized that I needed the benefit of her experience. One day I confessed that I was finding the minute by minute demands of quadriplegia exhausting. I told her how I was continually bursting into tears and was filled with guilt at finding it all such a struggle.

She smiled sympathetically, 'I wondered when you'd admit to having problems,' she said. 'I've been expecting it. Don't worry. You wouldn't be normal if you didn't find it impossible at times. You mustn't be so hard on yourself.'

She reassured me that it was common for the husband or wife of a paralysed person to feel overwhelmed by the new situation. There was after all a great deal to adjust to.

'At the moment you're both going through dramatic personality changes,' she said. 'It's very unlikely that your changes are going to match Frank's – you have different problems. So as well as adjusting to the paralysis you both have to adjust to each other's new character. It's quite a lot to do all at once.'

I recognized the logic of Penny's words and felt comforted.

'Just because you're finding life difficult at the moment it doesn't make you a useless individual. Remember that,' she said. 'It's important.'

I had needed someone to spell that out. My feelings of self-worth had been rapidly evaporating as I failed to meet the impossible standards I had set myself when we returned home. I had felt such conviction in my own capabilities at first. I had envisaged myself caring for Frank night and day, seven days a week. But it hadn't worked. It was impossible. Despite Robin's help with the nursing I was permanently exhausted. I had started to feel completely inadequate. Penny tried to help me to take a more forgiving view of myself.

Brian Gardner from Stoke Mandeville was a regular visitor to Boxford House. He would check Frank for physical problems and liaise with Penny regarding the progress of his physiotherapy programme. Brian was still keen for Frank to sample the regime at Stoke Mandeville and continued to mention it at every visit. We both remained stubbornly opposed to the idea but unexpectedly Frank's chronic staphylococcus infection forced the issue. Routine tests showed that the bug had reached unacceptably high levels in his kidneys and he needed an intravenous course of antibiotics which had to be administered under closely-monitored hospital conditions. On learning this we finally climbed down. If Frank had to go into hospital anyway it might as well be Stoke Mandeville, as a non-specialist unit.

It was arranged that Frank would spend a week there in late July during which time he would not only receive his antibiotic course but would sample the facilities Stoke had to offer him.

I drove him there with the same sinking feeling I had experienced when I delivered eight-year-old Jonathan to boarding school for the first time. I tried to keep cheerful, making bright conversation. Beside me Frank slumped silently in the passenger seat, he seemed consumed with despair at the dreadful prospect of spending a whole week back in hospital.

The atmosphere at Stoke surprised me. The buildings were very modern, there were no hospital smells and house plants lined the wide passages along which noisy cheerful young paraplegics were doing wheelchair wheelies. There was lots of noise and laughter. Frank had asked for a side room and we were shown through a mixed ward housing patients in the early after-stages of spinal injury. The unit is set up to cater for people as they progress from being critically ill through all the subsequent stages until they have become as independent as possible and are ready to face the outside world. In the later stages of a Stoke rehabilitation programme the patient lives in an adapted bungalow and only calls for medical assistance if necessary. The level of independence that will be attained, of course, depends ultimately on the site and nature of the spinal injury and Frank would never have been able to progress as far as this final stage.

Even on that first visit I could sense the air of optimism about the place. There seemed to be an attitude that anything the patient might possibly be able to do for himself or herself should at least be attempted. I wasn't sure that Frank was ready for this approach. We had cosseted him so much. I was afraid Stoke might come as a rude awakening to him! Before I left him I asked the ward sister about the laundry facilities. She gaily told me that Frank could use the machines in the utility area at the end of the ward. Help! I thought. Frank couldn't work a washing machine before his accident. There wasn't much chance he'd be able to do it now he was paralysed from the neck down. I never did find out how she envisaged him managing it!

Having established him in a pleasant side room with a television I decided to leave him to it, rather than prolonging the agony of a farewell. I spent the journey home worrying because it was Wimbledon week, and I remembered that Frank hated watching tennis on TV. Would anybody change the channel for him?

The parallel with my anxieties when I left Jonathan at boarding school struck me again. I told myself to stop worrying but to no avail. I hardly slept a wink; I was so terrified that he might not be receiving the ministrations that he had come to expect at home. But I returned the following day to find that all was well. He had enjoyed his physiotherapy and was in good hands. He was also starving, and anxious for something other than hospital food! There were no restrictions placed on our movements so I transferred him to the car, and drove into High Wycombe to buy some Kentucky fried chicken which we ate parked in a field nearby. This was not the sort of strict hospital regime I'd been fearing at all!

The week continued with no problems and with the aid of the antibiotics the staph. infection was brought back under control. I noticed on my visits that most of the other patients were only in their teens, the majority paralysed in motorbike or riding accidents. I shuddered when I first saw them – the thought of being crippled with your whole life still in front of you was appalling – but by the end of the week I was able to return their smiles. There was always a happy feeling in the wards, despite the terrible injuries the patients had suffered.

If Mr Gardner had hoped that this week in their care would tempt Frank to undergo a full period of rehabilitation, he was disappointed. Frank regarded his stay at Stoke merely as a temporary diversion. In his mind, to submit to rehabilitation would be to admit to being disabled. He had already chosen to try and ignore his disability and live in the outside world. He wanted to get back to work.

Back home, Robin resumed the nursing after his brief break. He had been working tremendously hard since his arrival. I had employed a succession of relief nurses to help him but we now felt that what we also needed was a personal assistant to Frank. Someone to act as his driver, make telephone calls, et cetera, and who could be trained to carry out simple nursing tasks if the need arose. I decided to ask Peter Windsor if he had any ideas how we might locate such a person.

The weather that summer remained good and Charlie and Jenny Crichton-Stuart suggested that we try taking Frank on a short summer holiday. It could act as a dummy run for his first trip abroad, we could see just how feasible it was to stay in a hotel and give him more experience of coping with air travel. Alan Jones had been to see us again and offered us the use of his plane, a Japanese Mitsubishi he called 'The Rice Rocket'.

We decided on Cornwall. The children and I were decidedly more excited about it than Frank was. We had been forced to cancel our annual two weeks in Marbella and the school holidays seemed very long without the prospect of a break. A week down by the sea promised to be fun and Charlie booked us all into what he thought would be a suitable hotel. Pauline, Sarah and I were to drive down with Claire earlier in the day and check it out first. We had to be sure that the wheelchair would fit in the lift and through the doors and that there were power points in suitable places and adequate room in the bedroom for all the bulky equipment that would have to travel with him. Only when we rang to say the room was ready for him would he board 'The Rice Rocket' at Kidlington, our local airfield. Special permission had been obtained for him to land at the RAF Coastal Command airfield at St Mawgan.

It was not feasible to transport the cumbersome air-loss bed and we had acquired an inflatable bed called a rhoho which consisted of a mattress of interconnected black rubber cones which had to be blown up using hand bicycle pumps. Pauline and I unrolled it in the hotel bedroom and set to work with our pumps. Halfway through the operation we were interrupted by a chambermaid who took one look and retreated from the room in enormous haste and embarrassment. We were perplexed by her reaction for a moment but then fell about in fits of laughter as the truth dawned. In the chambermaid's eyes we were obviously a rather kinky couple.

Charlie and his family arrived later in the afternoon and in the early evening Frank, Jonathan, Jaime and Robin flew down to RAF St Mawgan and drove over to the hotel with no problems. The weather was lovely, the hotel comfortable and we had a nice dinner in the restaurant on our first evening – Frank's first meal in public. I felt people's eyes on me as I spread a napkin on his chest and lifted a spoon to his mouth but I determinedly ignored them. We had to face strangers' reactions to Frank sooner or later. This was one more step in the right direction.

The following day we pushed Frank's wheelchair to the hotel garden and spent a few hours watching the children swimming and building sandcastles on the beach below. He seemed to enjoy it but by the end of the day he was growing restless.

'I feel conspicuous,' he complained. Inevitably people were staring at him. Some of them may have recognized him.

We returned home prematurely to Boxford the following day leaving the children to finish their holiday with Sarah and Pauline and the Crichton-Stuarts. However, our prime mission had been accomplished. Frank had made two flights and spent two nights away from home with no major difficulties. A trip abroad no longer seemed an impossible dream. Now he set his sights on going to Hungary with the team on 10 August. It was a new circuit, completed only that year and Frank, like everyone in motor racing, was anxious to see it.

While I had been at the British Grand Prix in July, Prof. Watkins had had a chat with me and suggested we might pay a visit to a hospital in Hungary which had built up a world-wide reputation for the rehabilitation of paralysed patients using hydrotherapy. 'It's far too soon for Frank to be directing his energy towards motor racing,' he cautioned. 'He should be using this first year to regain as much fitness and independence as possible. If he doesn't, I think both of you will regret it later. It will be too late to start thinking of improvement next year.'

Every time I had seen him since Frank's discharge Prof. had repeated the same message. Under duress we agreed to 'take a look' at the Hungarian centre. At least it meant Frank could now tell those who doubted the wisdom of the trip to Hungary that it was partly 'for medical reasons'.

We were terribly lucky in having such generous friends. People seemed happy to make their helicopters or planes available to us so that Frank could delay having to negotiate Heathrow in a wheelchair for as long as possible. This time Count Zanon, a good friend and a sponsor of the team, was going to collect us at Kidlington in his Falcon 20. Frank, Robin and I would travel with him to Budapest.

I had a lovely weekend in Hungary. The flight was smooth, and when we had settled Frank into his hotel I toured Budapest with Lisa Dennis, the wife of McLaren's chief, and we even took a boat trip on the Danube.

The black spot of the weekend as far as Frank was concerned was to be his tour of the rehabilitation clinic which had been scheduled for Saturday after practice. The visit was complicated by its being a hideously hot day. The temperature was in the upper eighties and Frank was in danger of overheating. Robin's ingenious remedy was to use a house plant sprayer. He squirted it continually during our tour, enveloping Frank in a fine fog of water vapour. Frank started throwing baleful looks around and Robin got the giggles which he tended to do rather a lot. We were off on the wrong foot from the first moment. Our guide was a charming doctor whom Frank chose for some reason to ignore. In my heart I knew then that rehabilitation here was already a lost cause. He had made up his mind he didn't want to come. It was too far from home, too far from his family, and worst of all, too far from the factory.

Dutifully I pushed him around the hospital and tried to phrase sensible questions about the programme there. Frank's stony face and the sound of Robin alternately spraying and giggling made it quite an ordeal and I heaved a sigh of relief when the door to the last ward closed behind us. The programme was similar to the famous conductive therapy programme used with cerebral palsied children. At the centre of the programme was the huge, elaborately equipped hydrotherapy pool in which a vast variety of exercises and massage were undertaken. It had been interesting for me even though that interest was only academic.

The following day saw a much more relevant experience from Frank's point of view when the Grand Prix produced another win for Nigel with Nelson taking third place. The two drivers were not such good friends by this stage of the season which came as no surprise to anyone. They both badly wanted the World Championship and it wasn't easy for either of them to be fighting it out with a team-mate. Privately I quite enjoyed all the in-fighting and back-biting, the aggravation and complaints. It was all part of the sport. There wouldn't be the same edge and excitement without it.

We returned home to find that Peter had managed to find someone to fill the role of Frank's assistant. Ian Cunningham, a young Scot with a passionate interest in motor racing, came down for an interview and seemed eminently suitable. He started work in September.

Prof. Watkins was disappointed at our rejection of the Budapest centre but he had no intention of giving up his crusade to get Frank into a rehabilitation programme. He continued campaigning relentlessly. He acknowledged Penny's skill but pointed out that one physiotherapist, however able, could not hope to achieve as much as a team, particularly when that team had access to specialized equipment.

'It's not just the physiotherapy,' he argued. 'A specialized unit could help you deal with the practical problems you're coming up against – advise you about the latest gadgets.'

Frank was still not tempted.

'I don't want to waste any more time being quadriplegic, Prof.,' he declared. 'I've got a business to run.'

But I was beginning to waver. Frank had not improved as much as I'd hoped. During his three months of immobility in the ITU his muscles had wasted more than we'd realized and many of the small joints in his hands had stiffened, apparently irretrievably. His head remained floppy and needed support, while his attempts to bring his hand to his mouth were still well short of the mark. Also, he was still having to be catheterized, as his bladder had not responded satisfactorily to tapping on the pubic bone. According to Prof. we only had another six months before all chances of improvement had gone. Suddenly, it seemed not such an unthinkable idea that he should go on this 'assault course' as Prof. Watkins termed it. Frank was becoming more and more resistant to Penny's attempts to get him to exercise. Perhaps somebody else would have more success with him. If it would benefit him I felt he should tolerate being back in hospital for a while.

I found it hard to think objectively about it. My judgement was becoming clouded. What were my real motives? Was I simply rationalizing my own need for a rest? Was it for my own advantage that I wanted him to go? Or would it really do Frank good? The decision had to be the right one.

We were told of a private spinal injury unit, the Paddocks, near Princes Risborough. The reports were favourable and Prof. Watkins fixed up an appointment for me to visit the unit at the end of August. I was instantly impressed. The directors of the centre seemed very keen to have Frank as a patient and were prepared to make all sorts of adjustments to fit in with our requirements. They offered to convert a large room into a bedroom cum office for him in which they would install his own telephone lines. They would schedule his treatments so that Ian could drive him down to Didcot in the afternoons. Alternatively, they would be happy for him to hold meetings at the unit. They suggested that he go from Monday to Friday for three months, coming home at the weekends.

I was introduced to the physiotherapy team. One after the other they extolled the virtues of the regime they had drawn up for Frank. By the end of their lecture I was convinced that under their care and scrutiny Frank would reach unthought of levels of independence. I had been promised that not only would he be able to feed himself, but he might well learn to clean his teeth, shave himself, and assist with his own dressing.

No one up till now had ever presented me with such an optimistic picture. I drove home believing that the Paddocks had a lot to offer us. Selling Frank the idea though, was a daunting task and it did not help that both of us knew that ultimately he had no choice. He was, as he had already acknowledged, entirely in my hands. I spent sleepless nights soul-searching but the answer I came up with each morning was always the same. The promised long-term benefits outweighed the disadvantages of spending three long months in hospital. Frank resigned himself, grudgingly, to the inevitable. In September he entered the Paddocks as a 'weekly boarder'. Alone at home I had my first full night's sleep since my trip with Susie to Bath back in April.

I wanted to put the period of Frank's absence to productive use and I decided to install a chair lift at Boxford House. The builders moved in straight away and began the laborious process of knocking holes in 18-inch-thick stone walls. I hated watching them. It seemed like desecration – the destruction both of history and the dreams we had nursed of living here in grace and style. But it had to be done. It would mean that Frank could sleep upstairs again and be given baths. I planned to convert the guest bedroom where Robin had been sleeping into a preparation and physio room. In the evenings Robin could bring Frank up in the lift, prepare him for bed in the guest bedroom and then wheel him down the corridor to the master bedroom. There I could take over his supervision until Robin came to collect him again in the morning. The change would serve two purposes: it would give me back some privacy, and Frank would have a more varied routine and would not have to live, eat, and sleep in the dining room any more.

I was able to buy a small thatched cottage near the village pub for Robin to move into. It would allow him more independence as well as providing us with more space. The builders were about to break through into the guest bathroom at home and we had a three-day schedule for moving Robin into his new home. Robin, Pauline, Sarah and Tony, the gardener, worked all hours with no outside help. Miraculously we managed to put in a new kitchen and bathroom, decorate, carpet and curtain the cottage all within the time limit.

I visited Frank nearly every evening. He was a good hour's drive away. I would leave home at six p.m. so that I arrived in time to feed him his dinner and would stay until he was being settled down to sleep at around eleven. I hated the return drive to Boxford. In early October we had a lot of heavy fog which slowed me down so that sometimes I didn't get home until the very early hours. At times it felt as exhausting as looking after him at home but I could not let him down, I had promised to be with him and did not want to put a single obstacle in the way of him getting everything possible from this exercise. If he needed me I would be there.

At first I made my visits with some trepidation, fearing I would have to carry the can for whatever he disliked about the Paddocks. But slowly I relaxed. It became obvious that Frank had very few complaints and was enjoying the luxury that the unit offered. It was extremely well-staffed and Frank's every whim was pandered to. The nurses there, unlike his carers at home, were able to jump instantly to attend to him every minute of the day. He was able to ask fresh staff for every little wish without being conscience-stricken. At home he was aware of the pressure we were under and had often felt guilty at his heavy demands.

Penny went in to see him a couple of times and felt that physically he was making a little progress – his biceps were considerably stronger and he could now get his hand halfway to his mouth. But she observed his enjoyment of his new indulged lifestyle with misgiving. She warned me that it would be impossible for him to come home and just slot back into being part of a household if he enjoyed the service at the Paddocks for too long.

'He's being spoiled,' she said, shaking her head. 'It will make problems later on.'

I had apprehensions about his return myself. Robin and I couldn't appear fresh on duty with smiling faces when there were only two of us to nurse him every hour that God sent. In early October Frank arranged to take leave of absence from hospital for two days in order to travel to New York for a Mobil press conference. Robin was unable to get an American visa in time so Penny and I were to act as care attendants for the trip. This time there was no opportunity for a lift in a private plane and we arranged to travel by Concorde. For the first time we experienced the difficulties faced by disabled air travellers using scheduled flights. The airport staff seemed to make no distinction between customers who used wheelchairs for minor problems and those, like Frank, who are unable to get out of them.

We had asked to board before the other passengers so that Penny and I could lift Frank into his seat with some privacy and dignity. The airline staff had agreed but then forgot, and we were faced with taking him on with the plane already half-full and creating an obstruction with his bulky wheelchair. They suggested that Frank should get into one of their own lightweight wheelchairs and they would wheel him onto the plane and then he could get into his seat. They couldn't seem to comprehend that he was totally unable to move from chair to chair. Nor could Penny get through to them that their push-on chair had no head support or straps and that he would fall off it.

Patiently Penny explained that he would have to be lifted on board, at which two helpful stewards stepped forward and grabbed Frank under his arms – the very place that it is vital NEVER to attempt to lift a spinally injured patient. Not only extreme pain but serious damage can result from such handling. Penny was by now furious, 'We can lift him ourselves,' she said between gritted teeth. 'We are trained to do it properly. Please leave it to us.'

Looking rather disgruntled the stewards stood back while Penny grasped Frank under his ribcage and I supported his buttocks and thighs. Then in full view of a craning audience of passengers we carried him into his seat at the front of Concorde. I felt as though we were exhibits in a circus freak show. I'm sure Frank did too. It was an unpleasant journey and I was constantly aware of people scrutinizing us, some covertly, others quite blatantly. It was a humiliating experience for all of us. We needed to empty Frank's leg-bag but were unable to because of the lack of privacy.

Deplaning presented us with the same wheelchair transfer problems in reverse. I was fast beginning to wish we had never set out on this trip. By now Frank's joints were beginning to stiffen up from the hours of sitting, all of us were weary and the final straw came when my suitcases failed to appear on the carousel. I resigned myself to appearing at the Mobil press conference in my jeans and with no make-up.

However once we arrived at the hotel and were able to put Frank onto the bed and give him some physiotherapy my spirits revived. I love New York. It was Penny's first trip and we took it in turns to stay with Frank so that we both had an opportunity to walk around the streets and browse in the shops for a few hours. Mobil had been long-standing and very special sponsors. I would always be grateful for their support for both of us during Frank's time in the London Hospital. Predictably they gave him a wonderful welcome and we were superbly looked after.

Now that we were away from the pressures and the invasions of our privacy that had driven a wedge between us at Boxford I felt there might be a chance that we could re-establish our communication and intimacy. In this warm protective environment perhaps we could start talking again. Penny diplomatically left early the first evening so that we could be alone together for dinner. We were to share an enormous double bed and before she went Penny and I inflated the rhoho and positioned it on his side of it. I ordered dinner for both of us on room service asking them to include a glass of wine for me.

After we had eaten, Penny returned and the two of us spent an hour preparing and positioning Frank for sleep. As the door shut behind her I switched off the light and slipped quietly into bed beside my husband. It was the first time we had lain together in the same bed for seven months. Snuggling up to him I laid my arm gently over Frank's chest trying to recreate our one-time closeness. Suddenly I realized that I was lying on the urinary collection tubing. I rolled hastily away but it was too late. It had already become disconnected. I reassembled the apparatus, it was not complicated and did not take me long. Recapturing my mood proved more difficult.

A burning pain seemed to be searing through my whole body. It was no good. I couldn't have it back. I'd been deluding myself. I had wanted to feel my husband's body against mine, I had wanted to feel his arms around me. To recapture the sense of security I remembered so well. But it was impossible, we would neither of us ever be able to experience it again.

I ached with loneliness.

CHAPTER 17

*P*enny took Frank back to England alone. Robin was to meet her and assist at Heathrow. It was very brave of her, considering the difficulties we had encountered on our outward journey. But I think she appreciated my need to be alone – to take some time to sort out my thoughts and feelings.

I spent two days in total isolation. Nobody here needed me. Nobody knew who I was. I walked in Central Park, took a helicopter ride over the Manhattan skyline, joined a boat to Staten Island, and braved the height of the Empire State Building. I filled my mind with new experiences in an effort to escape the pain. When the sightseeing failed to achieve its aim I found my way to St Patrick's Cathedral and prayed. I made so many bargains with God in those two days. Offered so many exchanges, trying to convince myself he had not deserted us. I asked myself over and over again why it should have happened to us. Wondered whether there is some divine pre-ordained timetable that we cannot influence. Whether our fates are sealed the day we are born.

And if not – if we had free choice then could we have prevented it happening? My mind ran obsessively over all the chance events and decisions that had led to Frank's going to France that weekend. Originally he had intended to go to America in the week before testing. If he had gone it was unlikely he would have gone to Ricard. But we had been invited to a wedding in London during that same week and, at my insistence, that took precedence and the trip to the States was cancelled. Was the accident, then, partly my fault? If I had not been so set on going to a lovely wedding at Claridges would Frank not have broken his neck?

I watched the mass of people on Fifth Avenue scurrying about their business. Before the accident it had seldom occurred to me that people I passed in the street might be unhappy. Now I studied their faces looking for signs of sorrow and pain, wondering if any one of them might be carrying around a secret burden that weighed as heavily on them as mine did on me. I spent introspective hours comparing Frank's situation with other scenarios – wondering if there was anything worse in the world than being paralysed from the neck down. I pondered morbidly what it would be like to be told that your husband had terminal cancer – or to learn that your child was dying . . .

I fought to stop self-pity overwhelming me. It was so cruelly absurd that one minute bit of spinal cord should be so important. The effect of its loss was so out of proportion to the physical injury. Previously I had always thought of the human body as a truly remarkable piece of engineering – almost as living proof that God existed. Now I found myself railing at God for his incompetence. Even human designers installed back-up systems for emergencies. In buildings where a power supply was vital there would always be a generator that could take over if the main system failed. Why hadn't God taken such precautions? Where was the back-up system for the human body's main power line? Confused and angry I alternately prayed to God to help and cursed him for allowing this to happen.

I returned to Boxford after my two days of 'freedom' with a heavy heart and set about re-establishing my routine; caring for the house and the children during the day and visiting Frank at the Paddocks in the evenings.

Ironically, 1986 seemed destined to become the year of our greatest triumph as well as of personal disaster. Williams were now in an unbeatable position in the Constructors Championship. We would win the cup for the first time in five years with an all-time points record. Nigel had also been leading the Drivers Championship ever since his victory at the British Grand Prix and Nelson was second. There was little doubt in most people's minds that we would take both titles.

The Mexican Grand Prix was the penultimate race. If Nigel won it he would clinch the championship. The final race in Adelaide would become merely a scrimmage for the minor placings. Visitors to Mexico

232

required vaccinations and Frank would not be able to tolerate them so he was forced to miss attending. However he was invited to the BBC studio to watch the race on the monitors and to be interviewed by Steve Rider. But the hoped-for celebrations had to be delayed when Nigel lost first gear on the start line. He did manage to claw his way up to a fifth place but that only gave him two championship points. Not enough. Even so, he was still six points ahead of Alain Prost, with Nelson only another point behind so the odds were stacked in our favour. Recognizing this the BBC asked Frank to come back and assist Steve Rider with the commentary for the Adelaide race.

There was enormous interest in this race. There was every chance we were going to have the first British world champion since James Hunt, and the general public's interest in motor racing was rekindled. I heard housewives discussing the outcome in the supermarket check-out queue. Nigel had a happy way of remaining very unspoilt despite his enormous success and the publicity accompanying it. The public liked him and were willing him to win. In response to their enthusiasm the BBC were taking the unusual step of broadcasting the whole Australian race live at three a.m.

We were asked to present Frank at the BBC's Shepherds Bush studios at two a.m. He still needed a lot of sleep so we had put him to bed at eight the previous night and woke him at around midnight to get him dressed and ready. Ian arrived and helped him into the car and we drove up a deserted M4. As we approached the Hammersmith flyover we put a telephone call through over our Cellnet line to the pits in Adelaide. Frank asked Patrick about the race set-up for both cars, the choice of tyres, and so on. The reception was as clear as a bell. We wished the team luck as we proceeded to the studio. Previously Frank would not have wanted or needed me to be present during television interviews. Now however I had a role – to ensure that Frank's tie was straight and his hair smoothed down; the little grooming jobs he could no longer take care of himself, and also to jump in, off-camera to administer a drink or move his arms into a more comfortable position.

As we were ushered into the studio I noticed out of the corner of my eye, an ice bucket sitting in the background. From it, the top of a bottle of champagne winked out at me. Above Steve Rider's head was a large photograph of Nigel. In a corner, presumably ready to be substituted if necessary, another picture lurked – this time of Nelson who was still second favourite despite being one point behind Alain. One way or another everyone was expecting it to be a Williams night.

Steve Rider is enormously professional and decided to rehearse the post-race interview before going on the air. Ian and I pushed Frank up onto the dais beside him and Steve interviewed Frank as though Nigel had already won. I felt myself shiver. The premature celebrations seemed to me to be tempting fate.

In the early part of the race Keke Rosberg took over the lead from Nelson, leaving Nigel a close third. This did not cause Frank to be too perturbed. Even if he could not improve on this position Nigel would still win the world championship. At third race distance, Thierry Boutsen pitted his Benetton with a minor mechanical problem and was automatically fitted with new tyres. The used tyres were inspected by Goodyear, found to be in perfect condition and the Goodyear engineers accordingly advised their teams that the tyres would be likely to last the full race distance. However on lap 63, the right hand front tyre on the leading McLaren of Keke Rosberg shredded, forcing Keke to retire. The Williams engineers, watching on their television monitors immediately prepared to call Nigel in for new rubber. If Keke's tyres had worn enough to blow then it was very likely that everyone else's were deteriorating similarly.

Fate decided not to allow them time to act. On that infamous lap 64 of the Australian Grand Prix, Nigel's left rear tyre exploded at over 150 m.p.h. leaving Nigel to wrestle for his life with the snaking car, crashing up the escape road and hitting a concrete wall before coming to a halt. Nigel climbed unsteadily out of his cockpit and he and Keke walked disconsolately back to the pits together. The silence in the BBC studio was deafening. Disappointment was etched into Frank's face.

The BBC staff were obviously experienced at reacting to last minute changes of schedule. Within minutes Steve Rider was replanning his interviews based around a championship for Nelson, who was now leading the race. But ten laps from the end all that had to be scrapped too. Sensibly, after Nigel's accident Patrick immediately called Nelson in for a tyre change. It took longer than normal and Alain Prost, one of the few contenders to have changed tyres earlier, took the lead. He won the race and with it the championship. The whole BBC studio was engrossed in a frantic search for suitable Alain Prost photographs and alternative post-race interviewees. We found ourselves suddenly superfluous. We took our leave, once more passing the champagne which glinted mockingly at us from its long-melted bed of ice, and drove home in the quiet early hours of dawn.

As we reached the Hammersmith flyover I started unexpectedly to see the funny side of the débâcle, and began to giggle. Frank stared at me in astonishment then gradually his own grim expression changed. Unlike me he couldn't physically laugh any more but he could still smile.

'We can't change it,' he said philosophically. 'So bad luck Nigel. You deserved that one.'

Ruefully he added, 'Congratulations Alain!'

CHAPTER 18

*C*hristmas was approaching. I planned a party to coincide with Frank's leaving the Paddocks at the end of his course of treatment. His three months there had seen an improvement in his biceps muscle and he was now able to lift his hand to his face. Unfortunately the force of gravity did not allow it to stay there. Even so, he was beginning to attempt to feed himself using a leather band called a feeding splint wrapped around his hand, into which a bent spoon could be inserted. If we loaded the spoon he was able to literally throw its contents somewhere in the general direction of his mouth. The children, witnessing this for the first time, were speechless!

Yet his progress at the Paddocks had been nowhere near as dramatic as I had hoped. The most significant development during his stay there had been their success in training his bladder to respond to the tapping on the pubic bone. Hopefully daily catheterization was now a thing of the past. None of the other promised skills had come about, he still seemed a very long way from the promised goals of dressing himself and cleaning his own teeth. It looked as though that had been a pipe-dream.

Despite this disappointment I wanted our first Christmas at Boxford to be as happy as possible. Organizing the celebrations gave me something different to think about – something not directly related to the never-ending demands of quadriplegia.

In the last two days before Frank returned, and I took over the night shift again, I moved happily back into a world with which I was more

236

familiar. I paid visits to Covent Garden market for armfuls of lilies, white amaryllis, and euphorbia. With Christmas carols playing on the stereo I spent hours buried in the branches of a fifteen foot Christmas tree in the corner of the drawing room, painstakingly tying on dozens of burgundy balls with yards of burgundy double satin ribbon. Frank would return to a very pretty Boxford House.

Very pretty, but sadly, in Penny's words, 'wheelchair unfriendly'. The house had marvellous ornate ceilings which were Listed Grade II and we were not allowed to interfere with them. Ideally we would have installed a four person passenger lift, capable of holding Frank in his wheelchair plus an attendant. The preservation order meant that we had been forced to install a small chairlift instead which ran from a cupboard in the dining room to the first floor. Its limitations were very soon apparent. Frank had to be transferred onto the lift seat and harnessed in before commencing a slow ascent. Robin would scream up the stairs with the wheelchair to meet him at the top. In all, the transfer between floors took around fifteen minutes, by which time Robin was exhausted and Frank was grumpy. I felt tension, wonderfully absent during my Christmas preparations, start to grip me again. I had high expectations of Christmas and I planned the celebrations as though nothing had changed. It was unrealistic of me. Had I made concessions to Frank's condition, I would have found it easier.

The welcome-home party went well, but Frank had to go to bed early and it was obvious that further socializing this holiday was out of the question. We had several invitations but Frank had no desire to go out. He was tired in the evenings and it was a major hassle for all of us to prepare him for a night out. I declined all the invitations with regret and frustration. It felt as though the rest of the world was enjoying the festivities while we had become isolated. I was still trying to convince myself that things needn't change. Every time the true implications reared their heads I felt thwarted in my attempts to live a normal life. I wanted to laugh, dance and sing. The reality was emptying the urine bag.

One of the few bright spots of the holiday was when Frank managed to get a spoonful of his Christmas dinner to his mouth as Penny had promised him he would. He gave up once he had achieved it, and I fed him the rest of his turkey and plum pudding but it made me feel that all the hard work had not been for nothing. Up until then I had been inclined to think his stay at the Paddocks had been an expensive holiday whose main achievement had been to make him discontented that he did not have such good servants at home!

If Christmas was disappointing, then New Year's Eve was even more so. Twelve months earlier we had spent this night at the wonderful wedding celebrations of McLaren's Ron and Lisa Dennis. Their candle-lit marriage ceremony in a quiet church in the Kent countryside had been followed by dinner at Leeds Castle. After dancing until past midnight all the guests had been accommodated at the castle for the night. It had been a fairytale experience which I remembered with a pang as we prepared to welcome in 1987.

There was to be no dressing up this time and no celebrations. Frank had no wish to stay awake to see the New Year in though he did make one brave resolution. He informed me that he was going to attend every Grand Prix on the calendar starting in Brazil on 12 April. I was pleased that his determination was still as strong as ever but a little sceptical that it would be possible.

Robin, who had worked over the whole of Christmas, had taken a few days off and a female relief nurse and I struggled to get Frank into bed. He had put weight on while at the Paddocks and it really needed a man's strength to help move him now. I always dreaded the meagre time off that Robin took. It was proving very difficult to find a regular back-up male nurse who was suited to this kind of heavy nursing. I made up my mind it had to be a priority in the New Year.

Robin returned to work just as snow started falling at Boxford. I handed over to him gratefully, gave the children their lunch, then left them with Sarah and drove to the cinema in Newbury. *Crocodile Dundee* was showing. Everyone was raving about it and I thought I would sound out the cinema management to discover if I would be able to take Frank to see it. I was politely informed that regrettably it was not cinema policy to permit wheelchairs inside because of the risk of them causing an obstruction if fire broke out.

I decided to see the film myself anyway, I hadn't been to the cinema for ages. I enjoyed it but at the end, as the rest of the audience rose and trooped out, I stayed seated. Unlike them I felt no pull to get back home. I watched the movie a second time around before trudging out with a heavy heart to return to the house we had once cherished such hopes for and which had now become a nursing home.

My attempts at structural improvements to make life at Boxford more comfortable had backfired on me. Apart from the disastrously unsuitable lift, the longed-for privacy I had expected by moving Frank upstairs had turned out to be an illusion. Before, when the nursing

238

and physiotherapy had all taken place downstairs my own bedroom had provided a haven I could retreat to – out of bounds to everyone but me. But now that Frank was being prepared in the guest room, then wheeled along to join me to sleep, I had no haven. I found that Robin or a relief nurse were continually springing up at inopportune moments. I was always darting behind a cupboard door to finish dressing.

Again, I was guiltily aware that my own problems were only a pale reflection of Frank's. For him there would be no privacy for the rest of his life. He was as helpless, physically, as a small baby, and like a baby he could never be left alone in the house or allowed out of earshot of a carer. Where once he had liked nothing better than to go out for a solitary run, now he was rarely allowed time with his own thoughts. It was perhaps the most cruel loss of all. But he seemed to have come to terms with it in a way that I was failing to.

Over the next few months, to try and escape from people, I started to search out little corners away from the world. I had already discovered the cinema. Soon also I was visiting the local gym, or driving off for miles in my car, aimlessly, just enjoying being alone and out of reach. Usually I would come back after a few hours but later that year when the nursing shifts allowed, I would sometimes book into an impersonal hotel room for a night so I could be alone with my thoughts. Scuttling away from Boxford I hid from reality, pretending I was free from the tyranny of all the demands on me. It was becoming more than I could handle.

I found I was excusing myself from more and more of the nursing tasks. I wouldn't admit to myself that I didn't want to do them any more but I undertook them now only on Robin's day off. Penny, noticing this, looked at me hard one day and said, 'The novelty's wearing off isn't it Ginny?'

I was shocked. How dare she suggest that looking after a quadriplegic could be regarded as a novelty! But on reflection I realized she was right. The newness of the challenge when we first came home had fuelled me with energy to keep me going even when I was tired. Now, as day followed day, each time-consuming task had become a monotonous routine and it was hard to keep the same energy flowing. I developed an almost continual tension headache. I had weaned myself off painkillers while Frank was at the paddocks but now I started taking them again in quantity and my eyes once more yellowed. But I couldn't cut down. They were my crutch. It was the hardest winter I had ever lived through. God knows what it was like for Frank.

The weather had turned very cold and this caused him additional problems as having lost his internal thermostat he felt the cold severely. We heated the house to phenomenal temperatures to try and keep him warm. On occasion he demanded the central heating on full throttle, an electric blow heater and a gas fire all at the same time. It was like being in the Sahara desert. Everyone else was forced to strip off to t-shirts. We carried out our nursing duties with sweat pouring off our brows to the accompaniment of the sound of Frank's teeth chattering! His favourite place in the house became the kitchen where we would push him up close to the Aga cooker. On one occasion we pushed him too close. Unnoticed by us his hand was touching one of the oven doors and he sustained a very bad burn without feeling a thing. In some ways I saw now that Frank was even more dependent than a baby. At least a baby would let you know if it was being hurt. Frank, I realized with horror, could have actually caught fire and been completely unaware of it.

The arrival of spring relieved all of us, not least the children, who had often found themselves unable to stay in the same room as Frank when all the heat was on and for whom the weekends must have seemed endless. To relieve the boredom we established a little ritual of Sunday drives, heading into the Hampshire or Berkshire countryside to join the hundreds of other 'geriatrics' out for a meander through the country lanes. Unfortunately we still had to keep the fan heaters on full blast to stop Frank getting chilled, which meant that Claire and Jaime generally passed out asleep within minutes of leaving home, half-asphyxiated by the heat.

I would pull into a lay-by and either get out for a short brisk walk in the fresh air or, more often, would doze along with the children while Frank sat patiently waiting for action in the passenger seat. Considering how short of patience he had been in the past he showed remarkable restraint in only handing out minor bollockings on these occasions.

Another weekend activity was a short walk through the village with Robin and the children. Claire took great delight in being allowed, under supervision, to push her Daddy's chair. I usually opted to stay at home for a peaceful cup of tea and a look through the Sunday papers during these outings. One Sunday I was halfway through the colour supplement when the back door burst open and Claire and Jaime hurtled in, very distressed. They were both crying so hard that I found it difficult to decipher what they were saying but eventually Claire gasped, 'Daddy's fallen out of his wheelchair! Bring the car.'

240

I shot out of the house and into my car. The children flung themselves into the back seats and directed me to the scene of the accident. I found Robin sitting beside the road, propping up Frank, who had quite a bad cut on his forehead. Apparently Claire had been pushing the wheelchair while Robin idled behind with a crafty cigarette. One of the wheels had dipped into a pothole and Frank had been thrown face first onto the tarmac. It is impossible to lift a paralysed person from the ground singlehanded so Robin had hauled him to safety at the side of the road and sent for reinforcements.

Together we lifted Frank into the car and I drove him back to the house contemplating with horror the thought of falling face first and being unable to put out your hands to break your fall. We applied first aid to the cuts on his face while Frank tried to console Claire who was devastated. Amazingly, Frank was very relaxed about the entire incident. He refused to allow his body's betrayals to distress him.

We all had a lot to learn. Even pushing a wheelchair is a skill to be acquired. The paralysed body is very unstable. We had a chest strap to secure Frank in the wheelchair but usually he preferred us not to use it, just as he refused a full harness in the car (which meant that whoever was driving him was forced to take bends with one hand on the steering wheel and the other holding Frank upright). But without a chest strap he was forced to work on his posture which would eventually improve his stability. If he relied on a strap he believed he would not only get lazy about his posture but would look far more disabled.

Both the children and I tended at first to push the chair in the same way that you push a child in a pushchair. But Frank's lack of control over his torso means his balance is far more tenuous than that of a child. Jaime was next in line to learn that lesson the hard way. He was not allowed to push the chair outdoors but he enjoyed pushing Frank up and down the corridor. It was Robin's weekend off and although we had a new relief nurse, he had gone home for a couple of hours. I had just put dinner in the oven and poured myself a glass of wine when I heard a heavy thud in the passage. My heart in my mouth, I tore out of the kitchen. Jaime stood, petrified with fright, behind Frank, who was sprawled face down on the marble floor. This time the chair wheel had hit the skirting and had just toppled him out. As gently as I could, I turned him over and sat down behind him propping his head and back up against me. I considered our predicament – I couldn't move him anywhere on my own. I couldn't let go of him in order to telephone for help – there was no cushioning for his head on the hard floor. We just had to wait there for the hour until John was due to return. I persuaded Jaime to bring my glass of wine from the kitchen and sat in the corridor with Frank's head against my chest sipping my wine and chatting to him about this and that. It was rather nice I reflected. For once no one else was about, and neither of us was too tired to talk to each other as we often were at bedtime. We sat there for over an hour quite contentedly. We had only two problems: Frank, unprotected from the cold marble was becoming chillier by the minute; and the lasagne was quietly cremating in the Aga.

Shortly yet another complication developed as Jaime, ever the opportunist, saw his chance to do all the things he was not allowed to do, namely, getting the sharpest kitchen scissors out and cutting up Frank's racing magazines, sticking them to the walls and then adding his personal illustrations to the disaster with felt-tip pens!

At last we heard the car of the relief nurse scrunching up the gravel on the drive. The back door opened and a voice called out, 'Good evening everybody.' 'We're here, John,' I yelled back to him, giggling. His face, as he discovered us both cramped up together on the floor in an ungainly heap, was a picture! There can be a humorous side to quadriplegia. There are plenty of occasions when both Frank and I are amused by the predicaments his body lands him in. Sometimes smiling at disasters is the only way of coping with them.

Frank spent that year bravely soldiering on, coming to terms and adjusting to his different kind of life. His day started with basic nursing and dressing followed by a two-hour session of physiotherapy. Towards noon Ian would arrive at the house to drive Frank to his office where he would spend the afternoon working. A passenger lift had been installed at the factory and the floor surfaces changed so that Frank had easy access to most areas.

His managerial work was hardly affected by his disability. In recent years he had always dictated his letters rather than writing them himself so no adaptation was needed there. Signing them was abandoned – at least temporarily. He had a hands-off telephone installed. Jackie, who had replaced Alison as his secretary, obtained the numbers for him as she had usually done before the accident. The only difference was that now there was no receiver to hold. Once his post had been opened he was able to sort through it quite well using special pimpled gloves which adhered to the paper. By flicking his biceps he was soon able to shuffle loose-leaf papers about as before, although books and other bound documents presented more of a

242

problem. He could have used a special page-turner which would respond to him blowing and sucking down a tube but he wouldn't hear of it as he steadfastly refused to have anything to do with aids for the disabled. It almost amounted to a phobia with him. He was prepared to have people stand at his side turning pages for him but not a machine. Nor would he contemplate putting a disabled badge on his car. The idea appalled him. It was all part of his own idiosyncratic attitude to his disablement. He wanted people, as far as possible, to ignore his paralysis and to treat it as unimportant. How could they if they had it thrust in their faces with gadgets and badges? I understood that, though I felt he sometimes carried his philosophy to unnecessary extremes. Occasionally when I was in a cynical mood I would reflect that Frank didn't believe in gadgets. He believed in slaves.

Frank had not forgotten his New Year's resolution. The first Grand Prix of the season, at Brazil on 12 April, saw him there with the team. The inventory of people and machinery that had to be transported to every race was already long, comprising two race cars, the test cars, the drivers, mechanics, management, motorhomes, transporters and 15,000 kilos of spares. Now to the list was added Frank's standing frame, his extra wheelchairs, bath equipment, special mattresses and a battery of medical supplies that might conceivably be needed. The final and most important items on the list were Robin and Ian, without their nursing and support the trips would have been impossible.

To travel with the team again gave Frank's life a much-needed purpose and structure. His spirits steadily lifted as he became once more truly involved in the sport he loved. His participation changed surprisingly little. The main concession he had to make to his condition was to watch the practice sessions and the race on the TV monitors in the pits garages instead of from the pit wall.

Significantly he felt completely comfortable to be seen by these people – the motor racing *aficionados*. They knew who and what he was. He was Frank Williams. Amongst this rarified clique he was never subjected to the inquisitive stares that he received from the general public. Going to a restaurant, or the cinema or even shopping had become things of the past for us thanks to the furtive whispering glances that always greeted his entry. He had come to hate people's reactions to his appearance so much that he would no longer face them and, as a result, our world had become smaller.

During that season he was away at a race for four days every two or three weeks. In between times he kept up his office routine five days a week. On a non-racing day Ian would drive Frank home at about six p.m. and Robin or John would help get him out of the car and ready for his evening 'exercise'. John's arrival that year brought both me and Robin considerable relief. He had started work as a back-up nurse but had decided to stay on permanently. Soon after Frank arrived home John or Robin would usually put him into his 'standing frame', a wooden support designed to enable a quadriplegic to maintain an upright stance by the use of straps across the chest, waist, hips and knees. Not only does it relieve the boredom of spending one's life in the sitting position but it is physically beneficial to the user, allowing the kidneys to function better and reducing muscle wastage in the legs. It also helps keep the dreaded pressure sores away. Frank would religiously spend two sessions of an hour each in his frame every day, timing them to the minute.

The only drawback to the frame was that it was a fascinating toy for a small boy. Rather foolhardily I left Jaime briefly in charge on one occasion while I prepared supper. Soon afterwards I heard cries for help and rushed from the kitchen to find Frank suspended upside-down from the frame with his nose inches from the floor. Jaime had decided to experiment with the strapping and had undone every strap bar one knee support. Not surprisingly with his track record, Jaime is not Frank's favourite 'babysitter'. On the whole the children adapted well to the new situation and were eager to help when they could. Pushing the wheelchair was very popular – other tasks less so. The least sought-after job was page-turning. While he was in the frame Frank often read a magazine to wile away the time, and he liked someone in attendance to turn over the pages which meant doing it every couple of minutes for an hour or more. Each request was met with moans and groans and, as when his head itched and needed scratching, there was a rush as each child tried to exit the room first.

1987 was the year when our hopes of recovery were finally laid to rest. We both now knew and accepted that no further improvement would be made. Toes and fingers would not miraculously start to wiggle again. Our education in spinal injury had been gradual but thorough. Today people constantly surprise me by their relative ignorance. Acquaintances still say to me, 'How's Frank. Is he better?' Only the other day I heard someone, a quite intelligent man, say, 'Is Frank Williams *still* paralysed after all this time?' I forget how unaware I too was until knowledge was forced upon me.

Occasionally still when I spoke to him on the phone I would forget. For a brief moment I would find myself expecting him to arrive home behind schedule, and come into the kitchen and cuddle me as he used to, in an effort to avoid a confrontation over the burnt dinner. But steadily that year those moments got further apart as the new Frank edged out the old one in my mind.

From now on all we could do for Frank would be to improve the quality of his life by good nursing and specialized aids. It was over this point that we ran into our first major argument. I was very keen for Frank to have an electric wheelchair. I felt that having a chair that he could control himself would give him a small, but mentally very important, measure of independence. However, he refused, arguing that an electrically-powered chair looked too disabled – that dreaded word again. I protested that to my mind having a nurse pushing him looked far more disabled. But nothing I could say would persuade him to change his mind. Every day for months I tried subtly to bring the topic up in conversation to no avail. Eventually I dropped the subject rather than acquire more grey hairs over an issue that I was clearly not going to win. However I resolved that it was only a ceasefire. One day I will take up the crusade again and force him to try it out. I am still convinced it could be the single biggest breakthrough in the way his day-to-day life operates.

But the time was not right for a big confrontation. Our relationship was becoming strained anyway and my nagging was just exacerbating things. As the reality of his limitations dawned on him that year I found myself on the receiving end of Frank's frustrations. Every morning I would brace myself in preparation for the tirade of wrath that would inevitably descend sooner or later in the day, usually over quite trivial things like being a minute or two late with a drink. I tried not to take his angry words to heart. I knew it was what Penny called 'referred anger'. She had warned me I would be used as a scapegoat to express his feelings about his predicament. There was a limit to how much rage he could vent on his nurses or physiotherapists. They might walk out. But he could take it out on me, secure that I'd forgive him when the heat had died down. However, knowing the theory which explained Frank's hostility did not make his angry words easier to bear. It was hard. To get through the storm I had to grow some broad shoulders.

I had other problems too. The novelty had now worn off for Pauline and Sarah too. They were both ready to jump ship and I couldn't blame them. The atmosphere at home was far from congenial. It was planned that Sarah should go first and that Pauline would stay until a suitable replacement was found. She was going to travel around the world with her new-found freedom. I wished guiltily that I could go with her. Within a couple of months, I said goodbye to both girls and a new housekeeper, Kay, moved into Boxford.

Penny continued to work every day with Frank to build up the biceps and by the middle of the year he could get his hand to his mouth with much more accuracy than he had been able to manage at Christmas. He recovered some of his enthusiasm for the physiotherapy when the occupational therapists at Stoke Mandeville made a splint for his hand into which a pen could be fitted. He practised for hours and eventually was able to scrawl a recognizable and repeatable FW. It was a big breakthrough. He started to sign letters and cheques again and I happily tore up the power of attorney!

Steadily his ability to hold his body upright was improving. He had also started to 'push' the wheels on his chair. During his week-long visit to Stoke they had kitted him out with wheeling gloves, the palms of which were cut from the fabric which is used on the faces of ping pong bats, to give maximum adhesion. He couldn't, strictly speaking, push – but by literally dropping his hand onto the correct part of the wheel the chair would move about an inch. Progress was painfully slow. It took weeks before he could move from one side of the kitchen to the other. Finally he made it but he never seemed as delighted with his accomplishment as we were. Perhaps seeing Jonathan jumping into the empty chair and doing effortless wheelies as he screamed through the passages at Boxford House gave Frank a different perspective on his 'success'. However as he progressed to ever lighter wheelchairs, and finally to an ultra lightweight 'sports' chair, movement became easier for him though it was still limited. For the time being he could only go in a straight line, and only on a smooth surface. Even a misplaced floorboard would stop his progress with corners or slopes being quite beyond him.

Once he started to feed himself regularly I had to give our menus careful thought. Some foods stay more easily on a spoon than others. I tried to avoid any meals that would require too much intervention from me, so spaghetti and tagliatelli, once his favourites, were out. I became an ace at puréed vegetables. Without the triceps muscle he was still not able to keep his arm up for longer than a second or two and if he had not got the food into his mouth by that time his arm would come crashing down, and large quantities of rice, peas and

246

chicken would end up on the floor. Usually in order for him literally not to starve to death we would take over and feed him the last half of his dinner.

Frank, the children and I became well used to this rather untidy eating process and we sometimes overlooked the effect it might have on other people. One day a schoolfriend of Claire was visiting and I insensitively seated her next to Frank at the kitchen table. The poor little thing sat rigidly in her seat, not knowing where to look as Frank ate. She was completely put off the food in front of her and was obviously longing to get away. I leaned over to Claire. 'Why don't you all take your food and have a picnic in the playroom?' I suggested. I had learned a valuable lesson. Our children are accustomed to the problems of quadriplegia and now take most of them in their stride but other children do not. After that I always thought very carefully in advance how young visitors might react to Frank's disability and tried to avoid situations that might distress them.

We had decided early on that one of our priorities was to ensure that Jonathan, Claire and Jaime's upbringing remained as normal as possible. Neither Frank nor I wanted his condition to change the routine of their daily lives. Inevitably the accident did affect them but on the whole they adjusted well, each coming to terms with their new wheelchair-bound father in a different way.

Perhaps Jonathan suffered the most confusion over how he should react to the paralysis. Motor racing was getting increasing publicity on television in the eighties and Frank was a hero among the pupils at Jonathan's school

'Do you know who his father is?' other boys would ask. Jonathan would quietly bask in the reflected glory, then return home to witness the subject of the hero worship in the throes of being spoonfed, or perhaps something even less dignified. It was hard for him to balance the two images. He was always reluctant to feed Frank himself, and he looked embarrassed and uncomfortable when I insisted. I decided to let the subject drop, feeling he had a better chance of coming to terms with it if I didn't push too much.

Gradually Jonathan seemed to work it out although he still prefers Frank not to come down to school. Perhaps he doesn't want other boys to stare – he knows how Frank himself hates it – or maybe it is just that he wants to avoid shattering their image of Frank.

I think it has been tougher on Jonathan than on the other two. Claire, since day one, has not taken off her nurse's cap. She never flinches; happily scratches Frank's head when it itches; fetches and

247

carries and, in contrast to Jonathan, loves to show her Daddy off at school. She is intensely proud of his achievements and will not allow any criticism of him from anyone. In any argument she automatically takes his side. Against the pair of them no one stands a chance.

Jaime was only three in 1986 and could have had little memory of what it was like when his Daddy was not in a wheelchair. He accepted Frank's paralysis the most fully and easily. He would hurl himself into Frank's lap, and would rough and tumble, with sometimes disastrous consequences, without a care in the world. Only one thing worried me about Jaime's attitude. During that first year I started to notice that he was regularly starting sentences with 'When Daddy gets better . . .' Did Jonathan and Claire think this was a temporary plight too? Had we inadvertently let them drift into a fool's paradise? I realized we had not spoken to them of Frank's prognosis since he left the London Hospital.

'Do you think we ought to spell it out to the children – let them know the bottom line?' I asked Frank one day.

He thought about it for a moment or two.

'Good idea. I get the feeling sometimes they think I won't always be paralysed.'

The next day as I sat with them around the kitchen table I asked them bluntly, 'Do any of you think that Daddy is going to walk again?'

There was a silence. The older two looked at each other.

Then Jaime piped up. 'Yes I do.'

Claire and Jonathan were staring anxiously at me. I sensed they were hoping for reassurance but I couldn't give it to them. There was no way I could soften the facts. I had to be cruel to be kind.

'Daddy and I think you ought to know that he will always be in a wheelchair. He is not going to get better.'

I wanted to extinguish every glimmer of false hope. Only then I felt would they be able to accept it and make whatever adjustments in outlook that were necessary.

No tears were shed. They must have half-expected it. One by one, quite happily, they returned to their activities. I felt a great sense of relief. It had been the right thing to do.

I have never since heard the words, 'When Daddy gets better.'

CHAPTER 19

Frank fulfilled his ambition for 1987. He attended every race of the year. Quite early on it became apparent that travelling through the airports of the world on commercial flights was going to prove impossibly taxing for a quadriplegic. Our Concorde flight to New York had given us a mere taste of the problems that could arise. Early in the summer the company purchased its first aeroplane, a Lear jet, which enabled Frank to avoid the delays and discomfort of scheduled travel, and, importantly, afforded him privacy, away from the curious eyes of fellow travellers.

From the point of view of results, it was another tremendous year for Williams. For the first time since the Jonesy days in 1981 we won both the Drivers and Constructors World Championships, the latter conclusively from McLaren with 137 points to their 76. Nigel had a brilliant season, winning six Grand Prix, and was favourite to take the title when fate again cruelly robbed him of it at the last moment. This time he was badly hurt in practice for the Japanese Grand Prix and had to withdraw from both that and the final race. In his absence Nelson, who had only three race victories under his belt, but had accumulated an extraordinary number of points, took the championship.

Everyone should have been over the moon. The victories proved beyond doubt that Williams was still a name to be contended with. Whether Frank was paralysed or not, we could still produce results. As if in recognition of this, Frank was awarded a CBE in the New Year's Honours List. But despite everything the season ended on an unexpectedly downbeat note. Nelson was to leave to drive for Lotus, taking with him the prized number one tag. Even worse, our fabulous Honda engine was also leaving, to link up with McLaren. The immediate future at Didcot looked rather gloomy.

To compound matters, the situation was far from idyllic at home.

Penny had been right. The whole dynamics of our relationship had altered. Both Frank and I were having to get used to living with a very different person from the one we had been married to before, and though we didn't admit it to each other, neither of us liked the new person very much.

Frank's adaptation was the hardest to make. Since the accident he had been forced to let me take over the running of his home, his family and his life. The entire balance of power had shifted. And not only in material matters. In the old days if we ever had a minor tiff he had been prone to walking out of the door and leaving me to 'come to my senses'. Now he had to sit helplessly and watch as I did the same. I found myself walking away more and more frequently as the tension between us grew. Frank had no option but to sit and await my return. Faced with this reversal in our roles his only redress was to ensure that he retained the upper hand mentally. He constantly criticized me. He became almost obsessive about punctuality; his drinks, his meals, his standing frame, all had to be ready at the precise minute they were supposed to be ready or all hell broke loose. Scheduling his day was one of the few ways he could still exert control over his life now so it became vitally important to him and if I was five minutes late with his nine o'clock drink or even if it was in the wrong glass he saw it as denying him that control. As the year wore on the flak increased. Little I could do for him was right.

If he disliked this new Ginny – the capable wife who had such power over him, I was equally uncomfortable with the new Frank. We were both temperamentally unsuited to a change of roles. I didn't like having to be the strong one in our relationship. I didn't understand the reasons behind his irritable behaviour. He seemed like a stranger. I had lost every point of reference. I searched in vain in this new husband for something of the old one to cling on to. I missed the Frank I had lost, the wicked one, the funny one, the unpredictable one. The Frank who had looked after me, escorted me, who had got into the driver's seat when we went out in the car, who had sometimes walked into the house and said, 'F— the dinner. We're going out. You deserve it!'

There was such a gap in my life now. I longed for the little things. I missed his laugh. My Frank was always laughing. This Frank would never be able to laugh again. I missed him coming home from work at night and giving me a big kiss and hug as I stood in the kitchen. I missed the familiar smell of his body – the new mixture of medicinal smells that clung to him was so different. I missed standing alongside him as we cleaned our teeth in the bathroom at night. I missed lying in bed snuggled up next to him, both of us reading our books. I missed making love.

In normal circumstances it is hard to know how important sex is in your marriage. When it is there and it is good it isn't an issue. I would never have said that our marriage was based on sex but now that it had gone for ever there seemed to be a void in the heart of our relationship. Not so much a physical void, as a mental one. Sex had always been there. Dependable. Through it we had each gauged how the other felt. It had broken down fences and mended bridges. I tried to pretend to myself that its loss didn't matter but it did. I had always wanted him and that desire had not disappeared. Since the accident we had never been able to discuss sex, I think its absence was too frightening a topic for either of us to want to conduct a post-mortem on it. I suspected that we were both doing a brilliant cover-up job on how we really felt about losing that part of our lives. One of those discouraging leaflets that I had read in hospital (the same one that had described my plight as being like a widow without the freedom) had informed me gloomily that ninety per cent of married couples in our circumstances end up in the divorce courts. I found it easy to believe but I doubted that it was directly due to the physical lack of sex. It probably owed more to what loss of sex means – the loss of intimacy, of that unique knowledge of each other that makes the rapport between a man and a woman who love each other different from all other relationships.

That is why the thought of a shallow physical affair with someone held little appeal for me. Maybe Frank would understand an 'indiscretion' on my part but it wasn't what I wanted. If I thought about sex I thought about Frank. I didn't want to make a substitution. The one thing I wanted more than anything else in the world was to have my husband back but it was the one thing I couldn't have.

Confused and depressed, I became increasingly bitter and angry towards Frank. Inwardly I caught myself blaming him for having subjected us all to this torment. What right had he had to drive so badly that he could heap all this misery on his family? I listened receptively as a nasty little voice deep inside suggested it was the most selfish act that Frank had ever committed.

Why had he always insisted on driving, in his own words, 'like a hooligan'? What kink in his character had constantly impelled him to dice with death? I found myself recalling many hideous drives to and from parties with Frank. I relived the times I had spent gritting my teeth in the passenger seat and swearing at him to slow down before he killed us both. Threatening not to attend his funeral if I survived the seemingly inevitable accident, I used to shout at him in terror, 'Put the headlights back on' when he switched them off in the twisted country lanes approaching Boxford as we returned home in the early hours.

'I can go faster this way,' he would say, unmoved by my hysterics. 'I know the road. I can see the lights if any other cars are coming.'

'What about stray cows?' I would mutter, sick with fright. 'What about other drivers who think like you and switch their lights off too? What about our three young children who'll be left orphaned at home?'

How many times after surviving those trips home had I crept to the edge of the bed, seething with anger, wanting to get as far away as possible from this person who had subjected me to an unasked-for ride on the wall of death?

Yet I had always had a hunger for speed myself. It used to give me a sense of accomplishment to break my previous best time to the Cherry Blossom roundabout. Before the accident (though never since) I would regularly cruise at 110 m.p.h. hoping to beat Frank's ridiculous record. I never achieved it. There was never a hope. The reason lay in a crucial difference between our attitudes. I made allowances for the vagaries of other drivers and the hazards on public roads. Frank did not. What if, instead of predicting that he would kill himself, I had told him to imagine spending the rest of his life paralysed from the neck down in a wheelchair? Would it have made him more cautious?

It was something that I might easily have said. A week prior to the accident we had been watching the television news and had seen Margaret Tebbit, badly injured in the Brighton Hotel bombing, entering the Stanmore Spinal Injury centre in North London. The newsreader said that she had no power of movement below her neck. I hadn't been able to wipe the image of her from my mind for several hours. Later that evening, lying in bed as Frank came out of the bathroom, I had asked him if he could imagine such a dreadful thing happening.

'Whatever would it be like to be paralysed from the neck down?' I wondered.

Now with a shiver I remembered his answer.

'I would rather be dead,' he had said.

As the second year wore on I found it increasingly hard to maintain my initial momentum. In the early days I had found reserves of untapped energy and had poured it all into Frank's care. At that time if I had a headache or was tired it simply did not matter. Compared with Frank's suffering what was a headache? I had applied the same perfectionist principles to caring for Frank that I had applied to furnishing my house or entertaining guests. Everything had to be a hundred per cent right. I was going to show the world how it should be done. It had come as a nasty blow to both of us to find out as the months rolled on that I could not keep it up. Worse than that was that I realized with shock that I did not want to keep it up. I was guiltily aware of resentment bubbling away under the surface. I wanted my husband to be strong. When I had promised to love him in sickness and health I had been thinking of 'flu not quadriplegia! I didn't want to have to feed and bathe him any more. He had let me down. Why shouldn't I let him down too?

Much later I learned that what I was going through was part of a classic progression, well-documented by the professionals who deal with paralysis victims and their families. When someone dies it is common after the initial impact has worn off to go through a period when you blame them for leaving you. And for me, as for Frank, what had died, what we had both lost, was Frank's body.

Penny had an uncanny knack of sensing what was going through my mind. She turned to me one morning when we found ourselves alone and said, 'You can't rush it you know. You both have to allow yourself time to mourn. It is the only way you can come to terms with it.' I know now she was right but at the time I didn't believe her. I could neither forgive myself for my resentful feelings nor allow myself to grieve.

In their own way the husbands and wives of quadriplegics have as much adjustment to make as the victims themselves, but there is no support system for them. As my desperation built up I felt there was nowhere I could turn for help. Because Frank so much disliked being stared at in public we very rarely went out now. Our social life had virtually disappeared and I felt cut off from my friends. I couldn't have talked to them about it anyway. How could they possibly understand how I felt? When visitors asked, 'All right Ginny?' I would say, 'Fine' because it was what they wanted to hear. I couldn't expose my inner turmoil to them and watch them scuttle away unable to deal with it. I felt frightened and alone.

There was no one to explain to me that everything I was feeling was part of the normal recognized journey towards acceptance. Looking back, I feel let down about that. Spinal injury is not uncommon. Why is so little counselling offered to the families of people who are thrown into this strange and frightening world? Perhaps if we had gone to Stoke Mandeville we would have been offered counselling, though it had never been mentioned to me when they were trying to persuade us to go there. But certainly here at home I was given no support or advice by anyone other than Penny, whose prime task was to look after Frank's physiotherapy. I felt it would have helped us both if there had been somebody whose job it was to help me to adapt.

Not surprisingly Frank became cross and disappointed in me. I had shown such early promise. He found my defection from my duties now hard to comprehend. His needs were so colossal and my own must have seemed insignificant in comparison. It soon became a vicious circle. The angrier Frank became, the harder I found it to be a ministering angel. I probably would have survived even this stage without it developing to crisis point were it not for one thing. My lack of privacy. It was eating away at me now. There were strangers living under the roof that should have sheltered just Frank and me and our children. I wanted to make a cup of tea in my own kitchen without having to talk to other people. I wanted to read the newspaper when I wanted to read it, not when someone else had finished with it. I wanted to get into my own bed with no one watching and get some sleep.

It was not the staff's fault; after all, it was their job to be there. But I felt as though I was living in a commune, and I was not a commune sort of person. All around me I saw my home being eroded. It was like watching my dreams dying. Ugly black wheelchair scuff marks appeared on the wallpaper and skirting boards. A constant stream of people flowed in and out of the house, seldom pausing to wipe their feet. Rings from carelessly put-down coffee mugs appeared on my antique furniture. I tried to tell myself that it was trifling; that it didn't matter. But I couldn't help it. It tore me apart. It was not my house any more. I felt rootless. As though I didn't belong anywhere. I had lost all control over my life, my surroundings, my future.

I was close to breaking point. Because I was still doing the night shift I was rarely sleeping for more than three hours at a stretch. My nerves were taut and strained. My face had become blotchy and red with an itching nervous rash and all the skin was peeling from my lips. What I needed was professional help but I was unable to ask for it and wouldn't have known where to seek advice anyway. What would my GP say to my tearful self-pity when he was treating Frank who had a 'real' and severe medical condition? I felt he wouldn't be interested in my trivial problems. No one was. No one asked me how I was any more I reflected bitterly. The only greeting I ever got these days was, 'Hello Ginny. How's Frank?'

I was afraid that if I voiced my misery my doctor would tell me to, 'Pull yourself together', and I felt I would deserve it. I was overcome with despair at my own shortcomings. I disliked the dreadful self-pitying person I seemed to have become. But there was no escaping her. One day, totally despondent, I sat down and wrote a letter to the problem column of a women's magazine. I scribbled page after page, pouring out my feelings. How Frank's injury had taken over our lives and how I felt I couldn't cope with it any longer. How, although I was surrounded by people, I had never been lonelier in my life. I did not receive a reply.

It had been my last forlorn hope. I don't know what I expected a magazine psychiatrist could say to help me but when no answer came I sank even lower into my private hell. I had to escape. I couldn't live with this thing any longer. It wasn't Frank I wanted to run away from. It was the situation. To live with a quadriplegic you had to be a saint and I was not saint material. Arrogantly in the early days I had thought I might be, but I had been wrong.

One day in early 1988 when the children had returned to school I sat down on the sofa in the morning room opposite Frank in his wheelchair and said, 'I'm sorry Frank, I want to leave. I can't stay. It's not your fault. I just want my life back.'

He didn't display any surprise. I think if he had said, 'Oh Ginny don't go. I really want you to stay,' I would even then have changed my mind but he didn't. He just looked at me without expression.

'How do you feel about it?' I asked, stung by his lack of response.

He shook his head. 'Ginny, if that's what you want to do, then that's what you have to do.'

I felt hurt and rejected. It was as though I was nothing more to him than just another care attendant. His reaction suggested my departure would cause him some aggravation because he would have to look for another pair of hands, but that was all. If he didn't care any more than that, then I might as well go. The alternative explanation – that he didn't want to put pressure on me – did not occur to me.

My resolve was strengthened now and I started to make plans. I decided to move to London and I asked Frank if he would help me to buy a house. Unemotionally he agreed. It was as though a shutter had come down between us. I couldn't just walk out. It would have to be organized to create as little disruption to everyone's lives as possible. I would leave in September. Claire had started boarding school now so when she and Jonathan had gone back for the autumn term I would move to London with Jaime. From my new base he could go to school somewhere close by and I could start to build a new life. Frank would be all right I told myself. He had his nurses, his physios, his housekeeper. The children could spend time with him in the holidays. He probably wouldn't even miss me. It was an anguished decision, born of utter despair.

We mutually agreed to sell Boxford House. I think we would have sold it anyway. The heart had gone out of it. Our dreams had died there, and living within its walls we were constantly reminded of what might have been. It was time for both of us to move on.

The only people I told of our plans to separate were Charlie and Jenny. They did not seem surprised although Charlie did try to persuade me to stay. 'Once you've got your freedom you won't want it,' he predicted. 'You feel trapped now. You're behaving like a fly stuck on sticky paper. But what you're chasing is an illusion of freedom. You'll never be free of Frank.'

I refused to listen and when they saw that I was determined to go, Charlie and Jenny stood by me. They advised me not to talk about it in case the Press got hold of the story.

'People are not likely to be very understanding about this,' Charlie warned. 'You're going to get a lot of bad publicity. You are prepared for that aren't you? I think if you're going, you should make it Australia. London won't be far enough!'

The thought of what people would say when they found out had been preying on my mind. What sort of woman leaves her crippled husband? I guessed the Press would brand me a callous deserter. But even that was not enough to deter me. I really believed it was a question of my own survival now. The words nervous breakdown had never been in my vocabulary but I sensed I was ill and perilously close to some sort of mental crisis. For the sake of my children I had to stop myself going under. If this was the only way then, as Frank had said, it was what I had to do.

Within two weeks of my decision to go, I had bought two houses. The first, intended to house Frank and his entourage, was at East Ilsley near Newbury; another redundant rectory, in need of an enormous amount of modernization. The second purchase was a small house off the Fulham Road in London, also in a fairly unhappy state of decoration. It would take a while to get both houses fit to live in but they should be ready by September. In anticipation of the move I enrolled Jaime at a prep school in Belgravia for the autumn term.

I spent a busy couple of months organizing the work on both houses simultaneously, trying hard not to confuse myself or the builders. I had not told the children of my plans as I was afraid that they might try to change my mind. Time enough to let them know when it was done. In the Newbury house, Frank's bedroom would be on the ground floor. Robin would live in a flat above it with a voice-activated intercom should Frank need assistance in the night. I included a bedroom and bathroom for me there too, I might pay the occasional visit when the children were spending time with Frank, I told myself. Despite having no intention of living there I was surprised to find I was decorating this new Old Rectory with as much enthusiasm as the London house.

At the beginning of the summer Boxford House was put on the market. It sold immediately. It was too late now for second thoughts. We had to move out in August which was earlier than I had envisaged. Originally I had imagined us going our separate ways at this point but there were complications. The children were still on their school holidays and more importantly, although the house in London was finished, work on the Old Rectory was two months behind schedule. Frank could not live with builder's rubble. He would have to go into a hotel for the interim. I booked him and the children into a lovely hotel in Goring, undecided about my own plans at this stage.

Frank left Boxford for the last time two days before me. I like to leave my houses immaculate and I wanted to stay and complete the final tidying up before handing over the keys.

As Ian pushed him down the wheelchair ramp we had installed at the back door Frank's face remained impassive. I opened the door of the car for him, bewildered by his lack of feeling.

'Don't you care Frank?'

His reply took me aback.

'Emotion is weak Ginny,' he said, looking me straight in the eye. Even Ian flinched at his words. But why was I so shocked? Surely after knowing him for almost twenty years I should not have been surprised at his answer. There were only a handful of occasions in all that time when I had seen him display his feelings. Why was I still looking for a chink in his armour? I would never find it and perhaps it was just as well. Frank has always totally protected himself against weakness. It had sometimes made him seem cold but his lack of vulnerability was the very thing which had helped him fight his paralysis. Without it he would never have coped with it as well as he had done.

The following day, the children moved into the hotel to join Frank. The furniture was taken away to store. I remained in the empty house for one final night, with a hoover, a kettle, a duvet, and Fred. It was dusk when I finally switched off the vacuum cleaner. My lovely home was eerily quiet. In near darkness I walked the dog around the garden for the last time. I climbed up my daffodil bank and sat staring down at the house in the moonlight. Tears coursed down my cheeks and Fred anxiously licked them away.

With leaden steps I walked indoors and locked myself in my bedroom to try to sleep. It isn't true that you can die of a broken heart, if it were I should never have woken up the following morning.

The agent arrived at ten a.m. and I gave him the keys, climbed into my car and slowly drove away, leaving behind me the house which had seen both the happiest and unhappiest years of my life.

I hadn't thought what I would do next but I found myself driving automatically to the hotel in Goring. Frank was in his room, a large one on the ground floor, overlooking the swimming pool where the children were already happily swimming. We ordered tea. 'I think I might book myself a room for a couple of nights,' I suggested tentatively. 'Good idea,' Frank responded.

That evening we went into the restaurant and had a quiet dinner together. I was surprised to realize as I got into bed that night that I had given no thoughts to Boxford since my departure that morning. In spite of the pain of leaving I felt suddenly as if an enormous weight had been lifted from my shoulders. My intended couple of nights' stay became a month. Gradually over that month, in new surroundings which held no memories, the tension between us faded away and Frank and I became friends again. We had suffered enough. There was no need to fight. With the enormous responsibilities of running Boxford gone I started to relax and recover. In the hotel I was looked after. I did not have to organize anything. I could play with the children and allow myself a little pampering. I even had time to enjoy helping with Frank's bath. I started to feel happy again. My certainty of what it was I wanted in my future began to waver.

September was looming. Frank knew it and I knew it. Neither of us mentioned it or discussed it. I had committed myself. Jaime was due to start school in London. I told myself to be sensible – reminded myself how I had felt at the beginning of the year. Although I might be able to cope in a hotel environment it was a far cry from what would be expected of me if I went with him to East Ilsley.

The two elder children went back to boarding school and I prepared to leave too. My two and a half years of night duty were nearly over. The appointed day, Wednesday 14 September arrived. I packed my case and Jaime's and we went in to kiss Frank goodbye. He kissed me back, his face betraying nothing.

'Bye Ginny,' he said.

I put Jaime in the car and drove away from Frank for what I had convinced myself, six months earlier, would be the last time.

My abdication lasted two whole days. Steadily during that time the ties that bound me to Frank tightened and pulled, until by Friday I was powerless to resist them. However much I had hated my changed life, after forty-eight hours without him I knew without a shadow of doubt that Frank was still at the centre of that life. Charlie had been right. Now that the cage door was open I found after all that I did not want to fly away. At lunchtime on Friday I telephoned Frank at the hotel and we talked for several minutes about the progress of the work at the Old Rectory.

'Frank,' I said hesitantly, when there was nothing else left to say, 'Is it all right if Jaime and I come down for the weekend?' There was no more reaction than if I'd asked if a friend could come to stay.

'Of course you can. I'll get some rooms booked.'

I picked up Jaime from his new school and told him we were going back to the hotel. Since I hadn't ever told him that we were not, his reaction was predictably casual. On Friday evening we drove down the M4 to Goring. Frank was waiting for us with a pot of tea, a plate of biscuits and his familiar teasing smile. I realized that he had never been seriously worried that I would leave him. Wherever Frank was, whether in hospital, in a hotel room or in the new house at Newbury, was my home too. He had always known that. Maybe underneath I had known it too. Why else had I prepared a room for myself in his new house?

They say that it takes seven years for a paralysed person to come to terms with his loss. Perhaps it takes that long for the person's husband or wife to adjust to it as well. Those two short days of our 'separation' did serve a purpose. They gave me time and space to think. I had been able to step back from the situation; assess it with more objective eyes and see where I had gone wrong.

My mistakes were suddenly very obvious to me. For too long I had refused to believe that there was no hope of Frank's recovery. Instead I had constantly tormented myself with the illusion that one day he might get better. Then, even when I had admitted the truth to myself I fought against it. I had been so angry. So unwilling to accept. Had exhausted myself by continually rebelling at the injustice of it, wanting things back as they were before, instead of doing something constructive about the situation as it was. If I was to return to him I had to learn from those mistakes. I might never be able to fully accept what had happened to Frank but I could try. I could give the healing process a chance to start.

CHAPTER 20

I had to make some changes in my life if I was to avoid falling back into the mental state that had prompted my desertion. I had to look at the things that had made me most unhappy and see what I could do about them. If running away was not the answer, perhaps adapting was.

The loss of my home to others had been one of the things that distressed me most. For me it had been almost as big a problem, as hard to cope with as the accident itself. But that, I saw now, could be compensated for. What I needed was a little area of my life where I was in control and could recover my identity – my sense of self. Where I could have things as I wanted them and keep them that way, a space apart where I could get my head back on when the strain built up, and could for brief periods live a normal life. To outsiders it might seem like an indulgence, but I needed it. Without it our marriage was not going to be able to survive.

I decided to keep the house in London and to use it for that purpose. During term time I could spend a few days there with Jaime each week and return home at weekends and holidays. Frank was not keen on the idea at first, having got me back he wanted me to stay, but gradually he accepted the idea of my 'bolt-hole'. It has worked better than I could have hoped. My London home has been a lifeline. It has provided an outlet for my streak of perfectionism as well as returning me my privacy. I have filled it with flowers and porcelain. It is my territory, where I can come down to the kitchen in the mornings to make a cup of tea in my t-shirt without worrying that someone will see me. During the week, while Jaime is at school I live there almost like a recluse enjoying my own company. It is where, unknown to Frank, I wrote this book.

In the end my decision to take a certain amount of freedom has benefited Frank too. In some ways the existence we enjoy now is more similar to the one we used to have. In the whole of our married life before the accident Frank rarely spent a whole week at home. We were simply not used to being together all the time. Our relationship then thrived on absences as it does again now. Frank has begun to enjoy saying goodbye to Jaime and me for a few days – for him they bring peace and quiet as well as some space of his own, away from my demands.

For I have come to recognize that the demands are not all on his side as I had believed when I was at my lowest ebb. Often I am more ambitious for him to reach his goals than he is. If I think they are within his reach then I nag at him to try. I pester him to attempt turning book pages over so that he will once again be able to enjoy reading. I urge him to practise more than his initials using his writing splint. I know he could do it therefore I feel he should do it. It's hard for me to allow him to set his own level of achievement. He finds this understandably aggravating. Occasionally, I seem even to myself to resemble a pushy parent constantly pressing her child to try harder – 'It's for your own good'. He rightly berates me for my 'bossiness' and I think often breathes a sigh of relief as my car drives away on Monday morning.

Over these last two years, compromise and a relaxing of our demands on each other and on ourselves has provided an answer to most of our difficulties. I have slowly forgiven myself for not being Florence Nightingale and I hope that Frank has too. I do my best for him where nursing is concerned but I often fall short and I will not allow myself to feel guilty about that any more. I am not a nurse. I never had any inclinations in that direction and I'm sure Frank would not have married me if I had been that sort of person.

Frank's motivation in life has always been motor racing and he still has that. My motivation before the accident was centred on Frank and our life together, and that has had to change. Now I don't complain that we can't go to the cinema. I go by myself. If friends ask us out for dinner and Frank does not want to go, I go alone. It will never be as much fun without him but I am still determined to enjoy going to parties, making trips to the sea with the children, taking the dog for walks in the snow. Making a martyr of myself will make no one happy.

There is no point in me making the same sacrifices that he has been forced to make as a result of that momentary lapse in concentration on a French road four years ago.

I have slapped upon myself a Grade II Preservation Order. It is necessary if I am to survive the thirty or so years I hope we have left. Sometimes it may make me seem selfish but Frank understands my reasons. They are much the same as his for putting Formula One before everything. I think it is at least partly due to my new approach that since we moved to the Old Rectory our life together has settled into a new and happier pattern. Against all the odds our relationship recovered. It survived the battering of that stormy year. And as I became happier and less distraught so Frank also softened and was less critical of me. His anger at his appalling fate has gradually waned. Slowly we have each learned to like and live happily alongside our 'new' spouse.

Neither of us have any expectations of a miraculous recovery. Just living, for Frank, will always be a heroic fight. From the time he wakes up in the morning until he goes to bed at night, his life is a struggle. He still suffers constant pain in his shoulders and he lives in an icy world where he always feels cold. We have been fortunate in Frank's carers, Robin, Ian and John. Frank's ability to operate as normally as possible relies entirely on their expertise and he will always be totally dependent on intensive nursing.

He is still, as he was before the accident, meticulous about detail and for this reason is a hard taskmaster. He adheres to a rigid routine. His time for rising in the morning; his physiotherapy; his time in the standing frame; even the time his drinks are administered, are all part of a strict schedule. We all understand his need for this control better now than we did – there are so few ways in which he can take charge of his life and we try not to overreact when he becomes overbearing about something trivial.

'What did you say Frank? We're twenty seconds late with your hot Ribena? Oh no. You shouldn't have to tolerate that.'

Frank acknowledges the teasing with a smile.

Frank's adaptation to his paralysis has had to be different from mine. Mourning his loss will never heal his wounds. However many changes he makes in his lifestyle he will never recover, but he has found his own way of coping with it. To an astonishing extent he ignores his paralysis and as far as possible he continues to treat it as if it doesn't exist. He certainly does not psychoanalyse himself. Refusing to think about it for him works far better.

We shall never know whether Frank would have benefited from the normal term of rehabilitation in a spinal unit that his medical advisors wanted him to undergo. But I have few regrets that we didn't try it. His fate was sealed at the time of the accident. No rehabilitation or surgery in the world would have given him back any movement or sensation below the spinal level of C5/C6. And I cannot envisage that Frank with his philosophy of 'emotion is weak' would have even considered submitting to counselling to help him cope mentally with his injury. So while a year in hospital might possibly have made him a degree more independent than he now is, it would have only been a degree, and that has to be weighed up against a year of his life.

Undoubtedly I suffered without the counselling that might have been available to me within a spinal centre, but I do not think accepting Frank's quadriplegia would ever have been easy for me, even with full preparation. I don't think it could be easy for anyone. It is not the sort of eventuality most people ever consider having to deal with. Most women have imagined at some time how they would deal with widowhood, or how they would deal with cancer. Because everyone knows the possibility is there, you do consider what it might be like to cope with them. But you never consider dealing with paralysis – or I didn't. You never visualize what it might mean. The implications are unexplored even in your imagination, so the adaptation is perhaps that much harder.

Thankfully I have at last reached the stage, which I never thought would happen, where I can count our blessings. We are luckier than most people in our situation, we have a financial cushion and Frank can afford to look after himself well. I thank God daily for that. I shudder to think what our lives would be like had he had his accident ten years earlier.

People often ask me if Frank suffers from depression, and with my hand on my heart I can say the answer is no. He will not allow it. If he ever started feeling sorry for himself that would be as he once put it 'the start of the slippery slope'. Instead he does as he has always done – he buries his head in the sand and gets on with racing cars.

1988, as we had expected, was not a successful season. Nigel Mansell was joined by the Italian driver Ricardo Patrese and they struggled through the year in normally aspirated cars making no impression whatever against the force of the new Honda-powered McLarens. In June I went with Frank to the Canadian Grand Prix and enjoyed a few days in Montreal. I left the track after the race with Nigel, who had struggled to qualify for a ninth position on the grid only to retire at a quarter race distance with engine failure. As we made our way through the heavy post-race traffic to the hotel, he told me almost apologetically that he would be going to Ferrari in 1989. I couldn't query his decision. In his continuing quest for the Drivers World Championship an uncompetitive year like this had been a disaster. It was time for a change. I was very sad, he had been a good friend and we had loved having him at Williams. I told him I hoped perhaps when Williams were once more able to put together a competitive world championship package, we would see him in our car again.

Talks with Renault had been taking place since the early part of 1988 and by the end of the season they had signed contracts to provide Williams with engines for 1989 and 1990. The gap left by Nigel would be filled by the Belgian driver Thierry Boutsen who was leaving Benetton. Frank was looking forward to a rewarding relationship with a new engine manufacturer although he did not expect it to be easy in the first year – nor was it. It was inevitable that there would be teething problems. But there was always the following season, and the one after that to look forward to . . . They would make it to the top again.

That hope, that continuing striving towards the next success, is still the overriding concern of Frank's life. It is what motivates him. What he lives for. Compared with motor racing, as far as Frank Williams is concerned, quadriplegia will always be of secondary importance.

CHAPTER 21

Sometimes I dream that Frank is running through the Berkshire lanes. Everything is all right. Or I dream that he is making love to me. Early in the morning in that split-second between sleeping and waking I sometimes forget, as one might forget what day it is, that Frank is paralysed. Then the knife blade of reality twists sharply in my stomach jerking me back to the present. How must Frank feel in that same moment of semi-consciousness? What a nightmare to wake up to. To be a prisoner within your own body. Not even to be able to get out of bed until someone else moves you.

Frank also dreams. He says that usually in his dreams too he is running; he has made a magical recovery and everyone is astonished to see him returned to fitness and turns to watch as he races past them. The difference between our dreams is that his are in the future. He has recovered. I dream of the past. He has never had the accident.

We are, and always have been, two quite different characters. Frank has never wasted his time bemoaning the past. It is one of his many strengths. The past means nothing to him – whether it's a world championship won or lost, or a road accident that crippled him. It's yesterday. It's boring. Today and tomorrow are what count.

I, in contrast, am happiest with the past. My memories comfort me. I need them. I prefer the past to the future. That frightens me now. What happened to my dreams? I wanted us to grow old together. I wanted to die in Frank's arms.

266

We have both changed. Possibly in some ways we have both grown as a result of the experience. But if a fairy godmother offered to wave her magic wand and take us back to the way things were when I first married Frank I would not hesitate for a second. I would happily exchange the houses, the executive jets, the smart hotel rooms, the gold Rolexes for just one night in a scruffy bedroom anywhere in the world with the selfish, funny, unsympathetic, unreliable, charismatic man I married.

It is too hard to think in terms of never living happily and normally again, so I avoid it. Instead I look for nice things in every day; something funny Jaime does or says; lunch with a friend; listening to my favourite music in the car. I realize now as I never did before that each minute of every day is precious and you have to make the most of it. Small pleasures have taken on a new importance. I treasure them. And I try very hard to laugh. I laugh much more than I used to. It helps to stop me crying.

My acceptance will never be complete. Even now a day rarely goes by when I don't look at his changed, destroyed body and think, 'Oh no! Not Frank.' I shall go to my grave heartbroken over what happened to him. But it is no good wasting your only life on this earth by pining for what might have been. The grey clouds hanging over our heads will never go away. Some days they are more threatening than others. Sometimes they lighten to a paler grey. But they are always there.

And in our own ways we have both at last found a way to live with them.

Lightning Source UK Ltd.
Milton Keynes UK
UKHW021309250219
337978UK00013B/1953/P